A CYCLE OF
CHINESE FESTIVITIES

AN ILLUSTRATED CYCLE OF
CHINESE FESTIVITIES
IN MALAYSIA AND SINGAPORE

C. S. WONG
PHOTOGRAPHS BY RONNI PINSLER

Jack Chia — MPH Ltd
1987

An Illustrated Cycle of
Chinese Festivities
in Malaysia and Singapore

First published 1967 by Malaysia Publishing House Ltd
This edition published 1987 by Jack Chia — MPH Ltd,
Pan-I Complex #03-21, 601 Sims Drive, Singapore 1438

Edited by Peter Hutton and Steve Thompson
Graphic artist Tang Wai Ching
Typeset by Koford Prints Pte Ltd
Printed and bound by Singapore National Printers Pte Ltd

ISBN 9971-73-224-6

*(Preceding pages) A Tiechiu opera actor in
the role of the celebrated Judge Pao Kung,
who is worshipped as a saint by many
Chinese devotees in Malaysia and
Singapore.*

For my grandchildren
Wong Ch'iu-Man,
Wong Ch'iu-Yin
and
Wong Tat-Chung

Preface

This book is not a compilation nor a rehash of what has appeared in print on the subject. It is a new work, the first of its kind, on Chinese festivities in Malaysia and Singapore. The approach is new and the treatment is new. As such it is a new contribution to the study of Malaysian and Singaporean sociology and perhaps to their history and literature as well.

The book seeks to trace the origin of each of the festivals, traditions and beliefs in China and show their modifications, if any, on the soil of Malaysia and Singapore over the years, with a summing up of their environmental and other causes. For this undertaking, we have a threefold advantage: (i) we have celebrated most of the festivals, observed some of the traditions and shared many of the beliefs at one time or another; (ii) we have had recourse to primary Chinese sources; and (iii) we have had the good fortune to compare our experience in (i) and the sources in (ii) with what sinologues have written about them in English. What is even more important is perhaps the fact that we act as the mouthpiece of the celebrants, not as curious observers nor as superficial critics, but as one of them.

We have sought authority from Chinese classics as well as information from simple folklore books. To our mind, the simple folklore books are equally important because, as they reach a wider audience, they are bound to exert a greater influence on the daily beliefs of the average layman. Our investigation shows that the traditions are generally transmitted verbally from generation to generation and through the highly dramatized stage shows (and latterly the cinemas) and a host of embellished legends, many of which are without historical basis. But this characteristic is common to all mankind.

In our research and in the final preparation of this work, we are much indebted to a number of people for their co-operation. First

A Taoist priest leaps over a ritual fire during the festival of the 7th Moon, symbolically opening the gates of Hell and releasing trapped spirits who might otherwise cause trouble as "Hungry Ghosts". This ceremony was performed in grand style at the Pek San Teng temple, in Singapore, in 1981.

and foremost, we wish to thank Miss Jean M. Waller, Librarian of the University of Singapore, for her encouragement and permission to use the University's Library, and the staff of the University's Library, the Reference Section of the National Library of Singapore, the Penang Library and the Penang Buddhist Association's Library for their prompt attention and courteous service.

We are grateful to Dr N. K. Menon, J.P., former Member of Education for the State of Penang, and Mr Alan F. Young, former Secretary for Chinese Affairs, Johore, for having gone through the manuscript and for their many useful suggestions: Mrs Lim Wong Pui-Huen (林黄佩萱) and Mr Lee Kwai-Tong (李桂棠) of the Singapore University for helping in the preparation of the bibliography; Mr Chang Chin-Chiang (张清江) of the *Sin Chew Jit Poh* (星洲日报) and Mr Wu Yong (吴荣) of the *Sin Pin Jih Pao* (星槟日报) for writing out the Chinese characters and proof-reading them and for general assistance; and Mrs Wong Lin-Ken (黄麟根夫人) and Mr Yeang Hooi-Chee (杨开枝) for the arduous task of reading the proofs, the latter also for help in the preparation of the general index.

There are many others who have rendered us service in one way or another, and in the majority of cases due acknowledgement is made in the relevant text or footnotes.

Postscript   When the manuscript was in the press, it was announced in a *Singapore Gazette Extraordinary* that by virtue of an agreement made on 7th August, 1965, between the Government of Malaysia and the Government of Singapore, Singapore shall cease to be a state of Malaysia with effect from 9th August, 1965, and thereupon become an independent and sovereign state and nation separate from and independent of Malaysia.

However, as our monograph was completed long before the date of separation, this political division does not alter the facts and findings reached by us, nor is it likely, in the foreseeable future, to affect the main observance of any of the traditions and festivals by the Singaporeans and the Malaysians of the Federation of Malaya, Sabah and Sarawak. Nevertheless, the attention of the reader is invited to the qualified usage of the word "Malaysia" as is indicated in the explanatory notes on page 213.

Wong Choon San
National Library, Singapore
7th May, 1965

Contents

(Preceding pages) A pair of dragons frolic
during the annual procession held under
the aegis of the "Johore Old Temple" at
Johore Bahru. Dedicated to five tutelary
deities known as the Goh Lau Yiah, this
festival takes place during the 1st Moon.

Plan of This Work

This book is divided into three main sections: (i) an introductory section showing how the luni-solar calendar and the animal symbols are interwoven with the daily life of a large portion of the Chinese in Malaysia and Singapore; (ii) the New Year celebrations — from New Year's Eve to the 15th night of the 1st Moon — dealt with in seven different chapters; and (iii) the main traditional festivals within the twelve-month cycle of a lunar year, also in seven separate chapters, followed by an Epilogue, a retrospective review, with reference to the contributory causes of the festivals' survival, the disintegrating forces, the influence on other communities and *vice versa*, the fusion or assimilation of inter-communal cultures and their future trend in multi-racial Malaysia and Singapore.

Finally, before you turn to the other pages, we would like to say (with apologies to Voltaire): "We may not share in your celebrations, but we are prepared to lay down our lives for your right to do so."

Prologue

Believe it or not, this book was inspired by a dream. About the time of *Ch'ing Ming* (5th April), 1964, the author's wife dreamt that Mum came to the house with a food parcel containing eggs — or dumplings, she isn't quite sure now. Looking well and happy, Mum asked, "Why have you not paid me a visit — it's such a long time?"

Mum (the author's widowed mother) had died of grief on 15th May, 1944, at Bukit Mertajam, Province Wellesley, over the unjust imprisonment and torture of the author during the Japanese occupation of Malaya. At the time of her death, the author was still under detention at the Penang prison and, therefore, was unable to pay her a son's last respects. When the author was released on 21st June, 1944, he was one of the black-listed residents and had to be careful with his movements. At the end of that year, the author had a chance to go over to Bukit Mertajam with some Japanese. An attempt was made to venerate his mother at the cemetery there, but owing to incorrect timing the plan did not materialize. After the British re-occupation, the author managed to perform a son's duty at his mother's grave in the early 1950s. That was the first and last *Ch'ing Ming* observance till the time of the dream in 1964.

The author is not a believer in dream interpretations. However, it did strike him that there must be some reason for the dream, some explanation for it. Of course, a thousand and one explanations could be made through the process of rationalization. One of these explanations was a reminder to the author of his gross neglect of duty, of his failure to observe the *Ch'ing Ming* regularly. This the author accepted, not because it was the most sensible interpretation but because it was the most convenient excuse for the author to make a pilgrimage to Bukit Mertajam.

A colourful dragon pauses momentarily during the Goh Lau Yiah procession at Johore Bahru.

And this was done with affection and sincerity, with a roast piglet as the chief item of food offering, to the satisfaction of almost every member of the family.

Shortly after, we decided to do research on the *Ch'ing Ming* festival, seeking an answer to the writer's six Ws — who, what, when, where, why and how. When the investigation was afoot, it was found that the Chinese pay homage to their ancestors not only at the graveyard during the *Ch'ing Ming* and the *Ch'ung Yang Chieh* (9th Moon Festival) but also several times before the "spiritual tablets" enthroned at home. As we probed deeper we found that some of the festivals are inter-related, and that, to assess the true purpose and value of *Ch'ing Ming* and its allied festivals, we had to make a survey of all the other annual festivals which form a complete (twelve-month) cycle of Chinese festivities, a meaningful cycle of life itself.

To fulfil our mission, we have had to plan our investigation — call it a "study" if you are academically minded — in two stages. The first stage was to trace the origins of the festivals and, wherever possible, their evolution down through the ages in China. The second stage was to show their observance in Malaysia and their evolution on Malaysian soil, if any. A similar treatment was given to festivals of Malaysian origin.

There was not much difficulty in the first stage, as there is an abundance of material from Chinese and English sources available in the Library of the University of Singapore, the National Library of Singapore, the Penang Buddhist Association Library and the Penang Library. But as this book purports to be Malaysian in character, the problems confronting us at the second stage were rather complicated. Malaysia, formed on 16th September, 1963, comprises Singapore, Sabah, Sarawak and the former Federation of Malaya constituted on Merdeka Day, 31st August, 1957.[1] If the investigation was to be comprehensive, it meant field research work should be carried out in each of the component states and that each state should be dealt with under a separate section. This course was not feasible, nor desirable, because of the time and labour involved and the inevitable duplication of material, apart from the enormous expense which would have been incurred. The simple solution lay in narrowing down the scope to one representative state, with occasional reference to significant features in other states in the main text or the marginal notes for comparison or for emphasis, or for both. For this, Penang was our choice for manifold reasons. First, because it is the settlement wherein the festivals are held with great zeal. Second, because it is the home town of the author, where it is easy for him, already known for many years as a writer on "Matters Chinese", to establish contacts for purposes of interview and other inquiries. The third and most important is that it is the settlement in which the two principal dialect groups (often called tribes), the Hokkien and the Cantonese, predominate, and that, generally speaking, the observance by the Hokkien and the Cantonese is representative of the majority of the Chinese, though there are variants from the Tiechiu, the Hakka, the Hainanese and the Chinese from North China, such as the Shanghainese.

But though the formalities of observance of the various dialect groups are multifarious and diverse in detail, on the whole, the principles and background history of the traditions are nearly always the same. Even amongst the Hokkien and the Cantonese

1. The Federation of Malaya comprised nine states, Perlis, Kedah, Kelantan, Trengganu, Johore, Perak, Selangor, Negri Sembilan and Pahang, and the Settlements of Penang and Malacca. [With the formation of the Federation of Malaysia, Penang and Malacca both became states in their own right. Singapore later withdrew from the Federation, becoming an independent republic on 9th August, 1965.]

groups, there are different interpretations and divergent formalities, because they come from different districts or prefectures of the two provinces. To surmount this difficulty we made it a point to interview a cross-section of members of each group, corroborated, wherever possible, by textual evidence from newspaper reports and books and journals written by first-hand observers. Only then did we accept them as what appears to us to be the common or fairly widespread practice. You may not endorse our findings or some of the findings, and you may be absolutely right. But we are on solid ground too, for what we have put down in these pages is based on the actual practice of at least a group or groups of celebrants or participants.

Wesak Day   In recent years the global revival of Buddhism has gained its foothold on Malaysian soil as well, and some years ago the government of the Federation of Malaya, in pursuance of its tolerant and liberal policy, recognized Wesak Day (birthday of Lord Buddha, in May) as a public holiday throughout the country, and this is now also extended to Singapore. In 1964, Buddhist rituals were observed and processions held in the principal cities on Wesak Day, during which stirring speeches were made by ministers of the federal and the state governments and religious leaders from certain sections of the populace, and the celebrations in Penang, Kuala Lumpur and Singapore were given prominence in both the English and the Chinese press.[2] Wesak Day has become a very important religious festival for the Chinese and the Buddhists of other races in our midst; but as it is not strictly confined to the Chinese community, we have to omit it from the main Chinese traditional festivities.

However, there are certain interesting religious festivals peculiar to some of the states which we must allude to briefly in this introductory survey, mainly because they are too important to be left out of a work purporting to be Malaysian in character.

Sin Sze Si Ya Temple   In Kuala Lumpur there is the spectacular procession held annually on the 28th day of the 1st Moon under the aegis of the Sin Sze Si Ya (仙四师爷) Temple at Jalan Bandar (formerly High Street), originally built by Kapitan Yap Ah Loy (甲必丹叶亚来) in honour of Seng Ming-Lee (盛明利). Later other deities were added, including Bodhisattva Kuan Yin and Yap Ah Loy himself, who died on 15th April, 1885. In 1960 the procession was almost five kilometres long, with hundreds of miners, wearing gorgeous traditional costumes of embroidered silk, participating. There were also "fighting men" carrying sword or spear, reminiscent of Yap Ah Loy's men in battle for the recovery of Kuala Lumpur. Three statuettes were carried in the procession: Kuan Yin, Tam Kung Sin Si (谭公仙师 , of China origin), and Seng Ming-Lee.

When the statue of Ming-Lee passed, devotees burnt joss-sticks and joss-papers. At the end of the procession, a medium slit his tongue, and with the dripping blood wrote out prescriptions for the sick and forecast fortunes on sheets of sacred saffron paper, which had been blessed by the deified Ming-Lee, now popularly known as Si Ya (师爷), the "Adviser".[3] This procession is held annually, but every seventh year a grand celebration takes place. In 1902 the procession is said to have cost over $100,000, big money in those days, and to have taken an hour and a half to

2. See, for example, *ST*, 27th May, 1964, and 星槟 , 27th & 28th May, 1964.
3. STA, Clark.

A. *Buddhist priests chant during Wesak Day celebrations in Singapore.* B. *The Sin Sze Si Ya Temple in Kuala Lumpur.* C. *The military deity Chow Ta One Sway, one of the five gods venerated at the Johore Old Temple.*

4. *JMBRAS*, Middlebrook & Gullick, p. 22.

pass by. "The original purpose of the cult was no doubt to reassure the immigrant Chinese that they were protected against the disease and sudden death which were always near them," observe Yap Ah Loy's biographers. "In later days, it seems to have served to demonstrate the prosperity of the various clans."[4]

Kapitan Ming-Lee Ming-Lee came from China to Malacca in about 1850 where he was employed as a shop assistant but later sent to operate a mining company in Rasah, Sungei Ujong (later incorporated into Negri Sembilan). Sungei Ujong was then the main tin-mining district under the Dato Klana, but his authority was challenged by the Dato Shabandar (Bandar), who held half of the district. As a result there were frequent disputes over the ownership of the tin mines. Accordingly, the Chinese miners were divided into two factions, each siding with one of the rival Malay chiefs. Eventually Seng Ming-Lee became a Kapitan (better known as Shin Kap) of Sungei Ujong, ranging himself on the side of the Dato Klana. With Ming-Lee were Liu Ngim-Kong (刘壬光) and Yap Ah Loy. The clash of interests culminated finally in a big battle on 26th August, 1860, in which Kapitan Seng's party was defeated and the Kapitan had to beat a hasty retreat. Liu Ngim-Kong and Yap Ah Loy, though seriously wounded, escaped death. But the Kapitan was caught and beheaded. Chinese tradition says that as soon as his head was chopped off, white blood spouted out, which was construed to be a miracle. In consequence, his clansmen removed Ming-Lee's body to Malacca for interment, while a temple denominated Ho Seng Kung (和胜宫) was later built at Cheng in the suburbs of Malacca town. Another temple called Ch'ien Ku Miao (千古庙), the "Temple of Eternity", was

also built in Rasah, Negri Sembilan.

When Yap Ah Loy became Kapitan of Kuala Lumpur, he often consulted the spirit of Ming-Lee, his "Adviser", for guidance in his battles, and after he had recaptured the town of Kuala Lumpur in 1873 he built a temple in honour of the "Adviser", originally a small wood shack on the same site.[5] The "Adviser", a locally deified hero, is a very popular deity in Selangor, where we recently saw a new temple dedicated to him at Semenyih. The original temples at Rasah and Cheng, which we visited in January, 1965, kindly guided by Ong Sek-Pek (王锡璧) of Malacca, seem to have lost favour with the public.

Johore Old Temple   An annual procession is held on the 20th, 21st and 22nd of the Chinese New Year under the aegis of the "Johore Old Temple" (柔佛古庙) in Jalan Ngee Heng at Johore Bahru. A date on an old brass bell in the temple indicates that it was built before 1874-75, most probably very much earlier, in the form of a wooden shack. It is dedicated to five tutelary deities, each representing a dialect group amongst the Chinese: Tiechiu, Cantonese, Hainanese, Hakka, and Hokkien. These deities are known as the Goh Lau Yiah (五老爷), the "Five Venerable Ones", and their enthronement in one and the same temple is a tribute to the unity, amity and cordial co-operation of the five dialect groups in Johore. To the pride of Johore there was only one triad society, the Gee Hin (义兴公司), in that state, wherein no inter-triad feuds took place in the nineteenth century.

According to a Chinese source, in the days of the *kangchu* administration there was an annual sea gala, to which every *kangchu* (港主), or headman of a riverside, had to contribute at his own expense a decorated tongkang and a pair of lanterns during the celebration.[6] Nowadays, when Johore Bahru has developed into a modern town with a network of metalled roads, the regatta has been supplanted by a flag procession on land, with typical Chinese dragon and lion troupes participating. Guided by our friend Alan F. Young, formerly of the Malayan Civil Service and the last expatriate to hold the post of Secretary for Chinese Affairs, Johore, we visited the temple on 1st November, 1964, and in compliance with our request, Alan has kindly supplied us with a brief account of his impressions of a procession he saw:

"The festival of which the *Chingay* procession forms part lasts for three days and on the first day, the images of the five gods — the tutelary deities of Johore Bahru — are taken in procession from the temple in Jalan Ngee Heng to the Market where they are lodged for the duration of the festival.

"The main event takes place on the evening of the second day when the gods are taken round the town accompanied by a most spectacular procession. Each tribe — Hakka, Hainanese, Cantonese, Hokkien and Teochew — has its own section and they vie with each other for the most outstanding display. The whole procession, which presumably in earlier days was a torchlit one, is now illuminated by electricity — men and boys carry lights on poles, the power being supplied by generators mounted on lorries — thus the whole scene is as bright as day.

"When I witnessed the procession in the first moon of 1961 the items included several lion and dragon dances (one complete with a fire-breathing dragon), lorries carrying historical tableaux and flower girls, stilt walkers and numerous banner-carriers (but

5. JMBRAS, Middlebrook & Gullick, p. 15; *KL*, p. 9; 叶德来传，王植原，新加坡艺华出版有限公司 March 1958, pp. 28–29; and 南洋 (n.d.) in the collection of Tan Yeok-Siong. According to an inscription in the temple, it was built in 光绪初年 , that is 1875. We noted this date when we re-visited the temple in January 1965 with K.K. Lam of the *Straits Times*.
6. 马来亚潮侨通鉴 ed. 潘醒农 Singapore, 1950, p. 43.

none with the giant flags for which the Penang *Chingay* was noted). The air is full of the sound of drums, gongs, cymbals, etc., and the whole atmosphere may be well summed up in the Chinese phrase *je nao* (热闹), 'bustling with gaiety, noise and merriment'."

Kusu Island   The famed Kusu Island, about an hour's trip by launch from Clifford Pier, Singapore, is formed by two large rocks joined by a sand-spit at low tide.[7] On one rock or islet is a Chinese temple with a green-tiled roof, dedicated to Tuah Peh Kong, a locally deified hero. On the other is a *kramat* (said in some quarters to be that of a Malay saint, Syed Abdul Rahman), situated at the top of a narrow flight of steep, winding, uneven steps. These islets become a beehive of activity annually from the 1st day to the 15th day of the 9th Moon, when hundreds of Chinese make a pilgrimage to them in sampans flying flags of red, green and yellow on their bows. Before the pilgrimage, devotees have to refrain from meat-consumption on the previous day, and the traditional pork is forbidden in the food offering. The food items are in Malaysian style and consist of *nasi kunyit* (rice and turmeric boiled together to produce a saffron colour), boiled eggs tinted pink, fruits and flowers and chicken curry. The pilgrims first pray to the Tuah Peh Kong, offering a large portion of the food items. Incense-sticks and white candles (not the customary red candles) are lighted and the devotees ask for luck, health and the good things of life. At the same time, barren women also hang stones on the branches of a cluster of so-called "fertility trees", which are believed to bless them with fecundity. After a break for meals from banana leaves in Malaysian fashion — using their fingers to shuffle food into the mouth — the same pilgrims scale the steps leading to the *kramat* on the other rock (believed, by many, to be that of Fatima, daughter of the Prophet Mohammed). There new food offerings, including a comb of bananas (not those already used before the Chinese deity), are made and the pilgrims ask again for luck, health and the good things of life. After the day's enjoyable picnic and pious devotion, the pilgrims return home by the same sampans.[8]

Kuching's Mock Tomb   In Kuching, the capital of Sarawak, the all-important festival seems to be the *Ch'ing Ming.* An unusual story is told by T'ien Ju-K'ang (田如康) about how two dialect groups — one Tiechiu and the other Hakka — are united in paying respect to what purports to be their common ancestor.[9]

There are two groups of clansmen bearing the surname T'ien (田) in Kuching. One is the Tiechiu group, rich and influential; and the other is a Hakka group. A few decades ago, there was a desire between these groups to be linked up together as one big family group through a common ancestor bearing the surname T'ien. In consequence, a "mock" tomb — without any corpse — was built in 1925 in the Ch'ao An (潮安) Tiechiu cemetery, with an inscription on the monument relating to the origin of the T'ien clan (surname) in China. The inscription expresses the hope that all descendants of the T'ien clan may jointly do homage to this tomb for continuation of their prosperity. Since then it has been the tradition of the T'ien members of the Tiechiu and Hakka groups to make an annual pilgrimage to the "mock" tomb during the *Ch'ing Ming* festival as if they were doing homage to their common ancestor from China.

7. [Reclamation has increased Kusu's land area from 1.2 hectares to 8.6 hectares, and even at high tide the two rocks are no longer separated.]
8. SM, "Chinese New Year Supplement", 24th January, 1965; McKie, p. 227; and interview with Mrs Tan Hood-Kim of Singapore.
9. T'ien Ju-K'ang, p. 25.

A. Si Yen Ti Kong, the most senior of the five deities honoured during the Goh Lau Yiah festival. **B.** The Chinese temple on Kusu Island is famed for its dedication to Tuah Peh Kong. There is also a statue of Si Yen Ti Kong, however, an important figure in the vegetarian cult that draws thousands of devotees to the island each year. **C.** The Cheng Hoon Teng temple at Malacca, said to be the oldest temple in Malaysia.

The Wangkang of Malacca   There was the famous *Wangkang* (艎舡) festival in Malacca, which was first observed in 1856. A wangkang was what we call a junk — a war junk about the size of an ordinary sampan and ornamented with gold, silk and jewels. It was held at irregular intervals ranging from five to fifteen years. The last of the *Wangkang* festivals was held in 1933, when a procession took place, lasting from 27th November to 8th December (the 12th to the 21st day of the 10th Moon). The essential feature of the procession was the Chye Lian Kah (采莲脚 , the "waterlily squad"), formed by twenty-five couples wearing gorgeous white garments with red silk girdles and white hats. Barefooted, they marched two by two, each carrying a wooden paddle, which was swung to and fro to the rhythm of the Chye Lian song (the "waterlily song"). Immediately following the squad were a float in the form of a sampan and the five statuettes representing the Wang Yeh (王爷). The purpose of the procession was "to present to Heaven the people's request to inspect and pacify the universe." After the procession, which went round the town, the wangkang was finally set on fire and allowed to drift out to sea.

The festival is traceable to a legend of the Ming dynasty. During the reign of Yung Lo (永乐 , 1403–1424) there lived a high priest of Taoist persuasion, named T'ien Shih (天师), famous for his supernatural powers. To test his skill, the Emperor summoned 360 scholars of the Chin Shih (进士) grade to play music in the basement of the palace. When the music reached its crescendo, the Emperor ordered T'ien Shih to stop it, to which T'ien Shih replied that the musicians could be stopped only if death overtook them. Notwithstanding this, the Emperor insisted his order be carried out. Accordingly, T'ien Shih sprinkled some rice and salt on the floor and struck it with his magic sword, resulting in the beheading of the 360 scholars. On the same night, the 360 aggrieved souls appeared before the Emperor demanding restoration of their lives. As compliance with their request was impossible, the high priest captured the souls and confined them in a casket, which was thrown into the sea. Later this casket was found ashore by a beggar, who opened it, thus liberating the souls. On the advice of the high priest, the Emperor deified the souls as Ong Yiah (王爷), with the title of Tye Tian Soon Siew (大典巡守 , "Power of an Imperial Justice"), and decreed that they should be prayed to in whatever part of his domain they might visit. Five of them, Choo (朱), Hoon (桓), Tse (徐), Lee (李) and Pek (伯), found sanctuary in Fukien and have ever since been worshipped by the people of Changchou and Ch'uanchou, from where Chinese emigrants left in large numbers for Malacca in the seventeenth, eighteenth and nineteenth centuries; and with them took the *Wangkang* festival.[10]

Chingay in Penang   There are still innumerable religious festivals of purely regional interest: the festivals of the cave-temples in Perak; of the Thean Hock Kiong (天福宫), the oldest temple in Singapore; of the Ho An Kung (和安宫) of Trengganu; of the Chen Hsing Kung (镇兴宫) of Kelantan; and of the Cheng Hoon Teng (青云亭) of Malacca, the earliest temple in Malaysia. But it suffices, as a matter of historical importance, to recall one celebration in Penang in the nineteenth century to "Welcome the Spring" (迎春) during the New Year season, when a fascinating

10. MG, 26th November, 1933, cited by Chen Ta, pp. 249–251; Braddell, *Lights of Singapore*, p. 84; and interview with Ong Sek-Pek, who told us that an attempt to revive the festival in 1948 was abandoned owing to inadequate funds. [A modernized form of *Chingay*, held on the 3rd and 4th days of the 1st Moon, was introduced to Singapore at the beginning of the 1970s.] See also SCM, Pun Lun, wherein the *Wangkang* of 18th September, 1905, an even more impressive procession, is described; the legend given in SCM goes back to Li Shih Min (618–626) of the T'ang dynasty, but is otherwise the same as ours in many respects.

procession went round George Town. In the 1880s this event was recorded by a European missionary who, in spite of his prejudice, has left us a vivid description of a nineteenth-century *Chingay* (妆艺 or 装棚 , a "Chinese decorated float") for which Penang was to become famous at the turn of the century with its giant flags processions. Below is an extract:

"But still more fascinating was a like celebration at another season of the year in a festival designed, I believe, to pay honour to the art of husbandry . . . . Look! here it comes — a huge cart, dragged by buffaloes, bearing erect within it a lofty tree. From its branches hang lanterns, and here and there among the clustering leaves, as if borne on 'the circumambient air' itself, are little maids, draped in green and gold, with necklaces and girdles of flowers, standing in shoes of spotless white, with mimic jewels sparkling in their plaited hair, their figures motionless, and faces placid, so as to be without sign of fear, and scarcely of life. It is impossible to exaggerate the captivating effect of the sight — a scene, it seemed, not belonging to earth, but a sudden unveiling of a part of a new spirit world. Then would come musicians with gongs, bells, lutes, and pipes, and after an interval of glittering lanterns, another umbrageous tree, thus peopled, as it were, by pure and beautiful creations, with nothing of vulgar earth or ignoble flesh about them. How I can yet dream all these bright scenes over and over again!"[11]

11. Beighton, p. 169.

(Preceding pages) This ritual dance to the Generals of the Five Directions (besides north, south, east and west, China had a "central point") underlines the pre-eminence of the numeral "5". The dance took place during a procession to celebrate the birthday of Ma-Chor P'o, Goddess of the Sea, near the Thean Hock Kiong temple, said to be the oldest Chinese temple in Singapore.

PART I:
Introduction

CHAPTER 1:
The Calendar in Malaysian and Singaporean Life

The Chinese calendrical history has been the subject of animated discussions amongst the savants of China and sinologues of the West. Its history is so diffuse, so massive and so complicated that, according to Joseph Needham, a "definitive monograph on this subject" has yet to be written, either in Chinese or a Western language.[1] It involves intensive and laborious research in the ancient and mediaeval dynastic histories and a host of astronomical and calendrical treatises, and, at least, an elementary knowledge of the science of astronomy, astrology and also modern cosmology in order to interpret and explain intelligibly the varied and, often, fluid Chinese terms. Fortunately for our purpose, such an attempt is unnecessary: it suffices to render a simple and concise account, without entering, wherever possible, into debatable issues of purely academic interest, but with sufficient attention to the main features which still have an important bearing on the daily life of the Malaysians.

Chinese legendary history says that Huang Ti (黃帝) in 2697 BC caused the study of the stars by the astronomers at his court, and it was his minister Ta Nao (大挠) who prepared the first calendar, called the Chia Tzu (甲子) system.[2] But credit is generally given to Yao (尧), 2356 BC, another legendary ruler who is reputed to have made what is now known as the Hsia calendar (夏小正). Yao is said to have commanded his two astronomers, Hsi (义) and Ho (和), "to calculate the signs (presumably zodiacal), the sun, the moon and the constellations, and respectfully to deliver the seasons to the people."[3]

If we brush aside the legendary period, we know as an historical fact that there was a sixty-day calendar used by the people of the Shang dynasty (商纪 , 1766–1164 BC). This calendar was a day-count, taking sixty days to complete a recurrent cycle.

An altar dedicated to T'ien Kuan, Lord of Heaven.

1. Needham, vol. iii, p. 176.
2. 史记 by 司马迁，涵芬，1916 edition, vol. i, ch. 1, p. 2.
3. Soothill, *Hall of Light*, p. 57; and Wylie, (Scientific section), p. 162.

Each day was designated by a combination of two characters, each taken in serial order, from the T'ien Kan (天干, ten Heavenly Stems) and the Ti Chih (地支, twelve Earthly Branches) respectively.

The ten characters of the T'ien Kan are: 1. Chia (甲) 2. Yi (乙) 3. Ping (丙) 4. Ting (丁) 5. Wu (戊) 6. Chi (己) 7. Keng (庚) 8. Hsin (辛) 9. Jen (壬) 10. Kuei (癸).

The twelve characters of the Ti Chih are: 1. Tzu (子) 2. Ch'ou (丑) 3. Yin (寅) 4. Mao (卯) 5. Ch'en (辰) 6. Ssu (巳) 7. Wu (午) 8. Wei (未) 9. Shen (申) 10. Yu (酉) 11. Hsü (戌) 12. Hai (亥).

Thus the cycle begins with the Chia Tzu combination, followed by Yi Ch'ou, Ping Yin, Ting Mao, Wu Ch'en, Chi Ssu, Keng Wu, Hsin Wei, Jen Shen, Kuei Yu, Chia Hsü, Yi Hai, Ping Tzu, and so on until it ends with Kuei Hai at the sixtieth combination. The sixty-day cycle then starts all over again, commencing once more with Chia Tzu.

The ten characters of the Heavenly Stems were also used as personal names. When a child was born, it received the name of the day on which the birth took place. This is testified to by the list of Shang emperors, with the exception of Ch'eng T'ang (成汤), founder of the dynasty. From the second emperor, T'ai *Chia* (太甲), to the last emperor, Chou *Hsin* (纣辛), one of these ten Heavenly Stems was applied as a personal "epithet" to denote his birthday. A few names, chosen at random, are T'ai *Keng* (太庚), Yung *Chi* (雍己), Tsu *Yi* (祖乙) and Wu *Ting* (武丁).[4]

Reformation in Process   In the meantime, reforms set in to apply the sixty-day cycle to the year. This modification involved no difficulty, for it merely required six cycles of sixty days to make approximately a tropical (solar) year. To achieve this end, the sixty-day cycle was subdivided into six ten-day units called Hsun (旬). In order to adjust this sixty-day cycle to the 365-day tropical year, one to three ten-day units were intercalated.[5]

The same method of combining each of the ten characters of the T'ien Kan with each of the twelve characters of the Ti Chih was used for the designation of the year. The first day and the first year of the Sexagenary Cycle concurrently bore the designation Chia Tzu, ending with Kuei Hai for the sixtieth (last) year of the cycle. Then the same process was repeated in the new cycle and so on *ad infinitum*.

From an early era, not later than the latter part of the Chou dynasty (周纪, 1122–255 BC), the T'ien Kan was correlated with the Wu Hsing (五行, the Five Elements). These were metal (金), wood (木), water (水), fire (火), and earth (土). The T'ien Kan was also correlated with the Yin (阴) and the Yang (阳), the two opposite forces of the universe. Similarly, the Ti Chih, already used to designate the solar year, was also applied to the solar months. As early as the late Chou, the day and the night (both sidereal) were divided into twelve equal double-hours, and the Ti Chih was used to signify the twelve double-hours of each day. It is believed by one authority that animal symbols were created in the sixth century BC to correspond to the twelve characters of the Ti Chih.[6]

There were also twenty-eight Hsiu (宿) or Kung (宫), the "zodiacal constellations" or "lunar mansions", originated in remote antiquity, with which a set of twenty-eight animal symbols and the

4. Hirth, p. 72. A list of the Shang emperors is given in Matthews' *Chinese-English Dictionary*, 1166, Appendix "A" tables. See also Creel, *Studies*, p. 7, which says, *inter alia*, "We know (as, indeed, the *Pai Hu T'ung* related in Han times) that the Shangs used the ten cyclical 'stems', which were the names of the days of the ten-day Shang 'Week', as names for people . . . . ."
5. Needham, vol. iii, p. 397.
6. Needham, vol. iii, pp. 322, 397, 398, 405 fn.a.

Five Elements and the Yin (Moon) and the Yang (Sun) were associated. According to Leopold de Saussure, the zodiac gave birth to "the system of the five celestial palaces and to the equatorial method which characterizes the Chinese astronomy."[7] This system had great significance for the theory of monarchy in ancient China where theorists argued that as the pole star was the central point of the firmament, so the "Son of Heaven", being its counterpart on earth, should be the undisputed central authority. From this also arose the pre-eminence of the numeral "5": the five seasons (besides spring, summer, autumn and winter, China had a "mid-season"); the five directions (besides north, south, east and west, China had a "central point"); the Five Elements; the five varieties of creatures; the five musical notes of the Chinese pentatonic scale; the five internal organs; the five tastes and odours; and so on.[8]

To chart the seasons, the twelve months of the solar year, which were called Ch'i (气), were divided into twenty-four half-months or fortnightly periods, twelve of which were called Chung Ch'i (中气) or Ch'i-centres, whilst the remaining twelve were called Chieh Ch'i (节气) or Ch'i-nodes. This system was devised at an early era, and is known to have existed at least as far back as the latter part of the Chou. These seasonal divisions were called "Twenty-four festivals" (二十四气节) or Solar Terms, which are based on the summer and winter solstices and the spring and autumn equinoxes. For that reason, they were also known as "Astronomical Months".[9]

As the Chinese calendar is of luni-solar origin, that is to say, it regulates the solar seasons, the solstices and the equinoxes, and combines them with the lunations for the predictions of the full moon and the new moon, a system of intercalated months (synodic) called Jun Yueh (闰月) was devised. There are roughly 365.25 days in the tropical year (solar), whereas a synodic (lunar) month averages only 29.5306 days, with approximately 354 days in the entire year. This arduous task of combination was achieved by the simple process of inserting an intercalated (lunar) month in every three years (tropical), and two intercalated months in every five years, making a total of seven intercalated months in nineteen years called Chang (章), "a cycle of nineteen years". At the end of every Chang cycle, the Ch'i and the Shuo return to the same place (积十九年而气朔皆齐), i.e. the solar and lunar luminaries come back (almost) exactly to their relative original positions.[10] There remains, however, a surplus of 3.25 days. This surplus would disappear when the Chang was repeated eighty-one times (1,539 years), after which "the difference would be resolved and all would return to the original state" (积至八十一章然后盈虚之数终而复始).[11]

To an agricultural country like China, this luni-solar almanac was the time index for religious observances, for weather forecasts, for planting and harvesting in accordance with the seasons, for business transactions and social intercourse. As the entire peasant economy or wealth of the country depended on the calendar, the Son of Heaven arrogated to himself the sole right to promulgate it annually on a propitious day — a symbol of supreme authority.[12] China's pride in her early astronomical history may perhaps be excused when it is recalled that it was many centuries later that Meton, the Athenian astronomer (432 BC), discovered the famous Metonic Cycle (of nineteen years).

7. *NCR*, de Saussure, p. 453. The zodiac is the Chinese Huang Tao (黄道), or "Yellow Road".
8. Soothill, *Hall of Light*, p. 114 (see also pp. 32, 33 & 114 for amplification on the numeral "5").
9. Needham, vol. iii, p. 404; and 中国年历总谱, 董作宾, Hong Kong University Press, 1960, vol. i, p. ix.
10. 事类, 上海文盛书局, 1915 edition, vol. xii, ch. 7, p. 59. See also Chen Te K'un, vol. ii, p. 232, which says, in summing up, that the calendar maker in the Shang period was already aware that there are 365.25 days in a solar year, 29.531 days in a lunar month and that "in every 19 years there should be 7 intercalary months, making a total of 235 months".
11. 岁时, 陈元靓 in 丛书, Commercial Press Ltd, Changsha, December 1939, vol. i, p. 14.
12. Soothill, *Hall of Light*, p. 52, explains that it was essential that the calendar should be in the hands of one man . . . who could promulgate it with authority . . . . . If each feudal lord were to produce his own calendar, his ritual and spiritual allegiance would vanish also, the nation would be disunited and the forces of nature throughout the empire be disrupted.

*An elderly scholar displays a copy of the
T'ung Shu, the "Sacred Almanac", at
the Hong Hock See temple in Penang. For
a small consideration, he will help devotees
to search its vast stock of answers,
suggestions and forecasts.*

Accuracy in Eclipses One sure way of verifying the accuracy
of a calendar was its indication of eclipses and other stellar
phenomena. An eclipse is called Shih (蚀): a solar eclipse, Jih Shih
(日蚀), and a lunar eclipse, Yueh Shih (月蚀), meaning "the eating
up of the sun" and "the moon" respectively. In monarchical
China, the occurrence of such eclipses was construed as a sign of
misrule and an ill omen. When a sun eclipse took place on 23rd
November in the second year AD, Emperor Hsiao P'ing (or
Emperor P'ing, 平帝) promptly counteracted its supposed ill-luck
by granting a general amnesty to the criminals of the empire.[13] On
another occasion, when a sun eclipse was due, the sky was
overcast by clouds so that the phenomenon became invisible. As
the eclipse was not seen, it was interpreted as not having occurred.
Adopting this line of reasoning, the courtiers jubilantly went up to
the Emperor to offer felicitations, that Heaven, moved by his
virtuous rule, had spared him the agony of sighting the "eating of
the sun".[14]

In the Shang period, which laid the foundation for future
Chinese calendars, the eclipse occurrences were accurately made,
showing six lunar eclipses in 1361, 1342, 1328, 1311, 1304 and
1217 BC, and one solar eclipse in 1217 BC. However, about a
century or two later, minor miscalculations crept in. In 1198 BC
the official astronomers predicted a solar eclipse for the 1st night of
the 9th month, but it occurred during the daytime — a mistake of
only a few hours.[15]

In spite of minor discrepancies, the accurate observation of
the eclipses was fairly well maintained in the Chou dynasty
(1122–255 BC). There was, for instance, an eclipse of the sun on
29th August, 776 BC, and Chavannes, who had verified it,

13. Pan Ku, vol. iii, p. 74.
14. S.W. Williams, vol. ii, p. 73.
15. Needham, vol. iii, pp. 410, 422.

declared that it was accurate to the day. There were thirty-seven eclipses between 720 and 481 BC. Of these, twelve had been verified by E.H. Parker and found to be "fairly correct".[16] But during the two and a half centuries towards the end of the Chou dynasty, the calendar began to deteriorate, and Chalmers was unduly severe in his criticism, saying, *inter alia*, that "the rapid derangement of the months, and consequently of the seasons, towards the end of the Chou dynasty, most probably arose from the adoption of some erroneous system of intercalation, invented to supersede the troublesome observations of the stars from month to month . . . . ."[17]

During the period of the Former Han (前汉) dynasty (206 BC – AD 64), according to Homer H. Dubs, who has made a comparative study of the subject, there were 559 solar eclipses, of which ninety-eight or 17.5% were visible in some parts of China. Fifteen of these minor eclipses were not visible in the capital of China.

Of the remaining eighty-three solar eclipses, Chinese astronomers appear to have recorded fifty-five. To the unbiassed mind of Dubs, these records show a high degree of fidelity to fact, and he remarks, "It is but natural that the original records should have suffered errors of transmission; as a whole they are surprisingly correct."[18]

As we have shown, between the Shang and the Former Han periods there were minor errors and discrepancies from time to time. The principal reasons were that the Chinese astronomers and star-observers were handicapped by an inferior knowledge of geometry, and the lack of adequate scientific instruments, such as the modern giant telescope.

A typical entrance to a modern highrise apartment in Singapore. Some traditional customs have survived the transition from village to highrise: note the altar to Ti Kuan, the surrounding "lucky" plants (especially the pomegranate shrub, or ang huay, with its red buds) and the decorations of red ribbons and ang pau.

16. Couling, p. 153. The accuracy of the sun eclipse of 776 BC is also confirmed by Hirth, pp. 173–174.
17. Chalmers cited by Soothill, *Hall of Light*, p. 56.
18. Pan Ku, vol. iii, Appendix V, pp. 546–559.

Calendar Revisions To make confusion worse confounded, there were in ancient times a few calendars that began the year at different periods. The Chou dynasty feudal state of Tsin (晋) used the calendar, said to be that of the legendary Hsia dynasty (夏纪), and put the 1st month in the 3rd astronomical month (between 21st January and 20th February of the solar calendar); whilst the Chou dynasty feudal state of Sung (宋) used the Shang calendar, which began the year one month earlier, putting New Year's Day in the 2nd astronomical month (between December and January). The royal calendar of the Chou dynasty began the year in the 1st astronomical month (between November and December); whilst the Ts'in (秦) dynasty put New Year's Day in the 12th astronomical month (between October and November). The rulers of the Former Han continued the Ts'in tradition until in 104 BC the Han Emperor Wu (汉武帝) restored New Year's Day to the period it occupied in the Hsia calendar, in the 3rd astronomical month, where it remained until the time of the Chinese Republic.[19]

The method of reform in 104 BC was elaborated upon by another historian thus: "Thereupon they determined the points east and west, set up sundial and gnomons and contrived water clocks. With such means they marked out the twenty-eight mansions according to positions at various points in four quarters, fixing the first and the last day of each month, equinoxes and solstices, movements and relative positions of heavenly bodies and the phases of the moon."[20]

In the Posterior Han (后汉) period (AD 25–220), there were some adjustments to the reformed calendar of 104 BC. The best known of these adjustments came from Liu Hung (刘洪), described by Dr Leo Wieger as a "man of genius" who, having observed the solstices by means of the gnomon, declared that "the solstitial points were not fixed", that "the equator and the ecliptic were not one and the same thing", and that "the fraction to be added to the 365 days of the solar year was not exactly a quarter of a day."[21] Liu Hung's calendar was adopted during the period of the Three Kingdoms (三国 , AD 221–263) and also the Western Tsin (西晋 , AD 265–316) with adjustments and revisions. This was again rectified in AD 385 by Chiang Chi (姜岌) of the Eastern Tsin (东晋 , AD 317–419).[22]

Down through the decades, efforts to maintain the accuracy of the calendar were continued, and in the Sui dynasty (隋纪 , 581–617) and the T'ang dynasty (唐纪 , 618–906), both the Taoist priests and the Buddhist monks came to the fore in calendrical calculations, with Hindu teachers helping in the T'ang period.[23]

During the Sung dynasty (宋纪 , 960–1278), two new calendars were produced, one in 1191 and the other in 1274, but their predictions of the eclipses and other celestial phenomena proved to be inaccurate. In an endeavour to defend the astronomers, Ts'ai Yuan-Ting (蔡元定), a noted scholar and friend of the celebrated Chu Hsi (朱熹), made this naive remark: "Heaven is animated and free, turns around and stretches itself out as it pleases. Astronomy ought to ascertain these movements, but ought not to want to predict them. An exact calendar will never be made in advance. The good calendar is that which is made when the year is ended."[24] But a contrary opinion existed at about the same time. It came from the pen of Ma Tuan-Lin (马端临), also a distinguished scholar, who ascribed the mistakes and

19. *T'oung Pao* (通报), vol. viii, p. 399, cited in Pan Ku, vol. i, p. 154. The 104 BC calendrical reform is generally known as the T'ai Ch'u (太初) Reform. But see *JNCBRAS*, Kingsmill, p. 11, which is at variance with *T'oung Pao* relating to the commencement of the New Year: it states that this new calendar "which has since that period with slight modifications prevailed in China, commenced on the 24th December, 105 BC."
20. 前汉书 , ch. 21, translated by W.P. Yetts. Cited by Goodrich, p. 47.
21. Wieger, p. 106.
22. Wieger. pp. 125, 140.
23. Wieger, pp. 180, 193, 194; and Goodrich, p. 129.
24. Wieger, pp. 220–221.

discrepancies since the fifth and sixth centuries AD to the negligence of the astronomers and historians. Alluding to the period between 420 and 580 when China was divided into two empires, each having its own astronomical board and historians, Ma Tuan-Lin said that the two astronomical records showed serious discrepancies in the sun eclipses. "Now," the critic added, "as there are not two suns in the heavens, it is plain that to the negligence and ignorance of the historians we must attribute these errors and contradictions."[25]

The same calendrical problems confronted the Mongol rulers during the Yuan dynasty (元纪, 1280–1367), in spite of initial help given by a Persian astronomer named Jamal Eddin (also spelt as Djamar ud'Din), who was said to have prepared a second calendar, called Wan Nien Li (万年历), the "Ten-Thousand-Year Chronology", which was not adopted for general use. Kublai Khan also appointed a talented Chinese, Kuo Shou-Ching (郭守敬), to revise the traditional calendar. For the purpose Shou-Ching, who laid down the principles of calendrical computation, had several mechanical instruments made for astronomical calculation. These instruments remained throughout the whole of the Ming dynasty (明纪), and were seen and described by the Jesuit Matteo Ricci, who visited Peking at the beginning of the seventeenth century.[26]

Nor were the Ming rulers (1368-1644) spared similar difficulties in adjusting and maintaining their calendar, which proved faulty. Two calendars were prepared for 1370: one was the Ta T'ung Li (大统历), the work of Chinese astronomers directed by Liu Chi (刘基); the other was the Hui Hui Li (回回历), the work of Ouigour (Arab) mathematicians directed by Cheng A-Li (郑阿里). By 1595, a useful work called *Sheng Shou Wan Nien Li* (圣寿万年历), a complete treatise on calculation of times, with a so-called perpetual calendar and a compendium of all previous Chinese writings on the subject, was prepared by Chu Tsai-Yu (朱载育).[27] This again proved inaccurate.

The Jesuits   Summing up the unsatisfactory position of the calendrical history since the fourteenth century, Dr Hu Shih (胡适博士) said that there was a fierce controversy amongst the scholars which dragged on until the seventeenth century, when the Jesuits, trained in the scientific knowledge of Europe of the sixteenth century and the use of the latest mechanical devices, came to China to spread the Christian faith.[28]

One of their leaders, Matteo Ricci (Italian), who had learnt calendrical calculations from Christopher Clavius, principal author of the Gregorian Calendar, died in 1610. In his wake came James Rho (Italian), who took charge of the calendrical reforms from 1629 onwards, and Adam Schall, a German Jesuit skilled in astronomy, who was made President of the Astronomical Board (1654–1666) when the youthful K'ang-Hsi (康熙) mounted the throne, and in that capacity was entrusted to correct the calendar, which he did.[29]

This Jesuit-revised calendar was promulgated as the imperial calendar, and became the official calendar of China until its abolition in 1912 by the Republic of China, which adopted the Gregorian Calendar.[30] Another ban on the luni-solar calendar was inposed by the Nationalist Government of China in 1927, but it continued to be the calendar of the people and, as a compromise,

25. CR, vol. iv, 1836, p. 3.
26. 元史纪事本末，陈邦瞻，商务 (n.d.), ch. 7, pp. 105–110; Wylie, (Scientific section), pp. 1–20; and Parker, p. 301.
27. Wieger, p. 249.
28. Hu Shih, pp. 28–30.
29. Cronin, pp. 230-232, 276; Gowan & Hall, p. 190; Needham, vol. iii, p. 444 fn.g.; and Nourse, p. 190. There was a tendency for some nineteenth-century sinologues to ascribe the revision of the calendar to Fr. Verbiest, a successor of Adam Schall to the presidency of the Astronomical Board. (See, for example, Parker, p. 306; and S.W. Williams, vol. ii, p. 298.)
30. Hu Shih, p. 29, asserts that the Jesuit-revised calendar was promulgated in 1643 as the imperial calendar of the Ming empire. Whether it was the Ming emperor or Emperor K'ang Hsi who accepted the Jesuit-revised calendar, it must be stressed that the acceptance of the calendar is not derogatory to the calendrical history of China as a whole. "Even in the West, with all its mathematical development," declares Soothill, *Hall of Light*, p. 56, "it was not until AD 1582 that the Gregorian Calendar was adopted in Western Europe, and the Russians until 1917 remained 13 days behind in the solar year." And Goodrich, p. 47, observes in effect that the Chinese had noted the sunspots with some regularity since 28 BC, whilst Galileo, the first European scientist to discover them, published his work only in 1613.

A secondary altar in a temple in Tanjong Tokong, Penang. Note the forked divining sticks, or hooki, whose heads are shaped to resemble a dragon or snake. The diviner traces characters in a sandbox and this enables him to communicate with the spirit world. The snake's head attached to hempen cord is an exorcism whip intended to drive out evil spirits.

its name was changed to *Nung Li* (农历), the "farmers' calendar". Even the iconoclastic Communist regime recognized the importance of the *Nung Li* for the peasantry, for in October, 1950, the Central People's Government of the Chinese People's Republic declared that it would henceforth issue the calendar with suitable scientific information and instructions to the farmers.[31]

It is the pre-Republic Jesuit-revised calendar that has become the unofficial almanac of a vast number of non-Christian and non-Muslim Malaysians of Chinese origin from the time of their migration to the Malay Peninsula and its neighbouring regions. This large section of the Malaysians consists mainly of the *Baba-and-Nonya* class and the non-English-speaking and, often, the English-speaking groups in the Chinese quarter of the city, in the rural and coastal (especially fishing) villages, in the mining and quarry lands, in small plantations and estates in the hill areas. These calendar-users, both English-speaking and non-English-speaking, may broadly be classified under the three main cross-sections represented by Chinese associations or clubs: (i) the territorial associations, (ii) the clan (of the same surname) associations and (iii) the professional or occupational guilds — all of which employ the calendar in one way or another for festival celebrations and other purposes.

Traditions in Malaysia The calendar in use in Malaysia generally falls into three main categories. The first category is printed in daily sheets, in English and Chinese, giving the days of the week and the lunar and solar dates, often announcing — on appropriate dates — the "Twenty-Four Festivals". The second category is printed in monthly sheets, in English and Chinese,

31. Soothill, *Hall of Light*, p. 236.

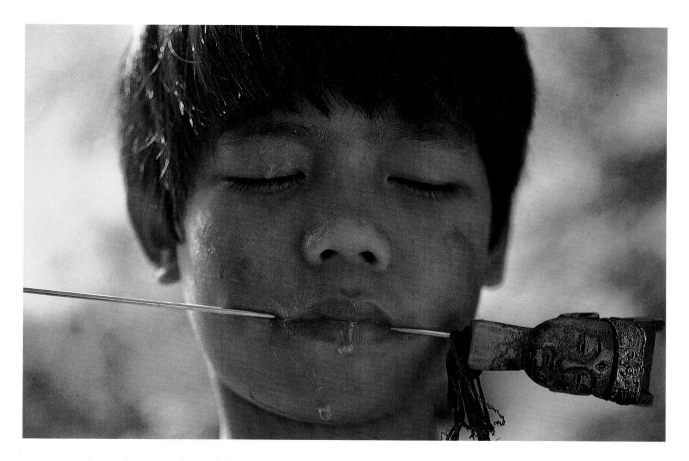

giving in tabular form the days of the week and the lunar and solar dates, with prominence to race days in Malaysia, and also important festive events like the Ch'ing Ming (清明). The third category is the annotated annual almanac, called in Cantonese the T'ung Sing, the "Sacred Almanac", printed in the Chinese language, which is imported from Hong Kong. This is a bumper almanac containing a wide range of information relating to the whole year's festivals, the different arts of divination, lucky and unlucky days in the lunar dates, weather forecasts, guidance to learning Chinese characters and many Chinese maxims, and is a sort of "bible" to many Malaysians of the old school of thought.[32]

The bumper almanac may correctly be said to have a bearing on the life of a vast section of Malaysian Chinese from the cradle to the grave. This is attested by the celebration of festivals to be discussed in Parts II and III. Besides that, there are other features and events which affect the daily life of this people. At birth, the hour (reckoned in the double-hour sense), the day, the month and the lunar year of a child are recorded and given to a fate-calculator or fortune-teller for the choice of a suitable name and, often, preparation of a horoscope even in later life. This is evident from an announcement on 10th October, 1964, in the advertisement column of the Nanyang Siang Pau (南洋商报), Singapore, by a Chinese Buddhist priest from Thailand that he would read a client's horoscope on being supplied his "hour, date, month and year of birth", and a written horoscope would be drawn up and forwarded to the client through the mail upon payment of a fee of $2.[33] In a proposed marriage, the hour, the day and the year of birth of both parties are studied to find out their congruity or otherwise; and, if congruous, a propitious day and hour are chosen

An eight-year-old divining youth offers his body for possession by a specifically invited patron spirit during a celebration of the birthday of Kuan Kong, God of War and Literature. The boy maintained his trance state for three hours.

32. JMBRAS, Topley, "Paper Charms", p. 64. Topley affirms that a copy of an almanac, which she calls a "book of esoteric information, invaluable in matters of worship", is found in most Chinese households.
33. See also 南洋, 24th October, 1964, in which a fate-calculator announces that if a client forgets his hour, date and year of birth, he may supply particulars of his [approximate] age, height and weight for divination.

for the pre-nuptial rituals (such as date of engagement and time for hair-combing ceremony on the eve of the wedding), for the wedding day and propitious timing for the post-nuptial ceremonies. And upon death, propitious days and hours are selected for the pre-burial, funeral and post-burial ceremonies. A very important point is the appropriate time (or exact timing) for lowering a coffin into the pit at the graveyard. Furthermore, persons whose horoscopes are not congruous with the day and the hour of this and other rituals at the graveyard generally turn their eyes away.[34]

In the observance of the annual festivals, the double-hours play an important role too. For example, in the Dragon Year (1964), the propitious time for sacrificial offerings to deities on New Year's Day was given separately: the God of Happiness (喜神) and the God of Rank (贵神) should be worshipped at the Ch'ou hour (1.00 a.m. — 3.00 a.m.), and the T'ien Kuan (天官, Lord of Heaven) at the Yin hour (3.00 a.m. — 5.00 a.m.).[35] To the religious devotees, the choice of the double-hours for making sacrificial offerings to the deities throughout the year is a serious matter.

As we have shown earlier, the ancient sixty-day calendar was divided into six ten-day units, called Hsun. The word *hsun* is familiar to all who read the Chinese language, for it is still used in Chinese books and newspapers published in China and abroad, including Malaysia, to connote a period of ten days. The expressions *shang hsun* (上旬), *chung hsun* (中旬) and *hsia hsun* (下旬) are daily seen in newspapers to signify respectively the 1st day to the 10th day, the 11th day to the 20th day, and the 21st day to the last day of the month, lunar or solar, as the case may be.

Irrational Beliefs When, for no apparent reasons, a boisterous din is created in the China Town area on a serene night, it may well be a lunar eclipse, and boys and girls and even adults and grandpas make a concerted effort to "save the moon from being devoured by some monster" by beating drums, old tin-cans, kettles and pans — an old traditional belief from China. The tradition was so widespread in mediaeval China that even Buddhist monks — whether they did seriously believe the "moon being devoured" or not we don't know — took part in trying to scare off the supposed monster. This is evident from the Japanese Buddhist monk's book, *Ennin's Diary*, being the record of a pilgrimage to China in the T'ang dynasty: "On the 15th day of the 10th Moon (in AD 839), there was an eclipse of the moon in the middle of the night. The masters in the cloister all went out and cried out and struck boards. At 3 a.m. the moon gradually brightened."[36]

S. Wells Williams recounted in his well-known book a total eclipse of the moon which occurred during a festival at Canton. In order to come to the rescue of the silver disc, the entire populace joined in creating the loudest possible noise, including the discharge of fire-crackers and firing a fusillade from guns.[37] If an eclipse were to occur on New Year's Day, it would be interpreted as an impending national disaster, such as the change of a sovereign or of the dynasty itself, and everything possible was to be done to avert such a disaster. This may be gathered from an imperial decree dated 3rd September, 1897:

"According to the *Ch'un-ch'iu* (春秋 , the Spring and Autumn Annals) it has been stated that an eclipse of the sun on

34. In China, such guests are "dismissed" at a convenient place some distance away, for their immediate presence may have a "bad influence on the fate of the dead". (See Crane, p. 208.)
35. *The Chinese Almanac* (天宝楼), Hong Kong, 1964.
36. Reischauer, *Ennin's Diary*, p. 150.
37. S.W. Williams, vol. i, p. 819.

the first day of the year betokens an impending calamity, hence the sovereigns of every dynasty which has preceded us have always made it a point, whenever an eclipse of the sun is prognosticated, to undergo self-abasement and humble themselves before Heaven in order to avert the wrath from above . . . . . Now, according to the Board of Astronomy, the first day of the 24th year of our reign (22nd January, 1898) there will be yet another eclipse of the sun. We are filled with foreboding at this news and hasten to seek within ourselves for sins which may have thus brought the wrath of high Heaven upon the land. We further command that the ceremonies of congratulation usually held on New Year's Day in the Tai-ho Throne-hall (太和殿) be curtailed and only ordinary obeisances be made, the place being changed to the Ch'ien-tsing Throne-hall (乾清宫) instead of in the Tai-ho Throne-hall. The banquet usually given to Imperial clansmen on New Year's Day must also be stopped, and when the eclipse occurs let all the members of the Court wear sober garments, and assemble in the inner Palace before the altar set up to Heaven to pray for forbearance and mercy to the country at large."[38]

But it should not be assumed, because of the irrational beliefs about the eclipse, that astronomical science in China was backward. The well-known scholar Ku Yen-Wu (顾炎武), writing in the *Jih Chih Lu* (日知录) in about 1695, affirmed that Chinese astronomers had known that "a solar eclipse is caused by the moon obscuring the sun and that a lunar eclipse is caused by the earth obscuring the moon" long before the advent of Western astronomy into China.[39] And the result of modern research confirms that the correct theory on eclipse was widely held in China as far back as Wang Ch'ung's (王充) time in about AD 80.[40]

Divinations   According to the *I Wen Chih* (艺文志) the traditional arts of divination are classified under six categories, three of which are connected with the calendar. One of these three categories, commonly used in Malaysia, is the application of the theory of the Five Elements in deciding a name for a child and forecasting a man's fortune. One theory says that "natural and human events are under the control of that element which happens to be in the ascendancy, but when its cycle is finished and it declines, it is followed by the next force in the series that can overcome it, and which, in its turn, flourishes and has its cycle. Wood can overcome earth; metal can overcome wood; fire, metal; water, fire; and earth, water again; so that there is an endless cycle of elements."[41] How the Malaysian fate-calculators apply this or other theories — there are many books on astrology and divination, such as the *Wu-Hsing Ta-I* (五行大义), the book on "Prognostication based on the Principles of the Five Elements" — is a "trade secret", which we have not been able to fathom. We know that they use the stem-branch combination of the day, month and year of birth and the double-hours — called *pa tzu* (八字), the "eight characters" — as the basis of reading a horoscope or forecasting a man's future. We also know that, in coining a child's name, the word composed of one of the radicals for fire, wood, metal, water and earth is invariably recommended if on the child's birth he lacks this particular element. If a baby was born at a time without the water element, his personal name would be chosen from a number of appropriate characters combining the radical *shui* (水 , water). One of these popular

38. MCM, vol. iv, no. 10, 4th March, 1905, p. 191. See Siren, vol. i, pp. 11 & 14, in which it is stated that the Tai-ho Throne-hall was normally used for great ceremonies on Chinese New Year's Day, the day of the winter solstice and the emperor's birthday, and that the Ch'ien-tsing Throne-hall normally served as an audience hall as well as a place for great ceremonies and festivals.
39. 日知录，顾炎武，vol. x, p. 4, in 万有，上海商务，October 1929.
40. Needham, vol. iii, pp. 410, 411, 413.
41. Fung Yu-Lan, vol. i, pp. 26, 162.

characters is *chiang* (江, river), e.g. the name of a former proprietor and editor of the *Straits Echo*, Penang, was Lim Cheng-Kung (Lin Ch'ing *Chiang*, (林清江), meaning "The River of Purity".

Traditional Physicians   To the traditional Chinese physicians, tolerated in Malaysia, the Yin and the Yang principles and the Five Elements are two of the important doctrines which they apply in diagnosing their patient's sickness. Briefly, some of the organs of the body, such as the abdomen, the lungs and kidneys, are Yin; whilst others, such as the heart and the liver, are Yang. The Yin and Yang must harmonize to maintain sound health. If there is an excess of Yang, it results in fever; similarly, if there is an excess of Yin, it results in chills. Even some drugs are classified under Yin and Yang. The Five Elements, earth, wood, fire, metal and water, correspond respectively to spleen, liver, heart, lungs and kidneys. The heart communicates with the tongue; liver, eyes; spleen, mouth; lungs, nose; kidneys, ears. If a proper proportion of these elements is maintained, good health is sustained; otherwise sickness ensues.[42] Explaining the *feng chi* (风疾 , sickness caused by wind), another source adds: "There are six heavenly influences, which descend and produce the five tastes, go forth in the five colours, and are verified in the five notes; but when they are in excess they produce the six diseases. Those six influences are denominated by the Yin, the Yang, wind, rain, obscurity, and brightness . . . . . When any of them is in excess, there ensues calamity . . . . . (An excess of) wind (leads) to disease of the extremities."[43]

Musical Notations   It has been pointed out earlier that the ancient five Chinese basic musical notes originated from the Five Elements. These five notes are Kung (宫), Shang (商), Chiao (角), Chi (徵) and Yu (羽), corresponding to C D E G A of Western notation. As the Five Li (also originated from the Five Elements) were laid down for the regulation of human conduct, so the function of the Pentagonal notes was to regulate human emotions. Briefly, Li (礼, propriety) and Yueh (乐, music) are two of the fundamentals of Chinese culture. The basic idea of Li lies in orderliness, whilst that of Yueh in harmony. The ancient Chinese, who composed music and laid down rules relating to rites and propriety, were directing their efforts towards the achievement of orderliness and harmony in order to produce good and beauty in the life of man.[44] An inquiry from a Malaysian flute-player of a traditional theatrical performance staged at the Ghosts' Festival brought forth an almost indignant reply: "Yes, we are aware of the five basic musical notes. We believe that the traditional music and the appropriate dramatic story on a stage do bring peace and prosperity to the realm. Did you not know that an ancient flute-player even summoned the phoenixes with his music? People of this generation who find pleasure in the Western cha-cha-cha and the monkey dance will never understand us — 'tis a pity indeed." Our flute-player was serious and he was alluding to Hsiao Shih (萧史) of the sixth century BC, whose instrument, accompanied by the singing of his wife Lung Yu (弄玉), is traditionally said to have caused phoenixes to come down from Heaven. There is a T'ang legend which lends weight to our flute-player's pride, for Ming Huang (唐明皇) is said to have played his flute to reproduce the melody which he had heard in the palace of the moon. The tune

This actor of the Lau Chet Kee Hiang Tiechiu wayang *troupe has spent the past sixty years as a strolling player, after receiving his early training in China. He still dreams of the day he will return to his native village.*

42. Wong & Wu, pp. 19–20. However, there seems to be some disagreement on the Yin and the Tang classification of the five internal organs. For instance, 高诱 , the commentator of 淮南子 , ch. 7, p. 99 in 诸子 , vol. vii, 北京中华 , 1954, asserts the belly is Yang and the heart is Yin and Yang.
43. *Tso-Chuan Chu-Su* (11. 41. 11b; tr. Legge, cited by Solomon, p. 12).
44. Couling, pp. 183–184; Chang Chi-Yun, pp. 9, 10; and CSA, Kluenter, pp. 49–59, in which it is declared that the five-toned scale of Chinese music at the present time corresponds to the Western notation d, e, f#, g#, a# (p. 55).

was written down by his musicians. Tradition says that this tune was a prelude to the inauguration of the musical play. With this as the genesis, plays and theatre to some Chinese are "not merely amusements but contain supernatural elements." This concept of supernatural elements was well demonstrated in a stage show relating to Pao Kung (包公), the famous incorrupt and impartial judge who was often aided by unseen agents to solve mysterious crimes. In the course of the play, an actor who enacted the role of Pao Kung became inexplicably possessed of occult power, and, in this state of possession, made vivid allusions to an actual murder that had occurred in a nearby village. Whereupon the curious audience went over to that village to investigate. In consequence, the murder was discovered and the culprit eventually brought to justice.[45]

Flavours in Food   If there be only one kind of sound, says an historian of the ancient records, there can be no music no matter how often the sound be repeated. Likewise, if there be only one taste, there would be no satisfaction. Therefore, if salt be added to what was salty, there could be no production of anything new. But if salt was added to what was sour, the resulting flavour would be new, and this harmony would result in new productions. As the judicious blending of the Five Elements produces harmony, so the clever blending of the five flavours produces palatable dishes. Illustrating this principle by means of soup, Yen Tzu (颜子), a celebrated disciple of Confucius, once explained: "You have the water and fire, vinegar, pickle, salt and plums, with which to cook fish. It is made to boil by the firewood, and then the cook mixes the ingredients, harmoniously equalizing the several flavours, so as to supply whatever is deficient and carry off whatever is in excess. Then the master eats, and his mind is made equable."[46] It is because Malaysian chefs have learnt the technique of mixing the five contrasting flavours that their cooking is amongst the best in the world, which has evoked appreciation from such connoisseurs at the Rt. Hon. Malcolm MacDonald, one-time British Commissioner-General for Southeast Asia, who declares that to eat Chinese food is to enjoy one of the most delicious of worldly pleasures. "Were I a skilled man of letters," he adds, "I would write a volume about it, and at every line of every page the reader's mouth would water. I would describe in detail the odd recipes and astonishing ingredients, the singular meats and unprecedented sauces, the mysterious appearances and seductive flavours of each dish."[47]

Popularity of the Calendar   To the pious vegetarians — and their name is legion — who take maigre food on specific days in the lunar month, the Chinese calendar is their invaluable guide. Swimmers, who are desirous of knowing the tides beforehand, seek guidance from the same calendar without reference to the daily tide-table reported in some newspapers; whilst every conservative householder knows from memory that during the *Ch'ing Ming* season there is always drizzling weather, and that during the *Kiu Ong Yiah* festival (九皇爷诞 (九皇大帝)) the weather is often inclement for a stretch of many days. Experienced Chinese mariners and fishermen are greatly helped by the new moon and the full moon in navigation and in the fishing enterprise; whilst connoisseurs of crabs — in Penang, at least — who relish the crab's

45. C.A.S. Williams, p. 191; and Eberhard, pp. 99–102.
46. Fung Yu-Lan, vol. i, pp. 35, 36.
47. MacDonald, pp. 337–338.

roe are confident that the best crab's roe comes on or about the 1st day and on or about the 15th day of the lunar month.

On one occasion when the writer was serving as a Chinese Affairs Officer, an *amah* who had a wage dispute with her employer came to the Chinese Secretariat to make a complaint insisting that she be paid in accordance with the lunar months, because her employer had agreed to let her off duty only on the 1st and 15th days of the lunar calendar. On the 1st and the 15th, *amahs* usually meet at the *amah's* "lodge" (association) for gossip and other private business transactions such as subscribing to, and bidding for, a tontine. In about 1950, the *amah* of an R.A.F. family in Singapore, in addition to her customary fortnightly day off, got one day's leave on the 7th day of the 7th Moon, celebrated the Ghosts' Festival with her *Tuan* and *Mem* on the 15th, obtained four days' leave at the Moon Festival, squeezed another day off on the 9th day of the 9th Moon and four days' holiday for the Chinese New Year, to the amusement as well as the discomfiture of Mrs Britton, her employer.[48]

A careful analysis shows that the life and being of all traditional associations is insuperably linked up with the luni-solar calendar, for in addition to the observance of the winter solstice (冬至 , 22nd December), the clan and the territorial associations also hold celebrations during the Spring Sacrificial Festival (春祭) and the Autumnal Sacrificial Festival (秋祭) connected with the Twenty-four Solar Terms — a traditional practice from China. It suffices to quote two examples. On the 15th day of the 3rd Moon (26th April) in 1964, the Shun Te Territorial Association (順德会馆), Penang, celebrated the Spring Sacrificial Festival with an interesting programme. At noon, representatives of the association went up to the Mount Erskine Cemetery to pay obeisance to the dead. At two o'clock in the afternoon, prizes and awards were distributed to deserving students — the children of members — at the association's premises at Love Lane. In the evening, a dinner was held, and the convivial gathering was enlivened by the association's own lion dance troupers. On the 13th day of the 9th Moon (18th October) in 1964, the Wu Clansmen Association (伍氏公所) of Singapore celebrated the Autumnal Sacrificial Festival. In the forenoon, representatives went up to the Chinese cemetery at Kampong Pek San Teng (碧山亭), off Thomson Road, to do homage to the Wu ancestors, and had a picnic lunch on the spot. In the evening the members partook of delicious Chinese food at a restaurant in the New World on a subscription basis.[49]

Last but not least are the twelve animal symbols. As to a vast number of Malaysians these animal symbols are easier to remember than the numerals, they become part and parcel of the Chinese way of life. This traditional mode of age calculation has often been challenged. But since each of the different animal symbols is separated by a period of twelve years, advocates of the system maintain that the appearance of a person is a decisive factor in pin-pointing his exact age. So it is the established custom in Malaysia that when two Malaysians inquire about each other's age, they invariably (if they converse in Chinese) reply: "Hare Year" or "Sheep Year" — which tradition was widely observed in China in the Yuan period (AD 1206–1367).[50] The history of these animals is dealt with *in extenso* in the ensuing chapter.

48. Britton, pp. 162–177.
49. 星槟 , 17th April, 1964; and 南洋 , 8th October, 1964.
50. 霞外攟屑 , 平步青 in 明清笔记丛书 , 中华 , Shanghai, November 1959, vol. ii, ch. 5, p. 277.

合胜貿易公司
HUP SANG TRADING CO.

新加坡小坡里士加律六十七號（即惹蘭勿刹）

67, DESKER ROAD, SINGAPORE 0820. TEL: 2965674 & 2946670

新加坡德福二巷門牌六號

6, DEFU LANE 2, SINGAPORE 1953. TEL: 2827561 & 2821811

龍鳳禮燭　紅白臘燭　各色雪梨　名香經營　自造

各種白臘　金銀紙料　諸君光顧　一律歡迎

歲次丙寅年
公曆一九八六年
1986

太歲姓陳名泰
大利東西不利北方

SINGAPORE PUBLIC HOLIDAYS 1986

New Year's Day	1st January, Wednesday
Chinese New Year	9th February, Sunday
	10th February, Monday
	11th February, Tuesday
Good Friday	28th March, Friday
Labour Day	1st May, Thursday
Vesak Day	23rd May, Friday
*Hari Raya Puasa	9th June, Monday
National Day	9th August, Saturday
*Hari Raya Haji	16th August, Saturday
+Deepavali	1st November, Saturday
Christmas Day	25th December, Thursday

一九八六年公共假期

陽曆新年	一月一日	（星期三）
農曆新年	二月九日	（星期日）
	二月十日	（星期一）
	二月十一日	（星期二）
復活節	三月廿八日	（星期五）
勞動節	五月一日	（星期四）
衛塞節	五月廿三日	（星期五）
開齋節	六月九日	（星期一）
國慶節	八月九日	（星期六）
哈芝節	八月十六日	（星期六）
屠妖節	十一月一日	（星期六）
聖誕節	十二月廿五日	（星期四）

CHAPTER 2:
The Twelve
Animal Symbols

A s we have indicated in the previous chapter, the twelve
Earthly Branches were associated with the twelve equal
double-hours as early as the late Chou, and it is believed
by one authority that the twelve animal symbols were created in
the sixth century BC to correspond to the Earthly Branches to
designate the twelve double-hours as well as the years in the
Sexagenary Cycle. In order to facilitate the explanation of the
origin of the animal symbols, we append below a chart, showing
the twelve branches, the animal symbols and the double-hours:

The Earthly Branches	Animal Symbols	The Double-Hours
1. Tzu	Rat	11 p.m.– 1 a.m.
2. Ch'ou	Ox	1 a.m.– 3 a.m.
3. Yin	Tiger	3 a.m.– 5 a.m.
4. Mao	Hare	5 a.m.– 7 a.m.
5. Ch'en	Dragon	7 a.m.– 9 a.m.
6. Ssu	Snake	9 a.m.–11 a.m.
7. Wu	Horse	11 a.m.– 1 p.m.
8. Wei	Sheep	1 p.m.– 3 p.m.
9. Shen	Monkey	3 p.m.– 5 p.m.
10. Yu	Cock	5 p.m.– 7 p.m.
11. Hsü	Dog	7 p.m.– 9 p.m.
12. Hai	Pig	9 p.m.–11 p.m.

The above chart is based on the table given in the *Sources of
Chinese Tradition* which observes, *inter alia*, that at least by Han
times these twelve branches had become associated with the twelve
animal symbols to designate the double-hours of the day and the
years of the Sexagenary Cycle.[1]

*Traditional lunar calendars like this are
found in homes and offices throughout
Malaysia and Singapore. Read right to
left, from the first month to the twelfth,
Western dates on the left, Chinese moon
days on the right.*

1. de Bary, Chan & Watson, pp. 21–22. [In
Singapore, the hare is more commonly referred to
as the rabbit, the sheep as the goat, and the cock as
the rooster.]

Origin of Animal Symbols   The next step is to find out the why-and-wherefore and the manner in which the twelve animals were selected. The answer to these questions is found in the Chinese book *Li Hai Chi* (蠡海集), written in the Sung dynasty (960–1126), which explains:

"There are ten Heavenly Stems and twelve Earthly Branches. The Stems are not correlated to the Animal Symbols but the Branches are, because Heaven issues the ethers which make the Earth. Men are associated with the Animal Symbols and the Branches and not the Stems because the father confers the essence of life, which takes form in the mother of whom a child is born. The child assumes his father's surname because the essence of his life originates from the father."[2]

The *Li Hai Chi* then goes on to show that the animal symbols were created from the double-hours represented by the twelve Earthly Branches in the following manner.

The first double-hour (11.00 p.m.–1.00 a.m.) is designated Tzu. During this period the power of Yin is at its zenith — stillness, the lowest ebb, hidden and dark. For this reason, the rat is associated with this Yin power, the rat being able to conceal its whereabouts. Opposite to the Tzu is the Wu double-hour (11.00 a.m.–1.00 p.m.), which represents the power of the Yang at its height — bright light, ease of movement, firm and robust. For this reason, the horse is associated with this Yang power, the horse being swift and fast.

The second double-hour (1.00 a.m.–3.00 a.m.) is designated Ch'ou. During this period of the Yin power, parents tend their babies with kindness and love, such as cooing and feeding the crying baby. The ox is associated with the Ch'ou, because cows are traditionally noted for licking their calves with parental tenderness. Contrasting the Ch'ou is the Wei (1.00 p.m.–3.00p.m.), the time for the rising Yang power and the observance of propriety. The sheep is associated with the Wei, because when a lamb sucks its mother's milk, its knees are bent in a kneeling position — a sign of decorum and filial piety.

The third double-hour (3.00 a.m.–5.00 a.m.) is designated Yin, the beginning of dawn or daybreak. It is the time when the power of Yang gains supremacy and becomes intense. The tiger is associated with the Yang power, because this animal is by nature ferocious. In diametrical opposition is the Shen (3.00 p.m.–5.00 p.m.), the time when the power of Yin begins to gain the upper hand, implying artifice. The monkey is associated with the Yin power because it is by nature crafty or cunning.

The Mao (5.00 a.m.–7.00 a.m.) and the Yu (5.00 p.m.–7.00 p.m.) are the opening periods of the sun and the moon, and the two animals become one — the hare being associated with Mao and the fowl with Yu. The doe licks the buck's hair, and through this sensitive touch conceives without intercourse, whilst the cock rides on the back of the hen, and contact is established without feeling.

During the period of Ch'en (7.00 a.m.–9.00 a.m.) and the period of Ssu (9.00 a.m.–11.00 a.m.), the power of the Yang rises and makes transformations. The dragon is at its best in transformation, with the snake taking the second place. The dragon and the snake are associated with the Ch'en and the Ssu respectively, because both are creatures capable of transformation.

During the period Hsü (7.00 p.m.–9.00 p.m.) and the period

2.   蠡海集・王逵 in 丛书・商务・December 1939, p. 19.

Hai (9.00 p.m.–11.00 p.m.), the power of the Yin is declining and should be safeguarded. For this duty of watchfulness, the dog is pre-eminent, with the pig taking the second place. The dog and the pig are calm creatures, hence their associations with the Hsü and the Hai respectively.[3]

It is likely that the choice of these animals was founded on the Yin and the Yang contrast, or, as Richard Wilhelm has put it, the "world of opposites". Perhaps a better phrase is the "diametric symmetry" used by Leopold de Saussure in delineating the twenty-eight zodiac signs. Whatever you may choose to call it, the "opposite" principles become abundantly clear when the list of animal symbols is re-grouped under the Yin and Yang columns:

Yin		**Yang**	
Rat	(11 p.m.–1 a.m.)	Horse	(11 a.m.–1 p.m.)
Ox	(1 a.m.–3 a.m.)	Sheep	(1 p.m.–3 p.m.)
Monkey	(3 p.m.–5 p.m.)	Tiger	(3 a.m.–5 a.m.)
Hare	(5 a.m.–7 a.m.)	Cock	(5 p.m.–7 p.m.)
Dog	(7 p.m.–9 p.m.)	Dragon	(7 a.m.–9 a.m.)
Pig	(9 p.m.–11 p.m.)	Snake	(9 a.m.–11 a.m.)

Yin and Yang Principles Why did the creator of the animal symbols strive to establish the Yin and the Yang symmetry? The answer, briefly, is that the Yin stands for the earth, the moon and the negative or female principle of shade, cold and inactivity; whilst the Yang stands for heaven, the sun and the positive or male principle of light, warmth and activity; and that all things in the universe are produced by the harmonious interaction of these two opposite principles (or forces).

At the beginning, there was oneness. According to Lao Tzu (老子), Tao (道, the Way) produced oneness. And oneness produced duality (the Yin and the Yang). Duality evolved into trinity (i.e. the Yin, the Yang and the Harmony arising from the interplay or interaction of these two forces). Trinity evolved into ten thousand (all) things, and the mode of all things is determined by the interaction of Yin and Yang. It is on the blending of the forces (of the Yin and the Yang) that their harmony depends.[4]

Elsewhere, it is stated that all that is produced by Tao is good. However, this goodness is not necessarily manifest to all and sundry, for Tao shows itself in different lights to people of different natures. The kind-hearted man who loves his fellow citizen discovers the Tao of cosmic events and calls it supreme kindness — "God is love". The wise man sees wisdom in Tao and calls it supreme wisdom. But the common the people who are borne and nourished by Tao do not realize it.[5] In fact, the workings of Tao are seen all through the universe — in the motions of the sun, the moon and the stars; the regularity of the seasons; the beautiful spring, the balmy summer, the harvesting autumn and the snowy winter; the cheerful twilight dawn and the scenic twilight sunset; and in the harmony of light and shade. That's the way of Tao, the beauty and rhythm of nature.

What applies to the cosmos also applies to men, for the universe is a macrocosm, and man, a microcosm. This has been well explained in the *Huai-Nan Tzu* (淮南子), written in the Former Han dynasty in the second century BC. According to this book, the spiritual component of man is received from Heaven, whilst his form and body are drawn from Earth. Heaven is round and

3. 蠡海集，王逵 in 丛书，商务，December 1939, p. 20.
4. 老子·ch. 42, pp. 26–27, in 诸子 op. cit., vol. iii. The English rendition is based on Fung Yu-Lan, vol. i, p. 178.
5. Wilhelm, *I-Ching*, vol. i, p. 321.

A brass dragon from a temple urn.

Earth is square, so a man's head is round and his foot square. There are four seasons, Five Elements, nine divisions of space and three hundred and sixty days. Man likewise has four limbs, five viscera, nine orifices, and three hundred and sixty joints. Heaven has wind, rain, cold and heat, and man likewise has (the qualities of) accepting and giving, joy and anger. Therefore, the gall corresponds to clouds, the lungs to vapour, the spleen to wind, the kidneys to rain, and the liver to thunder. Thus man forms a trinity with Heaven and Earth, and his mind is the master.[6]

In short, as there is beauty and rhythm in nature through the harmonious blending of the two opposite principles of Yin and Yang, there is the same beauty and rhythm in the life of man and other creatures. The way or course of Tao is eternal good, and if man acted in conformity with it there would be concord and happiness; and if he ignored it and acted in violation, then there would be discord and misfortune, sooner or later.

There is a secondary reason for the creator of the twelve animal symbols to establish the Yin and Yang rhythm. The calendar was calculated on the movements of the heavenly bodies, with Yang representing heaven and the sun and Yin representing

6. 淮南子（精神训）·ch. 7, p. 100, in 诸子 *op. cit.*, vol. vii. The English rendition is based on Fung Yu-Lan, vol. i, pp. 398–399.

the earth and the moon, and the ten characters of the T'ien Kan and the twelve characters of the Ti Chih were also chosen on the Yin and Yang principles.[7] It was, therefore, a logical sequel for the creator to select the animals in terms of Yin and Yang. It is true this selection is not invulnerable to criticism. For instance, we have noticed from other sources that the dog is positively a Yang animal;[8] and that from the *Li Hai Chi* itself the monkey is both Yin and Yang, because it gambols in daylight as well as at night.[9] In our view, to apply such criticism is not fair, because the selection of these two animals was made purely on the basis of the hours of the night and not on the attributes of the animal *per se*.

Similarly, when Wang Ch'ung (AD 27–c.97), the celebrated philosopher and critic, poked fun at the animals from the standpoint of the Five Elements, i.e. metal, wood, water, fire and earth, his criticism is branded by J.J.M. de Groot as "idle play with the cycles and Elements". A few examples of Wang Ch'ung's "idle play" suffice. The Wu hours which correspond to the horse are associated with the Fire element, whilst the Tzu hours which correspond to the rat are associated with the Water element. The Water element triumphs over the Fire element (because water extinguishes fire) — why then doesn't the rat expel the horse? The Yu hours which correspond to the cock are associated with the Metal element, whilst the Mao hours which correspond to the hare are associated with the Wood element. The Metal element is victorious over the Wood element (because metal is stronger than wood) — why doesn't the cock peck the hare? The Hai hours which correspond to the pig are associated with the Water element, whilst the Wei hours which correspond to the sheep and the Ch'ou hours which correspond to the ox are associated with the Earth element. The Earth element being superior to the Water element, how is it that neither the ox nor the sheep puts the pig to death?[10]

Criticisms apart, it is our view that originally there was no intention to attach any occult or symbolic significance to each of the animals. By inference from the brief reasons stated in the *Li Hai Chi*, at its best, only a few animals could have carried symbolic significance: the tiger being symbolic of ferocity; the sheep of propriety and filial piety; the ox of parental love; the horse of swiftness and endurance; the rat of sneakiness; and the monkey of craftiness.

Down through the ages, however, there have developed independently a number of occult and symbolic meanings invented for divination and other purposes. Some of these meanings have also arisen from anecdotes and stories. We have collected several of these, and some of them are recounted here in the order of the twelve animals for review and discussion.

The Rat   The rat is a Yin creature, with a life-span of three hundred years. When it reaches one hundred years, its colour is changed to white. A white rat is endowed with the power of divination and may forecast a man's luck and ill-luck for a whole year. It can also predict events occurring a thousand miles away. When there is tyrannical rule and the people are oppressed, the white rat manifests itself.[11]

The divining power of an ordinary rat may be gathered from the story relating to Ch'ai Tsai-Yung (柴再用). One day whilst he was seated alone in the guests' hall, a rat suddenly came forward

A tiger deity grips a meat offering in its jaws.

7.   蠡海集，*op. cit.*, p. 23.
8.   严陵方氏，稽燿钧，文曜钧 in 图书，上海中华，vol. 524, ch. 115, pp. 28–29.
9.   蠡海集，*op. cit.*, p. 15.
10.   论衡(物艺篇)，王充 in 诸子 *op. cit.*, vol. vii, pp. 31–32; and de Groot, *Religious System*, vol. iii, bk. i, pp. 987–988. (There are also observations and comments on the animal symbols in the 月令问答 based on the "Five Seasons". See 图书 *op cit.*, vol. 15, ch. 7, pp. 36–37.)
11.   图书，*op. cit.*, vol. 521, ch. 82, p. 51; 抱朴子，葛洪，ch. 3, p. 9 in 诸子 *op cit.*, vol. viii; and 灵征志 in 图书，*op. cit.*, vol. 49, ch. 175, p. 63.

and stood up, as if making a bow to him. Incensed at the antics of the rat, Tsai-Yung called out for his servants, but as no servant responded Tsai-Yung himself got up to chase the rat. At that very moment, a big beam of the hall crashed down on the platform where Tsai-Yung had been seated. But in another instance where a rat had prophesied the death of Wang Chou-Nan (王周南) in the Wei period (AD 220–277), its prediction went wrong and the rat itself perished.[12]

In a story from the famous *Liao Chai* (聊斋), a rat is called loyal because it continued to harass a snake which had devoured another rat; whilst Lu Hsiung, who had been appointed a military official, attributed his success to the auspicious presence of five rats hibernating in the oven of his house. One day Li Szu (李斯), the famous legalist thinker, noticed some rats nibbling the corn in the corridor of a granary, without fear of man or dog, and declared: "Man's perspicacity is unworthy of comparison to that of the rats."[13]

The Ox

The ox was transformed from the essence of a thousand-year-old giant pine tree. It is a Yin creature, possessing split hoofs. When it is sick, its sickness is caused by the ebbing Yin and the rising Yang, and because of this the sickly ox remains in a standing position. As it is a Yin creature, when it rises from the ground the hind legs stand up first; when it lies down the forelegs bend down first.[14]

In olden days the fate of the people depended on rice, and the ox was the king of the *padi*-cultivators. Because of this the nobles did not slaughter the ox without a good cause. In military affairs, an ox was slaughtered as a sacrifice to Heaven. Its hoofs were used for divination: if the two hoofs were scattered about, it was an ill omen; if the two hoofs stayed side by side, it was a good omen.[15]

The ox is a sign of longevity, because Lao Tzu rode a green ox when he passed through the barrier at the mountain, the life-span of a green ox being a thousand years. A man of the feudal state of Sung (宋人) was fond of benevolent and charitable acts, which were carried on for three generations. Then without rhyme or reason the horns of the family's black ox changed colour to white. When Confucius was consulted, he remarked that it was an "auspicious omen".[16]

The Tiger

The tiger is a Yang creature, being born in the 7th month when the Yang (celestial) ethers are formed. As the Yang rises on the 7th, the length of a tiger from head to tail is seven feet, and its stripes are a miscellany of the Yin and the Yang.[17]

Whilst one source says it is the "ruler of wild animals", another calls it the "divine dog". As the chief of all animals, the tiger could attack and devour demons of every description. Experience shows that if a person drank the cooked juice from the tiger's skin and wore the tiger's claws, all evil could be repulsed.[18]

The tiger's span of life is a thousand years; upon reaching the five-hundredth year, the tiger's skin becomes white. A white tiger has black stripes and a tail longer than the body; it does not eat living things, nor does it trample upon grasses. When a ruler is virtuous, the white tiger manifests itself.[19]

A story was told in the Han period that a tiger had sacrificed himself for the gratification of Emperor Ching (汉景帝 , 156–141

12. 太平・小说丛书大观・上海扫叶山房印行・vol. xxxvi, ch. 440, pp. 2, 5.

13. 聊斋・蒲松龄・商务・January 1963, vol. ii, pp. 651–2;稽神录 in 事类 *op cit.*, vol. xii, ch. 90, p. 57; and 史记・李斯传in 子史・上海锦章图书局 1922, vol. vii, ch. 136, p. 21.

14. 嵩高记 and 造权與 in 格致・陈元龙・1735, vol. xvi, ch. 86, p. 1.

15. 王制 and 晋书 *ibid.*, pp. 1, 3.

16. 关中记 *ibid.*, p. 8; and 列子 in 子史 *op. cit.*, vol. vii, ch. 136, p. 21.

17. 文曜钩in图书 *op. cit.*, vol. 520, ch. 61, p. 6.

18. 说文in 事类・*op. cit.*, vol. xii, ch. 88, p. 31; 图书 *op cit.*, vol. 520, ch. 61, p. 8; and 风俗通义・应劭・in 丛书・商务・December 1937, ch. 8, p. 200.

19. 抱朴子in 诸子・*op. cit.*, ch. 3, p. 9; and 陆玑诗疏 in 事类・*op. cit.*, vol. xii, ch. 88, p. 32.

BC). This emperor had a zest for hunting, but was unable to secure any tiger. So he made a grand sacrificial offering to the tiger, after which in a dream a tiger said to him: "As Your Majesty wants to obtain only my skin and claws, I shall die for you to achieve your end." True enough, a tiger was found dead on the next day at the place of sacrifice. His Majesty accordingly ordered the skin and the teeth to be removed. Later, the remaining carcase resumed the life of a tiger.[20]

The Hare   The hare is born of the Yin essence: its life-span is a thousand years. When it attains the five-hundredth year, its hair turns white. It may then transform itself into any object.[21]

This is shown in the story of a certain Mr Sui of Teng-Chou (登州有隋姓者), whose family was exceedingly wealthy. When he died, diviners suggested that he be buried in a certain mound. Upon a hole being drilled into the mound a white hare suddenly sprang out from it. It lay on the rock for a while. Then it transformed itself into a dragon, which plunged into the sea, leaving the mark of the scales and horn of a dragon on the rock.[22]

The white hare is a good omen and brings luck for a thousand years; whilst the red hare is the king of auspicious animals and manifests itself when virtue prevails in the world.[23]

But the ordinary hare is symbolic of crafty foresight, arising from an anecdote of the Warring States period (481–221 BC). Once Fung Huan (冯驩) spoke to Prince Meng Ch'ang (孟尝君): "A wily hare has three exits to its burrow, which enables it to avert any tragedy. Now you've only one exit and are unable to sleep with peace of mind. Shouldn't you provide yourself with two more exits?"[24]

The Dragon   The dragon is a Yang creature.[25] One source says it is the chief of the five kinds of living creatures, i.e. hairy animals such as the tiger, feathered creatures such as the bird, creatures with a carapace such as the tortoise, scaly creatures such as the pangolin, and the naked ones such as man; whilst another source says it is a divine creature, which is capable of transformation, and of rising up to Heaven during the vernal equinox and sinking beneath the river during the autumnal equinox.[26]

It is called the "Monarch of Things", capable of transformation and raising clouds. This was well elaborated by Kuan Tzu (管子), who said "the dragon lives in the water where it acquires the five colours of water and becomes a benevolent spirit. At its own wish, it can reduce its size to that of a silk-worm or caterpillar, or it can increase its dimensions to cover the whole world. If it desires, it can mount the clouds to go up or sink down to the deepest springs . . . . ."[27]

A divine creature, it is a sign of luck if seen by man and monarch. If a ruler is kind and virtuous, the green dragon manifests itself; and if there is calamity in the nation, the azure dragon manifests itself . . . . . When both the green dragon and the azure dragon manifest themselves at the same time, it is an auspicious omen.[28]

Whereas in China the dragon is a friendly and beneficent creature, it is a monstrous creature — a symbol of evil — in the West, where the victories of St Michael and St George over the dragons and their slaying by Siegmund, Sigurd, Arthur and Lancelot were hailed as crowning achievements.[29]

20. 李元独异志in 太平·*op. cit.*, vol. xxxiv, ch. 426, p. 38.
21. 晋书石勒载记in 子史 *op. cit.*, vol. vii, ch. 136, p. 21; and 抱朴子 · *op cit.*, ch. 3 p. 9.
22. 登州府志 in 图书·*op. cit.*, vol. 521, ch. 78, p. 38.
23. 图书· *ibid.*, p. 36; and 瑞应图in 事类·*op. cit.*, ch. 90, p. 56.
24. 战国策in 故事·香港广智书局·ch. 4, p. 236.
25. 朱子in 图书·*op. cit.*, vol. 525, ch. 127, p. 21.
26. 古今怪异集成·周教肃·中华·(n.d.) vol. iii, p. 87; and 山海经in 故事·*op. cit.*, ch. 4, p. 224.
27. 连山易in 图书·*op. cit.*, vol. 525, ch. 127, p. 21; and 管子 ch. 14, p. 237 in 诸子·*op. cit.*, vol. v.
28. 晋书吕光载记in 子史 *op. cit.*, vol. vii, ch. 138, p. 2; and 图书*op. cit.*, vol. 50, ch. 176, p. 1.
29. *JNCBRAS*, Read, p. 21.

Devotees bear an image of Sumo Kong, the Monkey God.

The Snake   The snake is of the same family as the dragon and may contract and expand itself; like the dragon, it is capable of raising clouds and travelling in them.[30] This is well illustrated in a story from the *Liao Chai*. Once a scholar named Fang (房生) and his friend went up to the Ox Hill (牛山) to visit a monastery. When they entered it a fragment of yellow brick suddenly fell from a rafter. As they looked up, they saw a small snake coiling on the rafter. It was as small as an earth-worm. After a while, it expanded into the size of a belt. The two friends were taken aback, but later realised that it was a dragon. So they hastened down the slope. As they were halfway down, they heard a thundrous clap, which caused a tremor in the hills and the valley. The sky was overcast with dark clouds and a huge dragon was rolling thereon.[31]

In the hills there was once a big snake, attired in official robes, and its name was Sheng Ch'ing (升卿). If you called it by its name, it would bring you luck. Generally speaking, the snake is a sign of ill-luck: if it entered a house, the inmates would be afflicted with illness; if you saw it casting off its slough, then it would be an auspicious sign.[32]

In Aesop's fable, a snake is likened to an ungrateful man; whereas in Chinese folklore, gratitude is an attribute of this reptile. Once the Marquis of Sui (隋侯) saw a wounded snake and ordered that medicine be applied to the injury. The snake soon recovered and slithered away. About a year afterwards, the snake carried an "illuminated pearl" in its mouth as a gift to the Marquis. The pearl, about an inch in diameter, was of pure white, and glowed at night as brightly as the moon.[33] It was thereafter called the "Pearl of the Marquis of Sui" (隋侯珠), the "Pearl of the Divine Snake" (灵蛇珠), or the "Bright Moon Pearl" (明月珠).

30. 尔雅 and 张华疏 in 格致 *op. cit.*, vol. xviii, ch. 99, pp. 1, 3.

31. 聊斋 · *op. cit.*, vol. ii, p. 750.

32. 抱朴子 *op. cit.*, ch. 17, p. 79; and 图书 *op. cit.*, vol. 50, ch. 178, p. 13.

33. 搜神记 in 干宝 · ch. 20, p. 2 in 学津 · 张海明辑 · vol. 150.

The Horse The Ch'ien (乾 , Heaven) is horse; it is represented by the horse because the element of Heaven is robust. Another version says the horse comes from the essence of the earth and was born in the 12th Moon, the result of the harmonious blending of the Yin and the Yang. Therefore, man rides the horse and travels far on his mission for the benefit of the world.[34]

The horse is symbolic of stamina, speed and reliability. Hence the horse ridden by Jan-Min (冉闵) was called the Chu Lung (朱龙), the "red dragon" that travelled a thousand Chinese miles in a day; whilst the horse ridden by Ts'in Shu-Pao (秦叔宝) was called Hu Lui Po (忽雷驳), the "sudden thunder beast". The nine horses used by Emperor Wen (汉文帝) of the Han period were so exceptionally fast and reliable that they were called Chiu I (九逸), the "nine leisurely (animals)".[35]

The pride of China is silk, the best fabric in the world. And the best silk came from the horse, according to folklore. In days of yore a man from the state of Shu (蜀人) was kidnapped, but his horse managed to escape. His wife declared in the presence of a crowd:

"If anyone can bring my husband home, I'll give my daughter to him in marriage." Whereupon the horse pranced and galloped away, bringing the missing man home. Thereafter, the horse neighed incessantly until the man found out the cause and said, "The oath was for a man, not a horse." But when the horse could not be appeased, the owner shot it with an arrow and exposed its hide in the courtyard for drying. Then of a sudden, the hide rose up, folded up the maiden and went off. A few days later, the corpse was transformed into silk-worms, which were called Ma T'ou Niang (马头娘), the "horse-head's bride".[36] A slightly

These horses are the mounts of the Generals of the Five Directions. Whenever the generals attend a festival, their horses must be groomed and supplied with fresh grass and water. Once the rituals are over, they will be burned in an au revoir ceremony.

34. 说八卦 and 说题辞 in 图书 *op. cit.*, vol. 522, ch. 101, p. 28 and vol. 520, ch. 90, p. 32.
35. 晋书冉闵载记 in 子史 *op. cit.*, vol. vii, ch. 136, p. 23; 西阳杂组 in 事类 *op. cit.*, vol. xii, ch. 89, p. 47; and 西京杂记 in 子史 ·*op. cit.*, vol. vii, ch. 137, p. 27.
36. 述异记 in 故事 ·*op. cit.*, ch. 4, p. 240.

different version says that the girl and the horse-hide were transformed into silk-worms. The cocoons were extraordinarily big and thick and yielded more silk threads than the normal cocoons. The tree was thereafter called Sang (桑), the "mulberry tree", because Sang rhymes with the word for "death" (丧). From that time onwards, the people competed in the cultivation of mulberry trees.[37]

The Sheep   The sheep is auspicious.[38] Other attributes of the sheep were given by Tung Chung-Shu (董仲舒), who said, "The ram has horns, but they are not used indiscriminately: it is well prepared, but its horns are not rashly used — this indicates chivalry. When the ram is held in captivity, it does not bleat; and when it is slaughtered it does not scream — this signifies heroism. When the lamb sucks its mother's milk, it bends its knees in obeisance — this implies filial piety."[39]

In former days when Kao Ku (高固) was the prime minister of the state of Ch'u (楚相), the sixth state was Canton. One day five rams which carried stalks of *padi* in their mouths appeared to offer luck to Kao Ku. From that time on, Canton was named the "City of Five Rams" (五羊城) — sign of good harvests.[40]

The sheep is symbolic of rank. Once Hsu Ch'ao (许超) dreamt that he had stolen some sheep and was sentenced to imprisonment. His diviner assured him that it was a good omen and that he would become an official of rank in the Ch'eng Yang (城阳侯). True enough, Hsu Ch'ao was promoted to be the Marquis of that city.

Another story tells of the Duke of P'ei (沛公). When he was a minor official, he once dreamt that he was pursuing a sheep and that his quarry had dropped off its horns and its tail. "You'll become a ruler," said his diviner, "for if the horns and the tail of the word 'sheep' (羊) are removed the remaining word becomes *wang* (王), a king or prince."[41]

The Monkey   The monkey is both Yin and Yang.[42] Its life-span is eight hundred years, at the end of which it becomes a baboon. The life-span of a baboon is five hundred years, at the end of which it becomes an ape. The ape's span of life is a thousand years.[43]

Because of this theory, the ancient Chinese applied the terms monkey, baboon and ape synonymously. One version says that the monkey is the "Duke of the Hills" (山公); another version calls it a "Time-reporting Monkey" (报时猿); and yet another version honours the monkey with the epithet of "Tailed Gentleman" (尾君子).[44]

It is symbolic of intelligence, arising from an anecdote during the time of the Three Kingdoms. In this anecdote Teng Chih (邓芝), the well-known archer, found that after being wounded the baboon was wise enough to pull out the arrow-head and apply certain curative leaves to the wound. When this process was repeated a second time, Teng Chih sighed and, throwing his bow and arrows into the stream, declared: "It's I who should perish."[45]

However, it was Master Liu (柳子) who once drew a distinction between the baboon and the monkey, saying that the baboon stands for benevolence, humility, filial love, charity and mutual love, whilst the monkey stands for viciousness, querulousness, selfishness, disorderliness and uncharitableness.[46]

37. 搜神记旧说 · in 图书 *op. cit.*, vol. 522, ch. 102, p. 31.

38. 说文 in 事类 · *op. cit.*, vol. xii, ch. 90, p. 52. The Chinese character 羊 stands for sheep or goat. To make a distinction, the characters 山羊 are used for goat and 绵羊 for sheep.

39. 春秋繁露 in 子史 *op. cit.*, vol. vii, ch. 136, p. 26.

40. 顾微广州记 in 说郛, 郑文宝, 上海文明书局 · 1915, vol. iii, ch. 4, p. 3. This original legend has since been dramatized. Some three hundred years before the Christian era, says this dramatized version, five genii clothed in radiant garments of five different colours, each bearing a straw grain, blessed nine times, arrived at the site of Canton city, riding through the air on five rams. The genii left, and the five rams were believed to have been turned into stone. Hence Canton is called the "City of Rams". (See Edward Lee, p. 6.)

41. 西阳杂俎 and 埤雅广要 in 事类 · *op. cit.*, vol. ix, ch. 59, p. 11.

42. 蠡海集 *op. cit.*, p. 15.

43. 抱朴子 *op. cit.*, ch. 3, p. 15.

44. 赵璘因话录 in 子史 · *op. cit.*, vol. vii, ch. 137, p. 28; 开元 in 图书 *op. cit.*, vol. 522, ch. 86, p. 15; and 陶谷清异录 in 子史 · *op. cit.*, vol. vii, ch. 137, p. 30.

45. 蜀志邓芝传注 in 图书 · *op. cit.*, vol. 522, ch. 86, p. 14.

46. 蜀志邓芝传注 in 图书 · *op. cit.*, vol. 522, ch. 85, p. 11.

The Cock The cock is associated with the "wood" element. The wood was exposed to the sun (Yang) and has taken the shape of a cock.[47]

It is an emblem for warding off evil. On New Year's Day, (the picture of) a cock was drawn upon or hung up on the front door and all evils dreaded its presence.[48] The cock is the transformation of Duke Chu (朱公); hence it is called Chu (祝), meaning harmony and amity amongst the feathered fraternity.[49]

The cock is a time-keeping creature, and when it crows, it does so three times — that is decorum. It crows punctually, rain or shine. Hence the poets compared the cock to a "Gentleman of Unwavering Principles" (不改度之君子). The highest tribute paid to the cock is that it has Wu Te (五德), the "Five Virtues": it wears a comb, indicating civility; its legs bear spurs, signifying military prowess; it fights in front, showing valour; it calls out to its mates to share its food, denoting generosity; and it crows with precision, implying reliability.[50]

Last but not least, its loyalty is demonstrated in a story of the Ming period when a travelling monk, who in 1641 had gone to the town of Nan Kuan (南关市) for donations, was suddenly attacked by a cock. The cock had flown up and alighted on the monk's head, fiercely pecking at him until the monk bled profusely from the face. When the attack was resumed a second time, the spectators became curious and reported the incident to the Magistrate. Sensing something was amiss, the Magistrate detained the monk for questioning, and it transpired that the monk had previously murdered and robbed an incense-stick vendor, the owner of the cock.[51]

The Dog The dog is a Yang animal, being born in the 3rd Moon, and is three feet high.[52] Insects are poisonous and harmful to human beings, and in the olden days hunting dogs, being Yang animals, were used to repel the insects.[53]

The sagacity and loyalty of a dog are proverbial, and many are the stories relating to them. There was the story of the Chu-Ko K'o of the state of Wu ((吴) 诸葛恪), who was about to attend a court assembly. Before he left the house, his dog bit at his dress trying to prevent him from going out. When this attempt was repeated, K'o ordered the animal to be driven off. K'o did not go far in his chariot when disaster overtook him.[54]

A merchant, who had gone to a district in Anhwei (安徽) to trade, chartered a boat to return to his own village. Seeing a butcher tie up a dog for slaughtering, the merchant paid the butcher double the price and took the dog aboard. During the voyage, the boatman robbed the merchant and wrapped him up in a blanket. He was then thrust into a big jar and thrown overboard. The dog instantly jumped into the water and directed the drifting jar ashore, where it appealed for help and the merchant was saved in time. Some days later the dog pounced upon a well-dressed man, biting at his throat, and when the merchant went near he recognised the man as the robber.[55]

During the period of the Warring States, a man named Li Hsin-Shun (李信纯) was very fond of his dog, called "Black Dragon" (黑龙). One day when Li Hsin-Shun was returning home inebriated from a convivial party, he fell dead asleep on a patch of bushy ground. It happened that at about the same time a Mandarin official, who was hunting in the vicinity, had set fire to

47. 马氏 ,*ibid.*, vol. 517, ch. 33, p. 48.
48. 荆楚in 四时宜忌 , 瞿祐 in 丛书 , 商务 , December 1939, p. 2; and 岁时记in 事类 ,*op. cit.*, vol. xii, ch. 87, p. 23.
49. 图书 ,*op. cit.*, vol. 518, ch. 36, p. 5.
50. 图书 ,*op. cit.*, vol. 517, ch. 33, p. 49.
51. 图书 ,*op. cit.*, vol. 518, ch. 36, p. 5.
52. 稽燿钧and 文曜钧 , 图书 ,*op. cit.*, vol. 524, ch. 115, p. 29.
53. 正义 *ibid.*, ch. 116, p. 36.
54. 晋书五行志 *ibid.* See Creel, *Birth of China*, p. 77, which says a dog was so used as an example of unswerving loyalty as early as the Shang period. The dog was so highly esteemed that a noble was named the "Dog Marquis", who was an ally or a vassal of the Shangs.
55. 聊斋 ,*op. cit.*, ch. 15, p. 801.

The hare is traditionally associated with moon mythology.

the bushes. Li's dog, which sensed the peril, ran to the scene to try to save its master. To moisten the bushes around Li, the dog ran to and fro to a nearby stream, wetting its own body and sprinkling whatever water there was onto the bushes. Finally it became exhausted and dropped dead by the side of its owner. As the bushes had been moistened, the fire did not scorch Li, who eventually woke up after a torrential rain. Li was surprised to see the dog lying dead by his side, but later found out what had happened.[56]

The Pig   The pig is a Yin creature.[57] The pig is symbolic of "black gold" (乌金), arising from a story of the T'ang period in which a pig-rearer of Hung-Chou (洪州) acquired riches through the sales of pigs. Another story indicates that the pig is a good omen. Once a certain Li Ch'u-T'an (李瞿县) had a dream in

56.   搜神记ch. 20, p. 3 in 学津 · *op. cit.*, vol. 150.
57.   礼记曲礼 in 图书 *op. cit.*, vol. 524, ch. 122. p. 59.

which he saw an exceptionally big sow. A diviner who interpreted the dream said, "The sow is the mother of litters of piglets. This indicates that you'll be appointed official of the granary." And it did come to pass.[58]

However, if a wild boar entered a private home, the family would lose the house; if it entered a garrison, the soldiers would suffer defeat.[59]

Generally speaking, the pig is by nature mean and reckless. It has big ears without intelligence and it brings misfortune. But a kinder story came from the Buddhist tale-tellers. One night when Monk Hsiang (僧姓香者) was asleep, he dreamt that a woman was kneeling before him in tears saying, "May the holy monk delay the tolling of the morning bell to save my life," and explaining that her master Chang San (张三) had already tied her up, but as her children had not yet seen the light, she pleaded for mercy. When this dream was repeated, Monk Hsiang woke up and instructed a servant to go to make inquiries at Chang San's house. There the servant noticed a sow in bondage, waiting to be slaughtered at the toll of the bell. When this was reported to the monk, he went over to the Chang home and requested that the sow be released temporarily. As the sow was liberated, she gave birth to a litter of more than ten young ones.[60]

Meanings and Interpretations   Now any of the occult and symbolic meanings above-mentioned and any other meanings may easily be read into the twelve animal symbols to indicate whether a particular year is to be auspicious, inauspicious or moderate. The same meanings may be associated with a person born in a particular animal year and also a particular hour. The data collected by us show that this trend did develop down through the ages.

Confucius was born in 550, 551, or 552 BC. In order to make the Sage's birth auspicious, a legend was created a few centuries later that one night Confucius' mother dreamt that two dragons had come from Heaven and stood by her side. As a result of this auspicious dream, she gave birth to Confucius.[61]

Emperor Kao Tsu (汉高祖 , 206 BC), founder of the Former Han dynasty, who overthrew the Ts'in house founded by the dictator Shih Huang Ti (秦始皇帝), was born a commoner named Liu Pang (刘邦). Though Liu Pang was essentially a man of brawn, he later proved a clever and wise administrator of his conquests. So the myth-maker set to work again to create a halo over this hero, saying that Liu Pang's mother once dreamt that a dragon had rested itself upon her body. In consequence of this dream, Liu Pang was born and, as the dragon was a lucky sign, became a ruler of men.[62]

There appears to be scanty textual evidence on the use of animal symbols to designate the year of birth of a person in ancient and mediaeval literature. In all the cases we have come across, the year in common usage was based on the stem-branch combination, which often causes a lot of trouble for the translator who has to find and give the corresponding year in the Gregorian Calendar. The case of Ming Huang, or Emperor Ming, of the T'ang dynasty (AD 713–755) illustrates our point suitably. A story was told that this Emperor was very fond of cock-fighting at the *Ch'ing Ming* festival and, to indulge in this game, had the best breed of fighting cocks in the realm. His predilection for cock-

58. 朝野金载in 事类 *op. cit.*, vol. xii, ch. 90, p. 55.

59. 图书 , *op. cit.*, vol. 49, ch. 174, p. 61.

60. 斋书下彬传in 子史 *op. cit.*, vol. vii, ch. 136, p. 24; 五行志in 图书 , *op. cit.*, vol. 49, ch. 174, p. 60 and 莱州府志in 图书 *ibid.*, vol. 524, ch. 121, p. 59.

61. 王子年拾遗记in 小史, 陈文烛, 涵芬 , vol. ii, p. 14.

62. 史记 *op. cit.*, vol. vi, ch. 8, pp. 1, 2.

fighting was ascribed to his being born in the Yi Yu (乙酉) year, corresponding to the "Cock Year" in 685. As 685 coincided with the first or second year of the infamous reign of Empress Wu (武则天 , 684–704), the same story-teller gave it another meaning, that "the cock year was emblematic of troublous times."[63] In another anecdote, it is stated that Chao Ju-Yu (赵汝愚) was born in the Mao year. As Mao corresponded to the "Hare Year", Chao construed the hare as a deity and refrained from using the hare as food until he died.[64]

According to P'ing Pu-Ch'ing (平步青) of the Manchu period, the employment of animal symbols to designate a person's year of birth was much in vogue during the Yuan dynasty (1206–1467), in which we find Kou Erh Nien (狗儿年) and Yang Erh Nien (羊儿年), meaning the "Year of the Puppy" and the "Year of the Lamb" respectively.[65] The Yuan dynasty may well be the period in which the animal-year tradition took root; this tradition has survived to the present day in China as well as abroad. Arising from the animal interpretations, there has evolved in China and Hong Kong a set of rules relating to marriages or proposed marriages between persons born under certain animal signs. A part of these rules has become proverbial, which consequently exerts considerable influence on the choice of conjugal partners. Six of these proverbs have been collated by V.R. Burkhardt in his popular work:[66]

i. "The white horse will not share a stall with the black cow," (白马不配青牛). Therefore, a person born in the Horse Year should not be married to a person born in the Ox Year.

ii. "The boar (pig) and the monkey are soon parted," (猪猴不到头). As a corollary, unions between persons born in the Pig Year and the Monkey Year are incompatible.

iii. "The sheep and the rat soon separate," (羊鼠一旦休). Which means marital contracts between people born in the Sheep Year and those born in the Rat Year tend to be short-lived.

iv. "The dragon takes to the cloud at the sight of the hare," (龙见玉兔云端去). As a consequence, if a person born in the Dragon Year takes a person born in the Hare Year to be his or her spouse, the matrimonial ship soon goes on the rocks.

v. "The golden cock dissolves in tears at the sight of the dog," (金鸡见犬泪交流). This is a warning against proposed marriages between people born in the Cock Year and those born in the Dog Year.

vi. "If the snake catches a glimpse of the tiger, it is as if it were wounded with a knife," (蛇见猛虎如刀断). If a person born in the Snake Year chooses a person born in the Tiger Year to be a conjugal partner, disaster soon follows.

There is another set of rules given annually in the annotated almanac which pairs the compatible animal years for marriage. They are the Rat and the Ox, the Tiger and the Pig, the Hare and the Dog, the Dragon and the Cock, the Snake and the Monkey, and the Horse and the Sheep.[67]

Malaysian Beliefs　In what manner and to what extent the China set of proverbs and the marriage formulae in the almanac have exerted their influence on the Malaysians is difficult to assess. As a rule, a fortune-teller, a priest or a vegetarian nun is consulted. However, partly as a result of the China tradition and largely as a result of their own rationalisation, the Chinese in Malaysia have

63.　岁时 op. cit., vol. ii, ch 17, p. 184.
64.　赵汝愚传 in 图书 , op. cit., vol. 521, ch. 78, p. 37.
65.　霞外攟屑 op. cit., vol. ii, ch. 5, p. 277.
66.　Burkhardt, vol. iii, p. 122; and Crane, p. 177. Citing Father Kennelly, Crane adds: "The companions of the bride, who are to escort her from her parental home to that of the bridegroom, must be born under the auspices of a cyclic animal living in peace with the animal that presided over the birth of the bridegroom. Were these animals at enmity with each other, the peace and prosperity of the future household would be endangered."
67.　The Chinese Almanac, op. cit., p. 2.

evolved a series of their own interpretations. A typical example of this series comes from Penang, and reads as follows.

Rat Year: A person born in the Rat Year is bold and daring if the birth occurs at night; but if the birth takes place in the daytime, he is very timid, like the rats which take to hiding in daylight.

Ox Year: A person born in the day is destined to toil and sweat for a living; but he is destined to live in clover if born at night. The reason is that when the ox retires in the evening, he is supplied with plenty of fodder and has an abundance of leisure to chew the cud.

Tiger Year: A person born in the Tiger Year is believed to be ferocious. If he is born after dusk, he is even worse; for it is then that the ferocious animal leaves its lair to prowl for victims.

Hare Year: Persons born in the Hare Year are moderate in everything, neither too good nor too bad, neither too rich nor too poor — moderate in talent and middle class in society.

Dragon Year: The Dragon Year is the most auspicious year. For the purpose of occult interpretation, dragons are classified under two main categories, "Big" and "Small". If a person is born a "Big" dragon, he has the world at his command — riches, luck, power, longevity, and perhaps a harem. If he is born a "Small" dragon, he has a smaller measure of these blessings.

Snake Year: The Snake Year is also auspicious because this reptile is reputed to be associated with the dragon. There were dragon and snake temples in China, and there is a so-called "snake" temple in Penang. There are others who abhor the "Snake-Year" person of either sex, arising from the Cantonese maxim, "Persons with snake-head and rat's eyes are treacherous."

Horse Year: People born in the Horse Year are destined to a hard life, bustling here and bustling there, like the beast in the jungle. If the birth occurs at night, the person leads a more stable and comfortable life.

Sheep Year: People born in the Sheep Year are good-natured. They are ideal companions in conjugal life. The sheep is the emblem of a peaceful retiring life in old age. Some authorities aver that the lamb is the symbol of filial love, for the lamb kneels in veneration when taking its mother's milk.

Monkey Year: A person born in the Monkey Year is prone to be fickle-minded and very often easily irritated. He is mischievous. He is also cunning, and highly susceptible to flattery.

Cock Year: Persons born in the daytime are proud, reassuring and full of confidence. Those born at night, the time for roosting, are tame and submissive, and are liable to be browbeaten.

Dog Year: A person born at night is destined to sweat and slog, like the poor dog keeping night watches whilst others indulge in sweet dreams. A person born in the daytime is fairly well-off.

Pig Year: "Fat like a pig" and "lazy as a pig" are attributes ascribed to a person born in the Pig Year. He is idle and brainless. He is a spendthrift, for he eats too much; and, being devoid of intelligence, he earns less than he spends. Like the Pig Spirit (猪八戒) in the famous Chinese novel, *The Western Expedition* (西游记), he is lustful and easily tempted by the fair sex.

Marriage Omens Stemming from this and other sets of interpretations there have evolved on Malaysian soil certain beliefs relating to the congruity or incongruity of proposed marriages

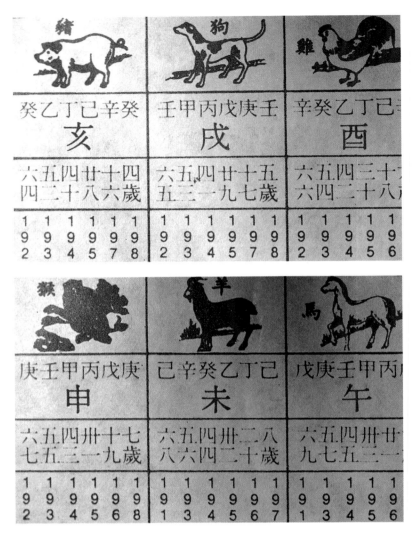

The twelve celestial animals depicted in a lunar calendar, together with the relevant cyclical years.

between persons born under specific animal signs:

    i. Matrimony between those born in the Dog Year and those born in the Rat Year is disastrous, for the dog invariably attacks the rat.

    ii. Similarly a marriage between persons born in the Cock Year and those born in the Snake Year is likely to go on the rocks for the simple reason that the bird pecks at the snake.

    iii. Whilst a boy born in the Snake Year is generally auspicious because of the snake's supposed association with the dragon, a girl born in the Snake Year has difficulty in getting a spouse because she is believed to be vicious and selfish.

    iv. A girl born in the Tiger Year is dreaded, because she is liable to cause the husband's premature death. To circumvent this possibility, a "tiger-girl" is usually wedded to an elderly man. On the other hand, a boy born in the Tiger Year is welcome in matrimony, because the ferocity of the tiger drives away evil influences.

    v. A girl born in the Horse Year is generally good and may enter into wedlock with a boy born under any animal sign; and *vice versa*.

    vi. A girl born in the Dog Year is likely to be loved by her husband, because everybody loves a dog, or rather, a bitch; and *vice versa*.

蛇	龍	兔
丁己辛癸乙丁	丙戊庚壬甲丙	乙丁己辛癸
巳	辰	卯
七五四卅廿十	七五四卅廿十	七六四卅廿
十八六四二歲	一九七五三一	二十八六四
1 1 1 1 1 1	1 1 1 1 1 1	1 1 1 1 1
9 9 9 9 9 9	9 9 9 9 9 9	9 9 9 9 9
1 2 4 5 6 7	1 2 4 5 6 7	1 2 3 5 6

虎	牛	鼠
丙戊庚壬甲丙	乙丁己辛癸乙	甲丙戊庚壬
寅	丑	子
六四卅廿十一	六五卅廿十二	六五卅廿十
一九七五三歲	二十八六四歲	三一九七五
1 1 1 1 1 1	1 1 1 1 1 1	1 1 1 1 1
9 9 9 9 9 9	9 9 9 9 9 9	9 9 9 9 9
2 3 5 6 7 8	2 3 4 6 7 8	2 3 4 6 7

vii. A boy born in the Dragon Year is considered most auspicious in marriage. Because of this, a "dragon-child" is invariably invited to perform the "hair-combing" (上头) ceremony on the eve of a marriage (Hokkien custom). But in the case of a girl born in the Dragon Year, she is said to have a characteristic weakness — lasciviousness. The ideal union of a Dragon-Year person is that with a person of the Cock Year, because the bird is believed to be a transformation of the fabulous phoenix, arising from the classical allusion "Dragons fly, Phoenixes dance" (龙飞凤舞), signifying a good omen.

viii. Persons born in the Ox Year are at loggerheads with those born in the Sheep Year, because oxen and bulls are proverbially stubborn, whilst goats (sheep) tend to goad others on the slightest provocation.

ix. A conjugal union between a Monkey-Year person and a Pig-Year person is tolerably good, because in the historical novel the Monkey Spirit (猴子 (孙悟空)) and the Pig Spirit are sworn brothers, in spite of the pig's lustful inclinations. On the other hand, the monkey and the dragon are estranged, resulting from a delectable anecdote of which we deem it worthwhile to give an abridged account.

Once upon a time a dragon's wife fell seriously ill and was told to eat a monkey's heart for treatment. Forthwith the male dragon came up from the depths of the ocean to go up to the nearest forest in search of a monkey. There, perching on a tree-top, the dragon espied a monkey. "Hail, hairy one, isn't that precarious?", the dragon accosted.

"No, I'm accustomed to it."

"Why remain up there? Cross the sea and you'll find fresh fruits and flowers aplenty."

"How can I get across?"

"Get on my back."

Whilst the monkey was seated astride on the dragon's back, the dragon dived down into the deep water. "Hey, where are you going?", asked the almost suffocated monkey.

"Oh, my dear sir, my wife is very ill and wishes to taste your heart."

Unperturbed by his predicament, the monkey promptly replied, "Illustrious friend, why didn't you tell me earlier? I've left my heart on the tree-top. Now, what a waste of time that we've got to go back for the heart."

The dragon swiftly returned to the shore; and as the monkey stayed put safely on the branch, the dragon said angrily, "Hurry up, little friend, I'm very impatient."

"What a silly dragon this is," the monkey thought to himself.[68]

Incidentally, this anecdote was invented more as a jibe at the irrational attributes ascribed to the twelve animal symbols than as a guide to the incompatibility of unions between the dragon-man and the monkey-woman or *vice versa*. It suffices to cite one more anecdote to show the inadvisability of taking the animal symbols or their primary, derivative and occult meanings too seriously.

When the ancients announced their intention to designate the years in the Sexagenary Cycle (六十花甲) with the names of the twelve animals, says this anecdote, the rat and the ox were the earliest to arrive at the assembly. As both the rat and the ox were keen to be first on the list of names, they had an altercation. "You tiny rat," said the ox derisively, "are you not too small for the honour?"

"Ah," retorted the rat, "what are you but an insignificant braggart? Let's parade before the judges; let these wise men decide as to which of us is really big."

So the two animals paraded themselves before the human judges. As the rat was small, it blew itself up to about double its normal size. The abnormal dimensions naturally attracted the notice of the judges. "What a giant rat!" exclaimed an excited judge. "This giant rat is really beyond comparison," commented another. "This is the world's biggest rat," the others cried in chorus.

At the termination of the parade the ox, baffled by the various remarks, mistook them to be the unanimous verdict of the judges. So before the final judgement was pronounced, the ox graciously threw up the sponge.[69]

Reckoning of Age   Before concluding, we have to divert to an allied subject — the custom of reckoning oneself one year older as soon as the lunar New Year comes, even if a baby was born on the last day of the out-going year. The explanation is simple: the Chinese reckon their age by the annual animal signs, and not by the aggregate of twelve solar months, as is the practice in the West.

68. The story is from one of the simple Chinese folklore books, which we have mislaid.

69. 笑话，沈文华，国光，3rd ed. (n.d.), pp. 61–63.

If Ah Kow (阿狗) was born in the Dragon Year (1964), whatever the date of his birth, he was one year old, like all his contemporaries born in the same year. He and his contemporaries became two years old as soon as the next lunar year (Snake Year) was due and three years old in the Horse Year (1966), and so on. This simple age calculation is a boon to the illiterate and semi-literate, many of whom have committed to memory the order of the animal symbols from childhood through a nursery rhyme (Hokkien): "It-Ch'u (一鼠), Ji-Gu (二牛), Sa-Hor (三虎), Si-To (四兔), Go-Leng (五龙), Lak-Chua (六蛇), Ch'ih-Beh (七马), Peh-Yeoh (八羊), Kow-Kow (九猴), Chap-Kei (十鸡), Chap-It-Kow (十一狗), Chap-Ji-Tu (十二猪)", meaning "First-Rat, Second-Ox, Third-Tiger, Fourth-Hare, Fifth-Dragon, Sixth-Snake, Seventh-Horse, Eighth-Horse, Ninth-Monkey, Tenth-Cock, Eleventh-Dog, Twelfth-Pig."

This nursery rhyme is made interesting through a kind of "hopping over the frog" game played by four or five children, one of whom becomes a "frog". Each of the other boys jumps crosswise, by rotation, over the frog's bent body, placing two hands on his back for the jerk. In the jumping process, the first boy recites the first phrase "It-Ch'u", followed by the second hopper who recites the second phrase, "Ji-Gu", who is again followed by the third hopper who recites the third phrase, "Sa-Hor", and so on until someone makes a slip in the rhyme. The defaulter then becomes the "frog", and the game starts all over again. The author still remembers this nursery rhyme because when he was about ten years old he used to play this game with other children living at Bridge Street, Penang, where the Hokkien dialect predominates.

*(Preceding pages) A flock of birds heralds
the arrival of a favourite entertainer in
Singapore's Chinatown at lunar New
Year, the grandest of all Chinese festivals.*

PART II:
New Year
Celebrations

CHAPTER 3:
Temple Visits and Sacrificial Offerings

To the Chinese, the lunar New Year is not merely the grandest of all festivals: it is withal the most solemn and the most religious season. During the season, which theoretically lasts for a period of half a month, sacrificial offerings are made to specific deities, on a grand scale, on specific days.

In Penang, the most popular deity is Kuan Yin (观音), known to Westerners as the Goddess of Mercy; and the best-known temples dedicated to this goddess are the Pitt Street Temple (the oldest), the Burmah Road Temple, the Hong Hock See (洪福寺) at Perak Road, the Phor Tay (*Bodhi*) at Bagan Jermal Road, the Penang Buddhist Association at Anson Road, and the Ayer Itam Temple. During the season, devotees, male and female, go to the temple of their choice.

Kuan Yin is prayed to almost every day during the season. On specific days, such as New Year's Eve, the eve of the 9th day (at about midnight in both cases) and the 15th day of the 1st Moon, exceptionally large crowds throng the temples with numerous varieties of cooked food, fruits and flowers to make votive offerings; and the suffocating fumes from the burning joss-papers, lighted candles and incense-sticks turn the places of worship into veritable smoke-houses, testifying to the zeal and devotion of the believers.

On New Year's Day and the days following, thousands of devotees make a pilgrimage to the Ayer Itam Temple, denominated Kek Lok Si (极乐寺 , Temple of Paradise), many in a holiday mood, but others, especially members of the fair sex, for devout prayers. The name Kek Lok Si comes from the term Sei Hong Kek Lok Sei Kai (西方极乐世界 , derived from the Sanskrit word *Sukhavati*, meaning "Western Paradise") as conceived by the Buddhists of the Ambitabha School, the "Pure Land Sect"

A. *The newly completed statue of Bodhisattva Kuan Yin at the Kek Lok Si temple in Penang — the largest and the most magnificent Chinese temple in Southeast Asia.* **B.** *A view of the pagoda.* **C.** *The sacred tortoise pond at Kek Lok Si.*

(净土宗). It is the largest and the most magnificent Chinese temple in Southeast Asia, possessing three distinct features: (a) the biggest and most imposing pagoda of its kind in Malaysia, (b) a sacred tortoise pond and two sacred fish ponds, and (c) the finest sculptural craftsmanship in its numerous Buddhist statues and statuettes. It is the only temple outside China glorified by an imperial sanction and an imperial set of Buddhist scriptures. Sprawling over an area of four hectares, ninety to one hundred and fifty metres above sea level, the temple, begun in 1891 and completed in 1904, consists of three main tiers of buildings where three principal shrines are constructed on rocks and cliffs: the Precious Hall of Buddha, the Hall of Divas, and the Hall of Bodhisattvas at the bottom section. In the last hall, the shrine of Kuan Yin is enthroned in the miniature Island of P'u T'o (普陀严). Here it is that the New Year pilgrims offer their prayers to Kuan Yin.[1]

Bodhisattva Kuan Yin Kuan Yin, meaning "to see and to hear all", is claimed by some authorities to be none other than Avalokitesvara, Lord of Love and Compassion, a male Bodhisattva from India. For this reason Kuan Yin was at one time represented by a male statue in China, especially before the T'ang dynasty (seventh to ninth centuries AD).[2] This explains why some Indians, especially of the Chettiar class, are occasionally seen in the Pitt Street Temple, not in the role of curious tourists, but as devout worshippers. To these Indians, the ashes from the incense-pot are sacred; and they apply this powder to their forehead as profusely as some ladies apply rouge to their cheeks.

It is stated in the *Lotus of the Good Law* (妙法莲华经) that Kuan Yin will appear in female form when that form is appropriate to the circumstances;[3] and it is mainly as a female Bodhisattva that Kuan Yin, the Goddess of Mercy, has won the hearts of Chinese devotees all over the world. In this connection, the most widely circulated version of her origin is the Chinese story of Miao Shan (妙善), the youngest and the most beautiful daughter of Miao Chuang Wang (妙莊王), a ruler.[4]

Miao Chuang Wang had three daughters, two of whom had been married happily into families of high social standing; but Miao Shan (a predestined Bodhisattva) firmly declined any proposal of marriage. As a result, her father drove Miao Shan out of the palace and confined her in a convent known as the "White Bird" (白雀寺), wherein the Abbess assigned her menial tasks. These she accomplished through the help of spirits and angels. Incensed at his daughter's determination, the ruler ordered the nunnery to be burnt down, but Miao Shan was unscathed. The ruler then ordered Miao Shan to be beheaded. No sooner did the sword touch Miao Shan than it broke into three pieces. Finally, the ruler ordered her to be strangled by a white belt. Suddenly, the sky was overcast with dark clouds and a white tiger appeared to carry her soul off to the forests. Her soul then went down to Purgatory, where she released several condemned sinners. When her soul returned to the forests, the T'ai Pai Hsing Chun (太白星君) transformed himself into an old man. This old man advised Miao Shan to practise Buddhist precepts in Hsiang Shan (香山), the Fragrant Mountain, and she did so accordingly.

Later Miao Chuang Wang was afflicted with an incurable disease. Miao Shan came in disguise to treat him. In order to cure

1. For a complete account see Wong, *Temple*.
2. This is evident from the famous painting of Wu Tao Tzu (eighth century), reproduced on p. 132 in *Epochs of Chinese and Japanese Art*, Fenollosa, 1912, cited by Johnston, *Buddhist China*, p. 275 fn.l.
3. Johnston, *Buddhist China*, p. 276, quotes an erudite Buddhist as saying that the true Kuan Yin is by nature both sexless and formless, but is capable of assuming, or of appearing to assume, all forms.
4. 搜神记 in 续道藏 series, 涵芬, April 1926, vol. 高上, no. 1105, ch. 3, p. 1.

him of the disease, she had to give up her eyes and her arms to prepare an ointment. After recovery, the ruler found out the truth and went to the Fragrant Mountain in person to offer his gratitude. At that moment, Miao Shan attained Bodhisattva-hood and "a thousand hands and a thousand eyes" manifested in the air.[5] This manifestation has since been known as "a miracle of the Fragrant Mountain" (香山显迹).

Apart from the festive occasions, Bodhisattva Kuan Yin is worshipped on the 19th day of the 2nd Moon, of the 6th Moon and of the 9th Moon, indiscriminately known as her birthday anniversaries. One main reason for her popularity is that she is also the Goddess for Children, to whom female believers, who are desirous of begetting children, especially male offspring, offer prayer. This belief in child-gift is traceable to a passage in the *Lotus of the Good Law*, of which the translation reads:

"If there be a woman, who desires a male child, and prays to Kuan Yin, the goddess will cause her to become the mother of a well endowed and highly gifted child; or if she desires a female child, she shall become the mother of one extremely beautiful, endowed with every gift and beloved of all."[6]

Chor-Su Kong Temple   On the 6th day, many Malaysians make a pilgrimage to the Chor-Su Kong (祖师公) Temple, better known as the Snake Temple, at Sungei Kluang, about ten kilometres from George Town, *en route* to the Bayan Lepas Airport. This temple holds a grand celebration in honour of its deity three times a year: 6th day of 1st Moon, 6th day of 6th Moon, and 6th day of 11th Moon. On these occasions, Chinese theatrical shows are performed on its stage, facing the temple, on the opposite side of the public road. At night, the neighbourhood is well illuminated, with food-stalls, fruit-stalls and miscellaneous goods-stalls lining the street and cars parked on the grass edge, and becomes the venue of pleasure-seeking villagers and city dwellers — nearly all in a holiday mood.

The temple is unique in that it gives sanctuary to a number of apparently harmless snakes, which increase in number on festival days. You see these curling reptiles on the rafters, around the twigs and branches placed on the altars, upon the candlestands, and underneath the incense-pots, coiling and entwining themselves in various postures. These reptiles are lethargic and are unlikely to bite; but it is extremely risky for the uninitiated to pick them up. They can lose patience if they are severely prodded. A snake expert has declared that they are a poisonous species, but so far no accidents have been known or reported.

The deity of the temple is Ch'eng Sooi Chor-Su Kong (清水祖师公), represented by a statue, draped in a yellow robe, enthroned in the central shrine. A short sketch of the deity is recorded in the temple's "account book" (帐簿), stating, in effect, that the Ch'eng Sooi Chor-Su was a Hokkien man of the Eng Choon district (永春县) during the time of the Sung dynasty. His name was Tan P'or-Chiok (陈普足), and he entered the Eng Choon Tuah Hoon Taoist temple (永春大云院) as a novice when he was a child. He died in the Ch'eng Sooi Cave (清水岩) at Aun K'ei district (安溪县) and was accordingly deified as the Ch'eng Sooi Chor-Su.[7] Another legend says that he was originally a mendicant monk in the Sung dynasty and a good friend of the

5. *Ibid.*
6. The translation from the 妙法莲华经 is by Beal.
7. An extract of this sketch is reproduced by 邝国祥，槟城，星洲世界，1958, pp. 51–52.

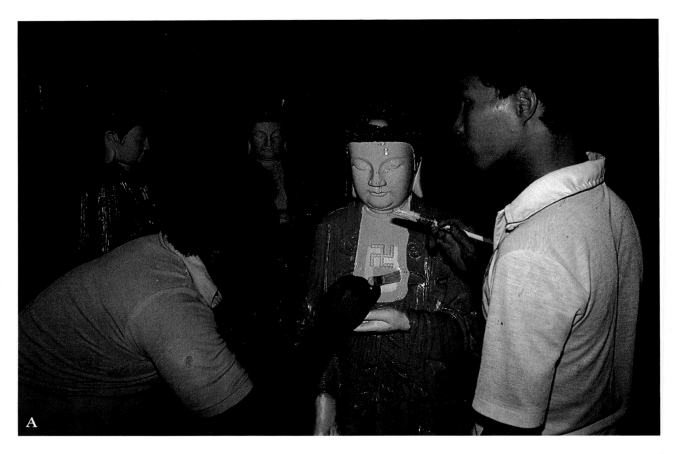

A. *Artisans restore a Buddhist statue in the Kek Lok Si temple, Penang. The temple underwent extensive renovation before the consecration of the new statue of Kuan Yin in 1986.* B. *The T'ai Shang Tao Chun, who appeared before Queen Pao Yueh Kuang in a dream.*

8. This information was kindly supplied to us by a teacher of a Penang Chinese School, a regular reader of the "Matters Chinese" column contributed by the author under his pen-name Wu Liu in the *Sunday Gazette*. This teacher cited 同安县志 ·ch. 24, as his authority. Yet another legend is given by Purcell, p. 133, which reads: "Ch'eng Sooi was a general who lived in the Siong (商) dynasty. He associated himself with Boo Ong (武王) and fought the tyrannical king of Tiu (纣王). All the generals who fought for Boo Ong were deified." (The Chinese characters are inserted by us for identification because these names are romanized in Hokkien dialect. This ancient legend is not impossible, inasmuch as "snake-worship" was already known in the Shang era.)

9. Low, pp. 99, 310.

celebrated Chu Wen Kung (朱文公 (熹)). Gifted with the power of exorcising malevolent spirits, the monk brought peace and happiness to the people of his time. Upon the monk's death, his admirers deified him as the Ch'eng Sooi Chor-Su. In the thirty-first year of Shao Hsing (绍兴三十一年 , AD 1161), a temple known as the Ch'ing Shui Yen Ssu (清水严寺) was built in the "White Clouds Mountain" (白云山) in his honour. Another temple dedicated to him was denominated P'eng Yen (彭严) in the district of Aun K'ei in Fukien Province. Annually, thousands of devotees went to this temple in the 1st Moon to offer prayers, which were always answered.[8]

When the Hokkien Chinese migrated in large numbers to Penang in the early days of the nineteenth century, they brought with them their Chor-Su deity. It was first enthroned in a small attap-and-plank dwelling in a sugar-cane plantation at what is known as Sungei Tiram. In those days, access to this shrine was by the rivulet, and devotees had to go there by boat or sampan.

In 1836, James Low, who had witnessed a ceremony in the 11th Moon, said the Chor-Su Kong was a sort of Aesculapius, whose image was carried over the fields to look for medicinal roots. The image was put in a small painted wooden or bamboo box with an open front, and a canopy overhead. The box was carried on the shoulders of four men, who went about at a quickened pace. Leading the party was a "physician". This procession was described by Low as "the search for Ceres or Proserpine".[9]

Low's account indicates the popularity of Chor-Su Kong in the 1830s as a healing deity. Funds began to pour in from all quarters, and by the middle of the nineteenth century a brick temple was built at the present site, which was donated by a

European. Some thirty years later, this temple was reconstructed and enlarged, and held in trust by a committee. A local legend says that as soon as the temple was ready for occupation, a number of snakes mysteriously appeared. These snakes are currently believed to be the "lieutenants" of the deity, i.e. they are at the beck and call of the deity. As such, they are reverently alluded to by devout believers as "blue dragons".[10]

Among the devotees who offer prayers to the deity for health, luck and prosperity, many plant a joss-stick or two in front of the "blue dragons", more as a gracious gesture than an actual act of worship. In addition to this, they purchase eggs to offer to the snakes, which are believed (by the credulous) to be able to prick a pin-hole through the shell of an unbroken egg and suck at the contents. Because of the action of these devotees, the Penang Chinese have been dubbed "snake worshippers" by superficial observers, especially tourists from Europe and America, who have an eye for the bizarre or what appears to be bizarre. Even some local European residents share such an unwarranted conclusion, as is manifest from the remark made by R.J.H. Sidney, "The snake is placed on a tray in the temple and worshipped", in *Malay Lands* (p. 227). There is perhaps no serious objection to this generalization; for, after all, serpent-worship (*nagas*) existed in China as early as the Shang period (1766–1154 BC). It was common in Egypt and among the Hebrews up to the time of Hezekiah. So was it in vogue amongst certain Indian and other Asian races.[11]

Snakes and Dragons   The temple-of-snakes tradition could have been inspired by the Nan-T'ai Temple (南台庙), commonly known as the "Temple of the King of Snakes" (蛇王庙) of Changchou (漳州) in Fukien Province. The statue therein represented a deceased monk, whose origin was obscure. Tradition had it that whenever anyone was bitten by a snake in the city, he could go to the temple to lodge a complaint. As soon as the plea was made, the pain caused by the wound immediately ceased. Moments later, the guilty snake would be seen, severed into halves on the roadside, or with its head chopped off in the vicinity of the temple — in consequence of the punishment inflicted by the King of Snakes.[12]

There were also temples of the Dragon King in China, which were favourite resorts of the people. Serpents (snakes) were regarded as manifestations of this deity. In the year 1874, a serpent was seen in a temple near the city of Tientsin (天津) wherein it ensconced itself beneath an altar. The priest of the temple welcome its presence, and Li Hung-Chang (李鸿章), the then Viceroy of the Province, paid a personal call to do homage to it as the personification of the Dragon King.[13]

The belief in the snake's association with the dragon is a matter of individual opinion; but if you extend your kindness to this species of reptiles you may, one day, be amply rewarded — who knows? There comes from China an old story, in which Sun Szu-Mo (孙思邈), a great scholar, had occasion to save the life of a "blue snake". It happened to be the son of a dragon. In appreciation of his deed, the Dragon King invited the kind-hearted Sun to his under-water palace and presented him with a thesis on "3,000 methods of making prescriptions in the Dragon Palace" and a set of books consisting of "30 volumes of precious prescriptions", which had never been seen by mortal eyes.[14]

10.   The presence of snakes in this temple is explained by a Chinese writer who says that the Ch'eng Sooi Chor-Su Kong was a monk from Aun K'ei of Fukien Province. This monk succeeded in subduing a blue snake-spirit in a duel of magical power. After its defeat, the snake-spirit became Chor-Su Kong's disciple and from that time onwards blue snakes assembled in his temple. The Penang temple is said to be a "branch" (分庙). (See 南洋三月记，郑健庐，中华 2nd September, 1935, p. 157.)

11.   Needham, vol. i, p. 89; and Johnston, *Lion and Dragon*, p. 387, fn.2.

12.   闽杂记，施可斋，申报馆印 , vol. iii, ch. 12, pp. 1, 2. This Chinese belief is not so preposterous as it appears at first sight, for in ancient Rome and even modern Europe snakes are believed by many to be incarnations of men's ancestors. (See Krappe, pp. 257–258.)

13.   Douglas, *Confucianism*, p. 277.

14.   沈汾续仙传 in 事类 , *op. cit.*, vol. xii, ch. 91, p. 62.

Furthermore, some snakes are endowed with as much intelligence and cunning as human beings, according to a fable by Han Fei Tzu (韩非子), the famous legalist philosopher of China. Once, two snakes of Ku Che (涸泽) were about to change their abode. "If you go ahead first, with me following behind," said the small snake to the big snake, "people are certain to notice the snake in you and kill you. But if I ride on top of you, people will say that we are divine beings." So when the pedestrians saw the double-decked snakes crossing the street, they respectfully gave way, muttering, "Ah, they must be divine creatures."[15]

God of Heaven   At about midnight on the 8th day, the Malaysians, those from Fukien Province in particular, make a big sacrificial offering to the T'ien Kung (天公), the God of Heaven, whose birthday falls on the 9th day. For this purpose, there is a special altar — a square or oblong table with four legs — carefully kept and reserved exclusively for this occasion. As this offering is made in the open air (skywards), this special altar is brought out and placed upon two rectangular stools, for the legs of this sacred table should not touch the ground lest the altar be defiled. The altar may be set up on the five-foot way, roadside, in the compound or garden or on the roof terrace of a bungalow, as the case may be.

On these altars are displayed a rich variety of eatables consisting of chicken, pork, fruits (mandarin oranges, pomeloes, water-melons and bananas), and candied fruits (sweetmeats) of varied colour called *bit chian* (蜜饯) in Hokkien — long slender sticks which are planted vertically into a special red wooden framework. Each of these sweetmeat sticks is decorated with a red-paper crown on the top. There are also rock sugar (sometimes moulded into the shape of a miniature pagoda) and "red tortoises" (红龟), which are wheat-flour cakes shaped like tortoises and stained pink.

Two important items are the roast pork and a pair of full-length sugar-canes, complete with foliage. The rich offer a roast pig or two; whilst the poor, at least, provide a small chunk of roast pork with the crispy skin. This viand is essential, because the roast pork is called *kim tu* (金猪), meaning "golden pig" in Hokkien. The two lengths of sugar-cane, each of which is festooned with a long stream of yellow paper, are poised one on each side of the improvised altar. They are burnt — at least some portions of them — in the bonfire of the joss-paper at the close of the ritual. A Chinese writer describes this as the Shu-Ch'ing (竖青) custom to symbolise evergreen or the youth and vigour of life.[16] Another significance is derived from the double pun of the Cantonese term for sugar-cane, called *kam che* (甘蔗). The first syllable is homonymous with the term for gold (金) and the second with the term for thanks (谢). Accordingly, it is construed as an offer of gold in thanksgiving. Moreover, amongst many devotees there is current a legend, which is recapitulated by Victor Purcell. In the Sung dynasty, the people of the Fukien Province were once mercilessly attacked by troops under the leadership of a cruel general, Yang Lu-Lang (杨六郎). The massacre continued till the eve of the 9th of the 1st Moon, when many who had taken refuge in sugar-cane groves were spared.[17] Thereafter, sugar-canes became a *must* in votive offerings to the God of Heaven.

The joss-papers are of a special variety called *t'ien chin* (天金 ,

15. 韩非子 (说林上) in 诸子 · *op. cit.*, vol. v, ch. 7, p. 127.
16. NM, vol. i, no. 8, June 1947, p. 165.
17. Purcell, p. 133.

An altar to T'ien Kung, the God of Heaven, at the Leng Hyam Twa temple, North Boat Quay, Singapore.

gold for Heaven), imprinted in gold in the centre of the sheet (about 30 cm × 30 cm); they are much larger than the ordinary variety (10 cm × 15 cm), which are imprinted in silver and called *yin chih* (银纸).

There is a pre-worship ritual peculiar to the local Hokkien community. All the members of the family, in their best attire, are present, and the eldest of them performs the ritual. He holds two effigies, one male and one female, and then waves them in the air, tracing an outline over a member of the family from the head downwards, first in front, then the back, and then on both sides of the body, muttering in the process the words: "In comes the good, out goes all evil." This same ritual is repeated for every member present. In other cases, every member of the family has an effigy, a male effigy for man or boy and a female effigy for woman or girl. The most senior member, who takes the lead, shows the other members what to do with the effigy (sometimes it is waved just three times in front of a person from the crown down to the feet). The elder usually performs this ritual for the smaller children who are unable to follow the adults. The effigy is made of paper, and a sheet of joss-paper with gold imprint is wrapped round it; this, in turn, is enclosed in a red piece of paper to serve as the outside cover. To all intents and purposes, these paper effigies are used as human scapegoats. For this reason, at the end of the ritual they are set ablaze in the bonfire of the joss-papers. The worship of the God of Heaven is followed by the discharge of fire-crackers, including in pre-war days the giant variety, about two centimetres in diameter, called *t'ien kung p'ao* (天公炮 , crackers for the God of Heaven).

After this sacrificial offering, the sacred altar is carefully removed and safely kept in a suitable place in the house, without allowing the legs to touch the floor, and away from general access to prevent any possibility of unintentional defilement by any member of the family. Devout believers who do not own or keep the sacred altar at home nearly all go to the Pitt Street Chinese Temple and the City God Temple at Bridge Street, where such sacred altars are provided in the courtyards, to make sacrificial offerings at about midnight.

The worship of the God of Heaven is done with meticulous care because it is the most solemn of all sacrificial offerings. An explanation given by a devotee who was once a staunch Kuomintang leader in Penang is that its solemnity started in about 1644 when the Manchus, after the occupation of Peking, were in hot pursuit of Prince Fu (Fu Wang, 福王) of the Ming house. Prince Fu, whose resistance had been suppressed, escaped to the Fukien Province where patriotic Chinese made sacrificial offerings to the God of Heaven, praying for the "overthrow of the Manchus and restoration of the Ming" (反清复明). Because every Chinese was anti-Manchu at heart, this tradition was henceforth observed annually to invoke divine help in the expulsion of the Manchu usurpers.[18] When this tradition was carried abroad, most Chinese forgot the anti-Manchu motive but continued to make solemn sacrifices to the God of Heaven praying for their own blessings.

The Jade Emperor   On the 9th day, the devotees make a pilgrimage to the temple known as "The Altar of the God of Heaven" (天公坛), which nestles on a summit at the foot of the Penang Hill. There are two ways to reach this temple. Once is by climbing up a granite path on a gradual ascent, which leads you to the front entrance. The other is by taking a short ride in the Hill Railway tram, which deposits you at the back of the temple.

Enclosed by four walls, the temple, though magnificent, looks rather small, especially when its spacious floor is occupied by huge statues. On the second tier of the temple is enthroned a giant statue representing the Yu Huang Ta Ti (玉皇大帝), the Jade Emperor, who is identified as the God of Heaven by the majority of the Chinese. On both sides of the Jade Emperor are enthroned the Pei Tou (北斗 , Northern Constellation) and the Nan Tou (南斗 , Southern Constellation), who are jointly worshipped for long life and riches.

As this pilgrimage is, in fact, a continuation of the worship started some hours earlier at home, devotees usually do not take viands and fruits with them. They just buy incense-sticks, candles and incense-papers with gold imprint from the temple authorities, light the sticks and candles and burn the incense-papers, followed by the traditional form of prayer or worship.

The Jade Emperor is said to have been born several millenia before our era, and was first invoked and popularized by Emperor Chen Tsung of the Sung dynasty (宋真宗 , AD 998–1022).[19] There was in the former world a kingdom by the name of Kuang Yen Miao Yo (光严妙药), whose king was named Ching Te (净德). The queen was Pao Yueh Kuang (宝月光). The king was getting old, and as he had no heir to succeed to the throne he became very sad. One day, in penitence, he ordered all priests in the realm to assemble at the palace to hold mass prayers whilst he devoted himself to pious meditation. This lasted for six months. Then one night, the queen, in a dream, saw the T'ai Shang Tao Chun

Offerings to the God of Heaven. **A.** *Traditional cakes and fruit — note the sugar-cane.* **B.** *Yellow paper to be burned.* **C.** *Gold and silver paper and various petitions to the God of Heaven are burned.*

18.   This inside story is not impossible or improbable, for one of the two cradles of the anti-Manchu Hung League was the Fukien Province, the other being Canton, the home of Sun Yat-Sen, the revolutionary leader who founded the Republic of China in 1912. See Schlegel, p. 4 ff., regarding anti-Manchu activity in Fukien. It is an historical fact that Prince Fu joined the anti-Manchu patriots. (See 中华民族抗战史，陈安仁，3rd ed., February 1947, p. 195 ff., and 清代史，萧一山，商务，3rd ed., February 1947, p. 17 ff.)

19.   搜神记in 续道藏，*op. cit.*, ch. 1, pp. 8–9. Our translation is an abridgement.

(太上道君) riding in a five-coloured dragon chariot with a child in his arms. The party, which floated in the air, arrived at the palace, illuminating the surrounding area with multi-coloured rays. Extending a cordial welcome to the party, the elated queen knelt down, entreating the T'ai Shang Tao Chun to let her have the child as heir to the throne. The request was granted.

Upon waking up, the queen had a miraculous conception, and at noon on the 9th day of the 1st Moon in the Ping Wu year (丙午岁), a prince was born. At the time of birth, rays of light radiated from the babe's body. A handsome looking child, the prince showed exceptional wit and intelligence when young. Upon growing up, the prince distributed the palace treasures to the poor and needy until hunger and privation were entirely removed from the realm and peace and happiness prevailed. Upon the king's death, the prince mounted the throne to become a model ruler. After a time, he relinquished the throne to devote himself wholly to a pious and religious life at the P'u Ming Hsiu Mountain Cave (普明秀岩山). An almost infinite period followed, during which he saved innumerable persons from poverty and disease and suffering souls from torture, both on earth and in Purgatory, in various guises, until he attained sainthood[20] with the title of Ch'ing Ching Tzu Jan Chiao Wang Ju Ts'ai (清净自然觉王如采).

The God of Heaven, who has been the subject of philosophic discussions by Chinese scholars, has been identified by Fung Yu-Lan[21] as the Huang T'ien Shang Ti (皇天上帝); whilst the Jade Emperor has been identified as Chang Tao Ling (张道陵) or one of his descendants by W.E. Soothill, one-time Professor of Chinese at Oxford University.[22] But to the common people of Penang, nay, Malaysia, the T'ien Kung and the Yu Huang are one and the same entity, regardless of academic theories and conclusions. As the worship of the T'ien Kung and the Yu Huang is mainly confined to the Hokkien Chinese, we have traced the source of the confusion to the Fukien Province where the people of Ch'uanchou (泉州) observed the 9th day of the 1st Moon as the birthday of Heaven; whilst the people of Amoy (厦门) observed the 9th day of the 1st Moon as the birthday of Yu Huang.[23]

Shang Yuan Chieh   The New Year carnivals culminate on the 15th day when two religious festivals are observed. One is the *Shang Yuan Chieh* (上元节), a festival of Taoist origin from China; the other is the worship of the locally deified Tuah Peh Kong (大伯公), popularly known as the God of Prosperity, for which Penang is famous.

The *Shang Yuan Chieh* is the first of the three festivals in the lunar year associated with the trinity known as the San Kuan (三官), which originated in the Han period.[24] The first member of the trinity is the T'ien Kuan (天官, Lord of Heaven). In Malaysia, he is enthroned on the pillar or wall on the five-foot way or verandah of every conservative home, represented by an oblong wooden board or a slip of red paper bearing four characters: *T'ien Kuan Tz'u Fu* (天官赐福), meaning "May the Lord of Heaven endow us with luck and happiness." Lighted joss-sticks are planted daily in the incense socket affixed to the bottom of his shrine. As his birthday falls on the 15th day, which is also the day when he comes down to the human world to record the merit and demerit of each person, conservative Chinese families make sacrificial offerings to him for his blessings.

20. *Ibid.*
21. Fung Yu-Lan, vol. i, p. 31, wherein 皇天上帝 is shown as the anthropomorphic T'ien.
22. Soothill, *Three Religions*, p. 75. Werner says Yu Huang was "born of fraud" and came from the brain of Emperor Ch'eng Tsung (*Myths*, p. 131).
23. 施可斋 *op. cit.*, vol. i, ch. i, pp. 6, 7; and 闽杂记, p. 116 in 小方, 王锡祺, 上海著易堂, vol. vi, 1891–1892. See 清录, 顾铁卿, 上海文化书局, 2nd ed., October 1943, p. 13, which shows this distinction: T'ien is Buddhist and is prayed to on the 9th day in Buddhist temples; whilst Yu Huang is Taoist and is prayed to on the same day in Taoist temples.
24. 李开先集, 中华, December 1959, vol. ii, pp. 646–647. See also 未平府 in 图书, *op. cit.*, vol. xvii, ch. 26, p. 22, in which it is stated that the *Shang Yuan* is "the day when the T'ien Kuan confers luck and happiness on those who remain indoors, eat vegetarian food and recite the (Taoist) canon."

The second is the Ti Kuan (地官, the Lord of Earth), whose birthday falls on the 15th day of the 7th Moon, called the *Chung Yuan Chieh* (中元节), and is celebrated on an extensive scale in Malaysia.[25]

The third is the Shui Kuan (水官, Lord of the Water), whose birthday falls on the 15th day of the 10th Moon, called the *Hsia Yuan Chieh* (下元节), which at one time was celebrated as a vegetarian day, during which everyone should observe ablution and meditation, offering floral tributes to the Taoist saints in order to receive mitigation for his sins and to attain long life. By the beginning of this century, however, the *Hsia Yuan Chieh* was seldom, if ever, celebrated in China.[26]

The Shui Kuan is not worshipped in the 10th Moon either, but the trinity (三官) is honoured at the same time on the 15th of the 1st Moon on a small scale and on a very grand scale in the 7th Moon. Because of the trinity's connection with the seas, there are group celebrations by the fishing fraternity and market traders, especially those who deal in maritime produce — an obvious survival of the T'ang tradition, when a decree was issued that during the *San Yuan* festivals (三元节, 15th day of 1st Moon, of 7th Moon and of 10th Moon) sacrifices must be offered to the San Kuan before putting out to sea for fish.[27]

In Penang, the celebration of the *Shang Yuan* festival is purely formal: a lengthy silk or cloth banner, red in colour, bearing huge characters in gold or in black, meaning "In celebration of the Shang Yuan Festival" (庆赞上元佳节), is hung up crosswise over the entrance to markets such as the former Chowrastra Market at Penang Road and the Prangin Road Market. At the Tanjong Tokong fishing village, a similar banner or two are suspended conspicuously overhead across the un-metalled street separating the attap-and-plank dwelling houses on each side of the highway to indicate the festival. After the usual sacrificial offerings, a feast takes place without pomp and grandeur.

The Tuah Peh Kong   The worship of the Tuah Peh Kong is an important religious matter in Penang. His origin is ascribed locally to Chang Li, but Kuang Kuo-Hsiang, a Chinese school headmaster and a newspaper columnist of Penang, maintains that originally Chang Li (张理) and his two sworn brothers Ch'iu Chao-Chin (丘兆进) and Ma Fu-Ch'un (马福春), who resided in the neighbourhood of Tanjong Tokong, were prayed to by local residents for protection against epidemics which were prevalent in the early days, and were deified together as the Tuah Peh Kong, a generic term for pioneering heroes.

According to Kuang Kuo-Hsiang (鄺国祥), Chang was the eldest; Ch'iu, the second, and Ma, the youngest: they were Hakka pioneers who had sailed from China together and landed at what is now known as Tanjong Tokong, long before Captain Francis Light's founding of Penang in 1786. It was their habit to meet often. Then of a sudden, Chang absented himself for a few evenings; so Ch'iu and Ma went to look for him and were astounded to discover him seated motionless in a cave beneath the huge boulder at Tanjong Tokong. Ascertaining that Chang Li was dead, they buried the body by the side of the boulder. Some years later, Ch'iu Chao-Chin died, followed subsequently by Ma Fa-Ch'un, and both were interred near the site of Chang Li.

The original shrine of Tuah Peh Kong was first established at

25. See pp. 119–120.
26. 李开先集，*ibid.*; 道经 in 岁时，*op. cit.*, vol. iii, ch. 37, p. 407; and CJ, Sowerby, "Lunar Calendar", p. 291. See also 考丘悦三国典略 cited in 清录，*op. cit.*, p. 19. It is to be noted that in 宋史方伎传，also cited in 清录 *ibid.*, the third Lord is given as 人官 (Lord of Human Beings).
27. 唐百官志河渠令 in 岁时，*op. cit.*, vol. iii, ch. 30, p. 343. To eat maigre food on these three days is called 三官素。(吴趙风土录，p. 2 in 小方，*op. cit.*, vol. vi.

A. *A statue of Yu Huang Ta Ti at the temple known as "The Altar of the God of Heaven" at the foot of the Penang Hill. Yu Huang Ta Ti is the supreme deity in the Taoist pantheon.* **B.** *A traditional altar to T'ien Kung.* **C.** *Stiltwalking entertainers take a break during* Chingay *festivities in Singapore.*

28. 槟城, *op. cit.*, pp. 58–59; 邝国祥 in *JSS*, vol. xiii, June 1957, pp. 53–58; and *SET*, 28th February, 1953. At first sight Kuang Kuo-Hsiang's claim that the trio were deified at the same time appears to be incongruous, as there is only one statue to represent the Tuah Peh Kong. Our theory is that it is possible that the earlier settlers did pay homage to and did intend to deify the trio. This seems to be borne out by the fact that there are three statues of the Tuah Peh Kong in the premises of the Poh Hock Seah at Armenian Street, Penang. But since only one bearded man, according to the local legends, manifested himself, it is not unlikely that from that time onwards the local residents deemed it practical to set up one statue instead of three.

A number of scholarly research articles on the origin of 大伯公 have appeared in the *JSS*: vol. i, December 1940; vol. vii, December 1951; vol. viii, December 1952; and vol. xiii, June 1957. According to Chen Ta, p. 254, immigrants returning to China brought Ta Pai Kung back for enthronement as Tu Ti (土地) in rural Kwangtung and Fukien.

29. *SEM*, 24th February, 1905. The popularity of the Tuah Peh Kong in Penang and Malaysia arises from the fact that he is believed to confer riches, etc. He is equivalent in this respect to China's God of Wealth (财神), to whom it is important to make a sacrifice during the period from the 1st to the 15th of the lunar New Year. (See *CJ*, vol. xii, no. 2, February 1930, p. 61.)

Tanjong Tokong not later than 1792, as is proved by the words inscribed on a granite incense-vessel, which still remains in the courtyard of the present temple. It was only in 1799 that a small temple was built. Later, funds were raised to build a brick temple with its back portion spanning the rocky cave.

A local legend says that in about 1862 an epidemic broke out in Penang, taking a heavy toll. One morning an old man was seen in the town holding a (magical) whisk in his hand. Whilst passing through the streets he waved the whisk at some of the buildings. On the next day, the old man appeared again to repeat the same performance, and the curious spectators pursued him when suddenly he vanished. It transpired later that the inmates of houses at which the old man had waved his whisk escaped the epidemic disaster. Another legend says that when the temple was renovated and expanded and given the poetic name "Sea Pearl Isle Temple" (海珠屿寺), a long-bearded man in a flowing robe manifested himself, descending from the hillock in the background and entering the new temple. This happened in about 1886 on the 15th day of the 1st Moon. A third story says that in about 1912 there was an attempt to retrieve the title deed of the temple, which had been mislaid. The trustees of the temple were at a loss to locate it when unexpectedly some members dreamt of the appearance of a hoary old man with a white beard telling them to take possession of the title deed from Mr X. On the next day, these people met and were surprised to learn that each of them had had the same dream. So Foo Tye Sin (胡泰兴, in whose honour Tye Sin Street in Penang was named) called upon Mr X, and explained the dreams to him. Whereupon that gentleman recalled that his ancestor had left a small box, which was kept intact in the attic. Upon the box being opened, the title deed was found.[28]

At the turn of the twentieth century, the Tuah Peh Kong became so popular that there were recriminations between the Hokkien section on the one hand, and the Hakka and Cantonese on the other, over the privilege of paying homage to the deity on specific days. This is evidenced by a notice framed up on the wall in the front hall of the Tuah Peh Kong Temple at King Street (mainly used by Cantonese).

In pre-war years, there was an annual procession — sometimes, on a grand scale — held in honour of the Tuah Peh Kong. In 1905, for instance, a grand and costly procession, called *Chingay* (妆艺), was held on the 14th, the 15th and the 17th of the 1st Moon. The *Chingay* was defined as "a sort of stage, borne on the shoulders of men, on which is a gorgeous representation of some historical scene,"[29] a decorated float, Chinese style.

It was a spectacular procession, consisting of twenty-six sections or units formed by groups of Chinese living in various sectors of the town. The components of each section or unit were: (a) A giant triangular flag, between seven and a half and twelve metres in height, made of silk. It varied in colour, red or green being more popular, with Chinese characters pasted or sewn on it. One side of the flag was affixed to a giant bamboo pole carried perpendicularly by a stalwart bearer, with half-a-dozen others taking turns. Great skill was required to balance the fluttering flag. A strip of silk, streaming from the top of the bamboo down to the ground, enhanced its gracefulness. (b) A pair of sizeable lanterns, painted in black or red Chinese characters, being borne aloft on

ornamental wooden poles painted in red. (c) A banner, half a metre by three metres, inscribed with Chinese characters to indicate the name of the section; the banner was supported at each end by a pole. (d) A band of musicians, varying from six to twenty in number, playing music on Chinese instruments.

The pride of each section was its artistic *Chingay*, which was drawn, for the first time, by a pony instead of being borne by men. There was great rivalry in preparing the most beautiful *Chingay* and in selecting the prettiest girl to become its occupant. In one *Chingay*, two blushing maidens sported jewellery worth about $100,000 between them, comprising ornaments, earrings, bracelets and rings on every finger, all set with sizeable brilliants. Great skill was shown in another *Chingay* wherein a bejewelled damsel was seen suspended perilously in mid-air "on nothing more substantial than the leg of a prostrate monkey".[30]

In the years after the second world war, the procession has become an almost insignificant event. It is called "Exchange of Lighted Joss-Sticks" (招 (请) 火仪式), held under the aegis of the *Baba* (Straits-born) Chinese of the Poh Hock Seah (宝福社). On the 14th day of 1st Moon, a special urn of the Tuah Peh Kong is carried in a small procession from the Poh Hock Seah at Armenian Street to the Tanjong Tokong Temple. In the temple, a sacrificial ritual is held at about eleven o'clock at night, at the time of the rising tide. The lights of the temple are then turned off, and about thirty members of the Poh Hock Seah start to burn the joss-sticks to allow the ashes to drop into the special urn. When the urn is filled with ashes and the last stick burnt out, the lights are turned on again. In the course of the ceremony, lighted joss-sticks are also thrown into the sea. Katharine Sim, a well-known English writer of books with a Malayan background, who witnessed this ritual in 1960, observed that the boisterous waves of the tide leapt "like live things, as if acknowledging the prayers of the people."[31]

On the next morning (15th), this special urn is taken back in procession to the Poh Hock Seah at Armenian Street. When the procession passes through a street where a member or an interested devotee resides, he is allowed to "exchange incense fire". In the exchange, some lighted joss-sticks are taken out from the incense-vessel in the devotee's house to be planted into the special urn and, in return, a cluster of burning incense-sticks from the special urn is put back into the devotee's own incense-vessel. This act is tantamount to the actual worship of the Tuah Peh Kong, whose blessings are invoked.

As the Tuah Peh Kong is believed to confer riches, luck and health, he is widely honoured in private dwelling houses. His portrait — a beaming old man with a flowing white beard — is enthroned in almost every private house in the predominantly Hokkien section of George Town. The belief is so deep-rooted that the words *peh kong* have become synonymous with luck. When the hundred-character gambling was rampant, the Tuah Peh Kong was usually consulted for forecasting the lucky numbers. In 1954, a statue of Tuah Peh Kong, enthroned in the premises of the Poh Hock Seah, was stolen for a day or two, presumably by hundred-character gambling enthusiasts for consultation, but was later returned as mysteriously as it had vanished.

Concluding Remarks   Thus, in this special chapter, we have given a panoramic survey of Chinese religious festivals in the New

30. *SEM*, 24th February, 1905.
31. Sim, *Journey*, p. 24. Katharine Sim, a genuine lover of the East, especially Malaya, is an accomplished artist and freelance writer. Amongst her other books are *Malacca Boy*, *The Moon at My Feet*, *Black Rice* and *Malayan Landscape*, in all of which she portrays the beautiful scenes of this country with a vivid and picturesque description, perhaps unexcelled by any contemporary writer.

Year season. The critical reader may notice that the Chinese under discussion are sometimes rather confused in their beliefs. If so, what of that? After all, the key to all religious beliefs is faith — blind faith, if need be.

There was, about two decades ago, a Malayan Chinese, who had started life from scratch and became a multi-millionaire banker before he died. His immense wealth was believed to have been acquired through faith in the Chor-Su Kong enthroned in the Snake Temple. Every year, this devotee made it his sacred duty to plant the first incense-sticks into the burner on the altar. There is a general belief that to be the first devotee is to have one's prayers answered promptly and favourably. You may scoff at the theory, but faith is a wonderful thing, and miracles or what seem like miracles did happen or are reported to have happened.

There is the well-known story of the Peking flower-girl, sole supporter of her aged father, who fell seriously ill and was getting worse. One day an elderly woman, a neighbour, who was going on a pilgrimage to T'ai Shan (泰山), the Sacred Mountain, told her that all prayers were favourably answered by the goddess T'ien Nai Nai (天奶奶菩萨) enthroned on the peak. The Sacred Mountain was a hundred Chinese miles away, taking ninety thousand paces to reach from the girl's humble abode.

Since it was unwise for the girl to leave her aged father, she waited every night until the old man was asleep. Then she went out into the yard and walked, carefully counting her steps as if she were making pilgrimage to the Sacred Mountain. When she was tired out, she knelt down on the floor, facing the mountain, saying "Please forgive me for not personally visiting your temple. Being only a girl, I am unable to go."

The girl repeated the walk for fouteen consecutive nights until, one morning, she had made ninety thousand paces. At just that time several pilgrims, rich and poor, had reached the temple at dawn, and were eagerly waiting for the door to open in order to be the first to burn incense. Amongst them was a rich palace attendant from Peking who stood ahead of the long queue; but as he entered he saw, with amazement, an incense-stick already burning in the pot, for which the temple caretaker was at a loss to give an explanation.

Undismayed, the rich man went again the following morning and, as soon as the door was opened, rushed to the incense-pot, only to find a lighted stick of incense therein. In front of the altar was the vague figure of a prostrate girl, which disappeared upon the rich man's hustled entry. Questions were asked. Finally, the elderly woman, neighbour of the flower-girl, remarked, "This could only be the pious florist in Peking. She must have sent her soul to pray for her father's recovery."[32]

32. Hume, pp. 72-74.

CHAPTER 4:
The Holy New Year's Eve

In the good old days, says a legend, when the ancient Chinese wore animal skins and ate coarse and simple meals, they were carefree, happy and contented, like Adam and Eve in the Garden before Adam succumbed to Eve's importunity. In course of time, they settled on a plain (the basin of the Yellow River) which yielded rich harvests. A community grew up and a model village was formed. Perfect harmony prevailed, for everyone loved his or her neighbour and there was no robbery or theft. The peace and quiet, however, was ruthlessly disturbed, on a wintry night, by a mysterious monster, which pounced upon several human victims and wantonly destroyed their property.

A council was held the next day, and precautionary measures were taken to prevent a second attack. Days passed and

A. *Traditional door gods, known as* men shen. *According to legend, Emperor T'ai Tsung of the Tang dynasty was harassed by ghosts and his ministers Chin and Hu volunteered to stand guard, which they did successfully. Later, portraits were made of Chin and Hu and pasted to the palace doors. Tradition continues, and each lunar New Year fresh posters of the two ministers are pasted on house doors to ward off evil spirits.* **B.** *A traditional New Year papercut and a jumble of used joss-stick wrappers make a colourful collage.*

weeks followed, but there was no sign of the mysterious monster. As time went on, vigilance was relaxed and the unfortunate incident was almost forgotten by the peaceful inhabitants. Then of a sudden, the mysterious monster descended upon the unwary villagers again, claiming a bigger toll of victims and demolishing a larger extent of property. A second council was convened; the same precautionary measures were again instituted; and vigilance was redoubled. Again, days passed and weeks followed. Nothing untoward happened, and the catastrophe was again relegated to the limbo of the past. Then the third tragedy occurred with even greater disaster. The victimized families began to probe deeper into the mysterious phenomenon. Investigation teams were sent out and advice was sought from all the sundry. When a grey-haired scholar, who had been living a hermit's life, was consulted, he ventured to suggest that he held the key to the solution of the mystery. "The mysterious invader," he explained, "has always made his sudden appearance at regular intervals."

"Regular intervals?" queried the host of impatient sceptics. "Venerable Sir, how do you explain it?"

"The explanation is simple," replied the sage calmly. "I've been watching the stars and heavenly bodies for years; and I keep records of their movement . . . "

"Venerable Sir," the impatient sceptics interrupted. "What have the heavenly bodies to do with the tragedies on earth?"

"Be patient," the sage said, without betraying any excitement. "Do be patient, all of you. According to my records, the mysterious plunderer came regularly at the time when some planets returned to certain relative positions."

As the sage spoke these words, he produced some diagrams and cryptic notes and passed them round for the perusal of his inquirers. The members looked at the diagrams and strange writings, and looked at one another in solemn amazement. "We confess we don't understand these drawings and words," the sceptics remarked, shaking their heads in despondency. We are still puzzled by your riddle."

"These are not riddles," the sage said, remaining as inscrutable as ever. "Spoken in terms of the sun and the moon, the mysterious monster whom you all dread has always repeated his attack after the sun has shown three hundred and sixty-five times."

"Yes, yes," the sceptics said in one voice. "But what does all this mean?"

"It simply means that the monster has set upon you regularly on the three hundred and sixty-fifth evening," explained the grey-haired recluse. "If all of you were alerted on that particular evening and took defensive measures, the monster could be easily repulsed."

Acting on the advice of the hermit, a council was held. Instructions were issued and intelligence men were sent out to collect information about the monster. A careful analysis and a close study of the available data disclosed that the monster was in mortal fear of three things on earth. They were noise, illumination and the colour red. On the suggestion of the grey-haired scholar, the monster was nicknamed Nien (年, Year).

On the three hundred and sixty-fifth evening, all preparations for defence were ready. The villagers, young and old, were armed with all manner of weapons. The houses were brilliantly lighted with bonfires and all solid objects were painted red. A din and bustle was created throughout the night, starting soon after dusk. The Nien was due; but the monster made himself scarce. No mishap occurred, and the suspense abated. Dawn came. Everyone was smiling; everyone was grateful; and voices of greeting and congratulation resounded in the air. The Nien was truly merciful; and celebrations were held. Subsequently, some religious-minded elders suggested holding a thanksgiving service regularly on every three hundred and sixty-fifth evening. All the gods from the highest to the lowest were prayed to and the ancestors were invited to participate.[1]

The aforesaid is one of the popular legends which related to the origin of the celebration on New Year's Eve, around which hovers a halo of sanctity. Down through the millenia, New Year's Eve has become the occasion for a grand national festivity.

Observance in Malaysia   In Malaysia, a fortnight or so before this festival, the majority of the Chinese are busy making preparations, and a small boom begins in almost every trade and prices are inflated in respect of commodities in great demand. Building contractors are consulted by house-owners for renovation and re-painting of their residences to present a "new look". Jewellery and gold articles are ordered, new suits and other items of habiliments are made or purchased, and even cars of the latest model are acquired by the wealthier section of the community. To attract customers, big commercial firms of alien proprietorship put up banners and neon lights of oriental colour, and special designs with Chinese dragons and phoenixes are printed on cigarette cartons and wine-bottle containers. As the festival day approaches, men and boys hurry to their barbers to have their hair cropped; whilst members of the fair sex, old and young, queue for their "perms". Seasonal fruits, special oranges, water-chestnuts, melon seeds, sausages, preserved ducks, salted pork, and cured livers imported from China and Hong Kong are snatched up, some for New Year presents made a few days beforehand, others for domestic use. Crisp and new currency notes are drawn out from the banks for purposes of making *ang pau* (红包) gifts. In Chinese firms, bonuses are issued to employees and accounts and debts are settled on New Year's Eve, and inability to do so involves a loss of "face".[2]

In every home a "spring-cleaning", preferably with bamboo leaves (to drive away evil spirits), takes place a couple of days before. On or about New Year's Eve, houses are brilliantly illuminated in place of the ancient bonfires. Doors and windows are left open till a late hour and even when the house is shut up for retirement, the verandah light is on.

Votive Offerings   In the forenoon a votive offering, followed by homage to the ancestors, is made to all the deities from ancestors, is made to all the deities from the God of Heaven to the God of Earth and, nearly always, the Kitchen God. When human beings are blessed with prosperity, longevity and offspring, they do not easily forget their deities, to whom they show, in their own traditional way, their gratitude. What occasion is more appropriate for this grateful gesture than on the expiry of the old year?

A moral may be drawn from the familiar story of Lu Meng-Cheng (吕蒙正), a famed premier of the Sung period. Before he

1.   异俗 · 国光 · May 1949, pp. 72–75. This is clearly a later interpolation, probably inspired by the legends on Shan Sao and Li T'ien (see p. 109). The Chinese moon averages only 29.53096 days and there are approximately 354 days in the lunar year. In order to regulate the lunar year with two equinoxes and the solstices, the Chinese insert an extra or intercalary month once in three years or twice in seven years, making a total of seven intercalary months in nineteen years. Strictly speaking, the mysterious monster in the story should have appeared on the 354th evening, or plus one month in the intercalary-moon year.

2.   星洲十年 ed. 关楚璞 · 新加坡星洲日报社 · Section V, p. 1077. In China, this tradition could be more tyrannical than law. A man who could not settle his debts had to go in hiding till New Year's Day. Even then, his creditor could pursue him with a lighted lamp in hand (to indicate that it is still night) when it was broad daylight, thereby causing incalculable disgrace to the unfortunate debtor. (See Bredon & Mitrophanow, pp. 81–82.)

The "spiritual tablet" stands on a special altar, either at home or in the clan temple: it is a central focus of ancestor worship.

3. 民新，黄华，上海正气书局，May 1948, ch. 3, p. 6. Another legend in local circulation says Lu Meng-Cheng bought pork on credit to make a food offering to the Kitchen God. Changing his mind, the butcher later snatched back the meat, already cooked, and threw a handful of sand into the soup. The Kitchen God thereafter petitioned to the Jade Emperor to help Meng-Cheng to come out first in the Civil Service Examination. Eventually Meng-Cheng rose to the rank of premier.

became known, he was a scholar of extreme poverty. On a New Year's Eve when every family was making sumptuous offerings to thank the deities, the best he could do was to offer a piece of charred wood (for chicken) and a bowl of pure water (for wine and tea) in prayer. At that moment a Bodhisattva, who had had a surfeit of rich food elsewhere, happened to pass by and, upon hearing the mention of "water", hastened into Meng-Cheng's house and gulped down the liquid to quench his thirst. Thereafter, with the blessings of the Bodhisattva, Meng-Cheng rose rapidly to the rank of prime minister and became rich.[3]

The Reunion Feast   New Year's Eve is the time for family reunion in all homes, called *T'uan Nien* (团年). It was also called *Wei Lu* (围炉), gathering around the family hearth. Every member of the family, wherever and whenever possible, makes it a duty to return to the family home. Nothing gives a Chinese of the old school greater pleasure than to hold a grand feast around the old, familiar hearth of the ancestral home with every member, old and young, participating. This rejoicing is appropriately designated *Ho Chia Huan* (合家欢). This custom, with its threefold object, has been immortalized by Su Shih (苏轼), a famous poet of the Sung period, in a set of poems. One is called "Pieh Sui" (别岁), when a feast was held to ring out the year. Another is called "Shou Sui" (守岁), when night watch was kept by everyone till morning. The third poem is entitled "K'uei Sui" (馈岁), in which Su Shih lamented his inability to attend the home reunion because of inevitable detention by official duties.[4]

When all are gathered at home in the evening, the reunion feast, usually a big affair, begins. In conservative homes the spirits of the ancestors are invited, and the feasting and rejoicing take place as if they were present. After this ceremonial feasting, some modern youths and Westernized maidens are inclined to attend pre-arranged dance parties or seek fun and merriment in the night-clubs and cabarets, where they remain till midnight when the Chinese New Year is ushered in with "Auld Lang Syne" after the fashion of the West; whilst the older members and younger children remain at home to observe what Su Shih called "Shou Sui". Children are encouraged to keep awake till late; for there was an old belief that if anyone, especially a child, remained awake on New Year's Eve, his span of life would be extended.[5]

Between 11.00 p.m. and 6.00 a.m., according to the propitious time given in the annotated almanac, the gods and deities are again worshipped to usher in the New Year. Red candles, incense-sticks and incense-papers are again burnt, often announced by the ritual of discharging a packet or two of fire-crackers, ban or no ban. In this sacrificial offering, vegetarian food (often uncooked), fruits such as water-melon, oranges and bananas, flowers such as pineapple-flowers, roses and orchids, and three cups of tea, each containing a red date, are placed on the altar. To each of these fruits and the pink pineapple-flowers, in particular, a slip of red paper cut out in design is significantly adhered, and almost every item in the offering is meaningful: representing luck, prosperity, success, longevity, completeness of life and an abundance of progeny.

The "Spiritual Tablets"   Homage is again done to the ancestors, who too are invited to share the family's anticipatory blessings and take part in welcoming the New Year. These ancestors are set up in the front hall of the house, taking the form of what is called the "spiritual tablets" (神主). Varnished in red, each spiritual tablet is made of an oblong piece of wood stuck vertically into a small transverse block at the base in order to balance its upright position. Upon the tablet Chinese words are inscribed in gold or in black to indicate the ancestor. Sometimes this tablet is represented by a sheet of red paper with the name of the ancestor. In recent years, there is a tendency amongst the wealthier class to supplant the wooden spiritual tablets by marble slabs of similar dimensions.

Traditional history says that the first spiritual tablet was erected in honour of a loyal subject of the Chou dynasty. The loyal subject was Chieh Chi-T'ui (介之推), who, with some others, had served the Marquis of Tsin (晋侯) loyally. When the Marquis of Tsin later decided to give awards to his faithful followers, Chieh Chi-T'ui refused the award on the ground that it was his duty to be loyal without expecting any reward. To avoid the honour, Chieh Chi-T'ui hid himself and eventually perished.[6] However, with a view to creating a halo of heroism around this loyal subject,

Simple portraits or photographs may replace the "spiritual tablet". Here we see an altar of photographs in the ancestral hall of the Cheng Hoon Teng temple, Malacca.

4. 苏轼诗 in 宋代名著选辑 · 绿窗书屋 ·Hong Kong, December 1954, pp. 17, 18.
5. 江震志 cited in 清录 · *op. cit.*, p. 113.
6. 春秋左传 (僖公二十四年) in 十三经注 · vol. vi. pp. 20–21.

a legend adds that whilst he was hiding in the woods a search party set fire to the woods to force him to come out, but unfortunately Chieh Chi-T'ui was burnt to death. The Marquis, on discovering the corpse, erected a tablet to his spirit, which he begged to accompany him home, wherein he caused incense to be offered to the tablet daily.[7]

To appreciate the custom of spiritual tablets, one must realize that a school of Chinese opinion used to maintain that a man had three souls. After death, one soul accompanied the corpse to its grave. The second soul resided in the spiritual tablet set up conveniently at home or in the temple. The third soul was either taken down to receive the sentence of the King of Hades, Yen Lo (阎罗), or sent up to Heaven as a reward for meritorious deeds.[8]

This traditional belief that a soul resides in a tablet is still held by many Chinese of the present generation. The tablet is composed of two parts, a vertical piece of wood and its horizontal base. On the obtuse side of the vertical piece of wood, the posthumous name of the deceased, the dates of birth and death and a character *chu* (主) are inscribed. The character *chu*, meaning lord or owner, is made up of two parts: the word *wang* (王), meaning a prince, at the base, and a single dot on the top. At the funeral ceremony, a special ritual is held to "spiritualize" the tablet. It is called *Tien Chu* (点主), the "dotting ceremony", and consists of smearing the dot over the word *wang* with vermilion ink or blood from the comb of a cock, preferably a white one.[9] Once this ceremony has been performed, the soul is believed to have taken up residence in the tablet, just as in the temples, the statues or images are said to be consecrated after the *K'ai Kuang* (开光), the "opening the light" ceremony.[10]

Where the spiritual tablet of an ancestor is enthroned at home, homage is paid to it several times a year. This tradition is founded in the Confucian doctrine of filial piety.[11] "Filial piety," said Confucius in answer to a query by Mang I, "consists in NO disobedience." Amplifying it later, Confucius added: "When the parents are alive, treat them with respect; when dead, bury them with respect and do homage to them with respect."

An Old Belief In paying honour to their ancestors, many unsophisticated Chinese entertained the belief that whilst the dead had to be served as if they were alive, they continued to look after the welfare of their family as they did in their lifetime, including protection, if required. The story of Li Pa (李霸) illustrates this belief. Li Pa was an official of the T'ang dynasty, and was incorrupt. Because of his probity, all underhand dealings of his subordinate officers were curbed, so they not unnaturally hated him. In spite of many years of official life, Li Pa remained poor. When he suddenly died of a violent illness, his widow and children were left penniless. So the widow cried by the side of his coffin, complaining that Li Pa had let down the family. A few days later, a voice said, "My wife need not be bitter and depressed. I'll take care of things." True to his word, the spirit of Li Pa frightened his former subordinates into contributing to his funeral expenses as well as to the coffers of his family.[12]

But this old-world belief has gradually changed, owing to the influence of Western civilization and culture. Nowadays, more and more spiritual tablets are kept in public places of worship — temples, clan associations, district associations, and so on —

7. Dyer, p. 31.
8. Burkhardt, vol. i, p. 2.
9. de Groot, *Religious System*, vol. i, p. 215, says that in Fukien Province at the time of performing the "dotting ceremony", these words are uttered: "I mark the word tablet 主 ; display spirituality, O Tablet." Another formula given on p. 218 is: "A point is placed on the character *tablet*. May the offspring become illustrious and prosperous, win the highest degrees at the State Examination and advance higher and higher in official service."
10. Reichelt, p. 160, says that the *K'ai Kung* ceremony is accompanied by an act of homage to the great spirit. Occasionally, a snake or some other reptile is inserted into the image through an opening in the back; sometimes the blood of a cock is smeared on the breast of the image. In the case of a Buddha or Bodhisattva, a heart or a gall bladder of silver or gold or some mixture of bitter herbs may be poured into the opening. Bredon & Mitrophanow, p. 49, call it an "induction ceremony" at which the priest inserts some tiny living creature, such as a young bird or a spider, inside the aperture of a statue with the silver or cloth replicas of the vital organs, then seals up this aperture and removes the paper mask left over the eyes. "The size of an image or its material has little bearing on its effectiveness," they add, "the one and only thing that counts is whether or not the priest has introduced the spirit of the god into its body."
11. Confucian Analects, Bk. ii, *Wei Cheng*, ch. v, the Chinese words being 孟懿问孝，子曰无违…生事之以礼，死葬之以礼，祭之以礼 .
12. 怪说，国光，reprint, November 1948, pp. 96–98.

instead of the ancestral home or the home of the descendants. The motive is more for venerating and perpetuating the memory of the dead than for invoking help from the ancestors. Many people have their tablets placed in the temple or association of their choice before they die, in the hope that the tablet will continue to be cared for as long as the temple or association exists. A higher scale of fees is chargeable for erecting the tablets in vantage positions.[13]

The Sin-Chew Custom Besides certain festival days, honour is paid to the ancestors on the birth anniversary (first, two or three years) and especially on the death anniversary (every year) of the parents and forebears. The death anniversary is denominated *Chi Ch'en* (忌辰). In the days of Imperial China, it was a day for private taboos, i.e. the day when a filial son would refrain from attending to worldly affairs and devote full time to the remembrance of his deceased parents. It was axiomatic that a *chun tzu* (君子 , gentleman) should mourn his beloved parents for life, and the annual day for taboos provided him the opportunity. During the T'ang period, an official was eligible for one day's leave to observe this "privately tabooed day",[14] called *Chi Jih* (忌日).

A classic example was set by the Marquis of Tsin, who alienated a big *padi*-field in Mien Shang (绵上 , in modern Hunan) to make provision for doing continuous homage (by posterity) to Chieh Chi-T'ui, the loyal minister who had declined any reward for meritorious service to the country.[15] This tradition, known as the *Sin-Chew* (神主) custom in Malaya, has been followed, as is amply indicated in the records of the Supreme Court where there are several cases in which the rich have made a clause in their will to set aside an annual sum for the purpose of what is commonly called "ancestor worship".[16] Unfortunately, when Choa Chong-Long of Malacca made a device for his *Sin-Chew* to be performed "four times in each and every year at the least, and as much oftener as the funds applicable thereto will admit", it was held by Maxwell, C.J., in 1869 to be null and void.[17]

But there are ways and means of circumventing this judicial decision, and a good lawyer certainly knows his job. Device or no device, the *Sin-Chew* tradition goes on. In January 1965 we made a tour of Malacca town and were privileged to examine the spiritual tablets set up in an ancestral shrine at premises Nos. 113–115 of the famous Heeren Street (now known as Jalan Tan Cheng-Lock), reputed to be Malaysia's most historic highway where generations of Chinese have resided. Rested against the partition-wall where the ancestral shrine is set up in the guests' hall is a portrait. Immediately in front of this portrait six wooden tablets — three in a row — are enthroned on a special altar, representing four generations of ancestors of the Ong Sek-Pek (fifth generation) family. By the side of these tablets are two mounted glass-frames, one of which contains a list of Chinese characters on a red sheet of paper, showing the birth and the death anniversaries of the ancestors to whom obeisance is to be paid annually on these days. This type of ancestral shrine is found in most Chinese homes of the old school.

13. *JMBRAS*, Topley, "Religion", p. 95, where she says that one of the (district or clan) associations charges as much as $1,000 for an ancestor tablet to be set up in the centre of the shrine, $500 on the left and $400 on the right. Freedman, p. 97, says a clan association permits a spiritual tablet to be placed in the centre of the altar upon a donation of more than $1,000 and that (pp. 213–214) another clan association ranges its charges from $100 to $300 per tablet according to position.
14. 礼祭仪 cited in 历俗，尚秉和，商务，April 1938, ch. 20, p. 261; 颜氏家训 (终制) ch. 20, p. 44 in 诸 *f. op. cit.*, vol. viii, which adds 四时祭祀...欲人勿死其亲，"the purpose of homage to ancestors in all the seasonal festivals is not to let them die"; and Yang Lien Sheng, p. 23.
15. 古文观止，商务，8th ed., November 1946, vol. i, ch. i, p. 18.
16. *Sin Chew* (神主) is translated by Roland Braddell, a prominent Malaysian advocate and solicitor and specialist in Chinese family customs, as "the spirit ruler" or "spiritual head of family". (Braddell, *Lights of Singapore*, p. 82.)
17. Withers-Payne, p. 243. For a full report of the judgement of Maxwell, C.J., se Kyshe, vol. i, pp. 216–222.

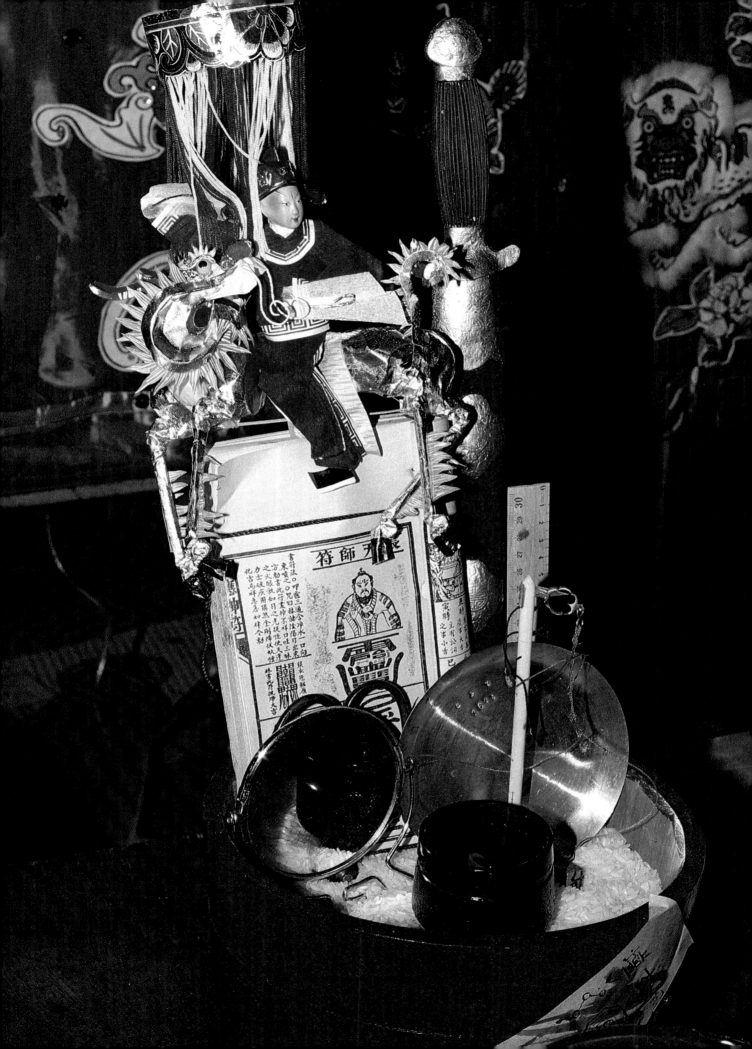

CHAPTER 5:
New Year Greetings

New Year Greetings to you. A universal Chinese form of greetings is "Kung Hsi Fa Ts'ai" (恭喜 (禧) 发财), wishing you to grow prosperous (with the in-coming year). Tradition says that it is an auspicious omen to begin the New Year well; and, if you do so, it foreshadows that everything you do throughout the year will be crowned with success, happiness and health.

This is one of the reasons why New Year cards are sent out and received a week or so before the New Year. As far as the Chinese are concerned, the tradition of card-sending originates from Emperor Kao Tsu (206–193 BC) of the Han dynasty (汉高祖). During this period it was also an essential practice to make New Year calls amongst the officials. The greeting cards were called the *pai p'ai* (拜牌), i.e. greeting placards or tablets. They were supplanted about one thousand two hundred years later by handwritten cards. These cards were presented at the time of calling but taken home by the visitors, presumably to be presented again and again at other calls.[1]

Nowadays, with the advancement of paper production and modern printing, artistically printed — and often multi-coloured — cards are used, and the common greetings are "Hsin Nien Chin Pu" (新年进步 , "Progress in the New Year"), "Kung Ho Hsin Nien" (恭贺新年 , "New Year Felicitations"), and "Hsin Ch'un Ta Chi" (新春大吉 , "Plenty of luck in the Spring"), with symbols of luck, success and longevity, like the dragon, the deer, the bats and peaches in the background.

Besides the outward and inward mails of felicitations, every Chinese home salutes you (and members of its family) with more wishes. If you look inside a Chinese house, you will see silk scrolls, wooden boards, and/or slips of red paper inscribed with lucky

A traditional New Year altar, which includes a bucket of uncooked rice, a weighing scale, a ruler, a mirror, a lit oil lamp, a pair of scissors, an almanac (open at a page showing the famous Taoist exorcist Teo Tien Sze) and a sword — all symbols of prosperity and progeny. The altar is an open invitation to all good influences, while the mirror and the sword keep evil at bay.

1. 通典 cited in 清录 *·op. cit.,* p. 2; and Eberhard, p. 39.

words and maxims posted up in different parts of the premises. Some silk scrolls depict legendary figures and moral stories, such as the Pa Hsien Ho Shou (八仙贺寿 , the "Eight Immortals") blessing a family with longevity, and the San Hsing (三星 , Three Stars) represented by three beaming old men signifying happiness, success and long life. The San Hsing are often represented by three porcelain statues: the statue carrying one or two infants represents Happiness; the central statue holding an emblem of authority represents Success; and the smiling statue carrying a long staff in his left hand and a peach in his right hand represents Longevity. Wooden boards are engraved with words like the *san to* (三多), an abundance of blessings, an abundance of years and an abundance of offspring; and the *chiu ju* (九如), meaning "May your life be lasting as the mountains and the hills, as the greater and lesser heights, as the streams which flow in all directions, as constant as the moon, like the rising sun, as enduring as the Southern Mountain, and as luxuriant as the pine and the cypress."[2]

Lucky Posters   The posters, renewed every year, are aplenty, especially in poorer homes. Over the lintel of a private residence, there is a wooden board, silk banner, or poster inscribed with four characters, *wu fu lin men* (五福临门), "may the quintuple blessings descend upon this household." The quintuple blessings are generally happiness, official success, longevity, joy and riches. They represent the *summum bonum* and *Ultima Thule* of human existence that only the poetic fancy of the mellow Chinese, wise in the way of the world, can invent for you.

Inside an unpretentious house where many families are herded together, perhaps through no fault of their own, there is the exhortation "Chia Ho Wan Shih Hsing" (家和万事兴), harmony in the house brings success in everything. There is also the desire to be blessed with "I Ts'ai Erh Hsi" (一财二喜), to get rich and to have two happy events, for example, a son's marriage and/or the gift of a male grandchild; and there is also the desire to be endowed with wealth and an easy and comfortable life, "Ch'ien Chin Pai Shun" (千金百顺). In the kitchen, apart from the renewed shrine of the Prince of the Oven (on or after New Year's Eve), the wish is for the presence of "Shui Lu Chen Pao Ch'i Chi Tsai Tz'u" (水陆珍宝 , 齐集在此), all the precious food obtainable on land as well as from the sea, in the hope that delicious dishes may be served therefrom. And upon the half-filled rice-jar is posted the words "Wu Ku Feng Sheng" (五谷丰盛), an abundance of the five cereals. Alternatively, the poster reads "Chu Mi Ying Weng" (珠米盈瓮), this jar is filled to the brim with pearls of rice. As the staircase is rickety and the wooden steps creaking, a poster assures you with the words "Shang Lo P'ing An" (上落平安), there's safety to go up and come down. Whilst the stinking and over-crowded cubicle on the first floor may cause tuberculosis and induce premature death, its poster at the door cheerfully claims that it's the "Isle of Taoist fairies and immortals" ("Hsiao P'eng Lai", 小蓬莱), where longevity and happiness exist.[3]

In the case of a business firm, the silk scroll or poster over the lintel usually reads "Wan Shang Yun Chi" (万商云集), trade and commerce of every description assemble here like the clouds. A merchant's sole aim may be reflected in the wish "I Pen Wan Li" (一本万利), to make profits ten thousand times over a capital

2. 辞源正续编合订本，商务 ·15th ed., February 1947. Our translation is adapted from Matthews' *Chinese-English Dictionary*, Harvard University Press, 1947.
3. P'eng Lai is one of the "Three Isles of Fairyland", the other two isles being Fang Chang and Ying Chou where immortals were believed to have drunk of the "Elixir of Immortality". These islands were said to be situated in the "North Sea" — Japan; and Shih Huang Ti (the first Emperor, 221–208 BC) was said to have sent an expedition with "a thousand virgin boys and girls" for the fairy realm, which failed to reach the destination. (Balfour, p. 25; C.A.S. Williams, p. 231; Giles, p. 48; and Dyson, p. 309.)

outlay. And to attain that aim, some may unscrupulously cut the throat of their unwary customers, to whom they extend a welcome in sugar-coated words, but at the same time they seem to assuage their own conscience with the poster containing the maxim "Ch'iu Ts'ai Cheng I" (求财正义), all wealth should be acquired only through righteous channels.

Single Characters   Sometimes, only one word such as *fu* (福 , luck or happiness), *lu* (禄 , official success) or *shou* (寿 , longevity) is inscribed on a silk scroll or a large sheet of fine paper. Each word is a symbol of human desire and is tastefully decorated in the hall or the guests' room.

The most popular word at one time was the character *fu* — and for very good reasons. An interesting legend says that in the Ming dynasty, a number of people had painted on their doors a bare-footed woman, with a lemon pressed to her bosom. When the reigning Emperor Hung Wu (朱洪武 , 1368–1398), founder of the dynasty, who was sightseeing during the Feast of Lanterns, saw the poster, he construed it to be a caricature of the Empress who had large feet and so he was greatly incensed. His Majesty, therefore, commanded that the word *fu* be distributed to every household, except the premises with the offensive painting. Later, an edict was issued to massacre all inmates in any house without the character *fu*. From that murderous incident onwards, the people deemed it a good omen to exhibit the word *fu*, and the custom has survived to the present day. Even up to the time of the Ts'ing (Manchu) dynasty, the word *fu* was distributed at the imperial palace to favourite officials of the court, and to the Hanlin scholars and imperial guards of the palace the character *fu* was specially written with a "double hook".[4]

Chiang Yee (蒋彝), of the *Silent Traveller* fame, narrates an interesting account in one of his books.[5] Opposite the site of his family house in China someone had constructed a towering three-storey building, which obscured the view from the Chiang home. This was interpreted, in geomancy theory, as an act "jeopardizing the prosperity" of the Chiangs. To counteract this, a brick screen-wall of tremendous height was immediately erected in front of the Chiang house. Facing the main gate was a stone pillar, and Chiang Yee's uncle caused the character *fu*, written by a popular calligrapher of the city, to be engraved thereon, so that everyone who had to come out of the gate would meet with luck and happiness.

Chinese Calligraphy   To be effectual, New Year wishes, it is believed, should be written in good penmanship; but so difficult is Chinese writing that only a few calligraphists, past and present, have really mastered the art. Specimens of good penmanship, which are reproduced for sale and for the imitation and practice of students, show a very high standard of art. It would be invidious to single out any particular master of the art, but mention must be made of Yen Lu-Kung (颜鲁公) and Liu Kung-Ch'uan (柳光权) of the T'ang dynasty, whose styles are known respectively as "the tendons of Yen and the bones of Liu" (颜筋柳骨), indicating elasticity and strength. Their styles and those of other masters serve as models of good penmanship.

Chinese calligraphy — a sister art of Chinese painting — demands full attentiveness, patience and the energetic and

4. Bredon & Mitrophanow, pp. 84–85. See also Burkhardt, vol. i, pp. 70–71; and 清史 · 小橫香 室主人 · 中华 5th ed., September 1930, vol. ii, p. 14.
5. Chiang Yee, p. 22.

弟子洪科 玉皇上帝 山殿

A. *The Pa Hsien Ho Shou, or "Eight Immortals", embroidered on silk: each holds a personal symbol.* **B.** *A housewife prepares the New Year's Day feast: note the altar to the Earth God, left.* **C.** *A Singapore street calligrapher discusses business with a client.*

constant practice of a learner. From the Chinese expression *shu hua* (书画) writing and painting, it is deduced that writing is a more exacting art. A beginner should, first of all, learn to write the big-sized word *ta tzu* (大字); thus exhorts Lady Wei (卫夫人) in the *Pi Chen T'u* (笔阵图); on no account should he start with *hsiao tzu* (小字), the small-sized words.[6] If he concentrates on the word first and then reduces it to written form, that writing tends to be good; if he hastens to write first and then recalls the word, that writing is bound to be poor. When the strokes are skilfully written with strength, the character becomes "bony" (多骨). When they are unskilfully written, the character becomes "fleshy" (多肉). Writing that has an abundance of bone and a dearth of flesh is called "sinewy writing" (筋书), and writing that has too much flesh and too little bone is denominated "a pig in Chinese ink" (墨猪). Writing with plenty of strength and plenty of muscle is "saintly" (圣); and writing devoid of strength and devoid of muscle is "sickly" (病).

The Great Master The greatest of the masters is Wang Hsi-Chih (王羲之 , AD 321–379), whose penmanship is said to possess "iron strokes and silver hooks" (铁划银钩), which connotes that the characters written by him were full of strength, buoyancy and grace. The proof of his writing may be inferred from the delightful anecdotes found in Chinese literature. When Hsi-Chih was twenty-seven years old, he copied out the *Wang T'ing Ching* (王庭经 , *Canon of Wang T'ing*) with such superb craftsmanship that a divine voice was heard in mid-air: "If your calligraphy could touch me so deeply, what may it not do to man?"[7]

On one occasion when Hsi-Chih noticed an old woman

6. 美术丛书 • 神州国光社 •Shanghai, series no. 2, vol. xxxix, under 书法粹言 Section, p. 2.

7. 图书会粹in 事类 •*op. cit.*, vol. vii, ch. 48, p. 52.

offering bamboo fans for sale, he took up a fan and scribbled some words on it, to the annoyance of the vendor. "My whole family depends on the sale of these fans," protested the woman. "Why did you spoil one of them?" "My good lady, your fan has not been disfigured. You've only to say that it bears the penmanship of Wang Iu-Chun (王佑军 , Hsi-Chih's alias) and ask for a hundred coins for each character." When the attention of the people in the market was drawn to this fan, there was a scramble for it regardless of the price. Later, the old woman begged Hsi-Chih to autograph a few more fans, but he dismissed her with a laugh.[8]

Hsi-Chih had a passionate craving for goose-meat, and when, one day, he learnt that a Taoist priest of the valley had a flock of geese, he hastened to the scene. Delighted at the succulent birds, Hsi-Chih requested the priest to sell them to him. But the owner declined to part with them for money. Instead, he suggested to Hsi-Chih to write out two chapters of the *Tao Te Ching* (道德经 , *Canon of the Way and Virtue*) in exchange for the entire flock. Hsi-Chih spent half a day to complete his part of the bargain and then wended his way home, a happy possessor of the basketful of geese.[9]

The roadside writers in Malaysia, who try to sell their posters a fortnight or so before the New Year (posters which are avidly purchased by the less affluent section of the community and put up at their residence after the annual "spring-cleaning"), produce works that are generally unworthy of the name calligraphy. But perhaps their penmanship suffices, for, after all, it is the spirit of the tradition rather than the material form that counts. At any rate, the main advantage of making New Year wishes, instead of making New Year resolutions as is the custom of the West on solar New Year's Day, lies in the fact that if the wishes were not granted one could, with complacency, put the responsibility entirely on the gods and deities; whereas when you make resolutions and break them, as many of you do, and often in record time, you have only yourselves to blame.

New Year Hospitality   Since the Chinese are expectant of blessings from the deities, they themselves deem it proper to set good examples by expressing their goodwill and extending their hospitality to all and sundry during the New Year, for is it not Confucius who said "Within the four seas all are brothers"? In the good old days, the door was open — and still is in many cases — to visitors of all nationalities and a host's popularity was judged by the number of calls, even without invitation. A European eye-witness reported in 1878 that the Honourable Mr Ho Ah Kay (胡亚基 (胡璇泽), also known as Whampoa, 黄埔) of Singapore was "besieged" for eight or nine days during the New Year by hundreds of people of various nationalities and the road to his mansion was jammed from morn till eve by numerous carriages heading to his "hospitable" gates.[10] The same hospitality is maintained by many a wealthy Chinese at the present day.

Inside a Chinese home, the guests are greeted with an overflow of auspicious symbols, represented by the cakes and fruits. There is the *nee-koay* (年粿 — Hokkien), the sweet, round (not spherical) cake made of pulut-rice, for instance, which is emblematic of eternal friendship because of its glutinosity. Its stickiness is suggestive of the theory of standing by one another through thick and thin — a universal brotherhood. *Nee-koay* means "the cake of the year", and if you consume it, all calamities

8. *Ibid.*, p. 53.
9. *Ibid.*, p. 52.
10. Vaughan, p. 43. According to the NYB of 1951 (section x, pp. 97–98), the Honourable Ho Ah Kay was an unofficial member of the Legislative Council in 1869 and later of the Executive Council as well. He was appointed a Justice of the Peace in 1871 and an Honorary Magistrate the next year. In 1876 he was honoured as a CMG and in the next year he became concurrently the Chinese Consul and Consul for Russia in Singapore. Hence his popularity in 1878. In April 1879 he was also made Consul for Japan. He died on 27th March, 1880, at the age of sixty-four.

are averted for the whole year. The Cantonese call this cake *nin kao* (the cake of the year), but because *kao* puns with the word for "high" (高), it is metaphorically construed to mean a "better life" in every respect than the preceding year.

Besides the cake of the year, there is the traditional octagonal tray containing eight varieties of sweetmeat and cakes in each of the eight outer sectors, called *pa kuo ho* (八果盒). In the central sector there is an abundance of the ubiquitous melon seeds (symbol of progeny). When a Cantonese host invites a guest to help himself with the melon seeds, he says "Yau Ngan" or "Yau Kam" (拗银 , 拗金), meaning respectively to pick up silver or to pick up gold.[11] The sweetmeat indicates the sweetness of life; the cakes suggest a higher level of living in the social and other spheres; and the dates, called *tsao tzu* (枣子), rhyme with the phrase meaning to have male children at the earliest opportunity (早子).

Oranges come under two principal categories: the *kam* (柑) variety, about the size of the California fruit; and the *kat* (桔 (橘)) variety, resembling the local lemon, slightly flattened on the top and the bottom. *Kam* is homonymous with the Chinese word for gold and also the word for sweetness (金 , 甘). As a corollary, oranges are emblems of what are sweet, auspicious and golden. Being fresh fruits, the oranges imply the gift of "new vigour and new lease of life" to the consumer. *Kat* is homonymous with the Cantonese word for luck. When you munch the juicy slices of the fruit, it is symbolic of your being blessed with *kat* (吉), plenty of luck or good fortune.

The circular or round shape has a meaning too. The Chinese word for circular or round is *yuen* (圆), which also means "satisfaction", or a cycle of life. In Cantonese, the word *yuen* puns with the syllable *yuen* in the expression *chong yuen* (状元), meaning a prince consort or minister of high rank in the old imperial days. Therefore, the circular shape of *koay-ka-pek* (*koay Belanda*), a Malayanized crispy, thin, rice-powdered biscuit known to local Europeans as a "love letter", connotes success in one's career or in one's cycle of life. When served, this biscuit is folded to look like the famous unfolded triangular Chinese fan. It is known as "love letter" probably because of the embossed designs on the cake, which resemble the secret code between lovers.

The groundnut or local peanut, in the pod stage, which is offered to the guests during the *yam seng* drinking bouts, also plays its part by virtue of its slender, cylindrical appearance. Normally it is called *hua sheng* (花生), the flower of life, and metaphorically it is called *ch'ang sheng kuo* (长生果), the nut of longevity. When a person partakes of the nut what else does it signify but a long, healthy and active life?

The Ang Pau Gifts   To cap it all, there is the well-known monetary gift, wrapped up in a red packet, denominated *ang pau* (红包 — Hokkien). This gift is made freely by the more affluent parents and elderly persons to their children and the children of relatives and friends and often to grandpas and grandmas as well during the New Year calls. Priority of calls is bestowed upon the most senior member of the family. If a senior member happens to be poor, the caller who could afford it usually makes a lavish *ang pau* gift, say $1,000 or multiples thereof. Conversely, if the senior member is a multi-millionaire, he may make generous *ang pau* gifts,

11. 新年，妾子匡，商务，1935, p. 83.

A. Mee koay, *a traditional New Year delicacy.* B. *The foot of a lion dancer crushes an orange — a ritual that brings luck.* C. Ang pau, *a red packet containing money, hangs temptingly in a doorway — from where it will shortly be snatched by a dancing lion.*

especially to his less fortunate kinsfolk. In the first year of their marriage, when a rich bridal couple makes the New Year calls visiting the chain of in-laws and relatives from one house to another, sizeable *ang pau* are anticipated and generally given to each of the kinsfolk. Conversely, if the newlyweds are in poor circumstance the wealthy parents, in the first year, may distribute *ang pau* worth a small fortune.

In more conservative homes — rather rare nowadays — the grandparents receive felicitations from their children, grandchildren and great-grandchildren. Each of the junior members offers, by rotation, a cup of edible bird's nest soup or a cup of tea, containing dragon's eye (*leng-geng*, 龙眼) and red date, sometimes with *ginseng* (人参), to the grandparents to wish them good health, vigorous and youthful life, a good ending and even more offspring. A similar tea-offering ritual is observed before the parents by the children. At the tea ritual the junior members, by rotation, kneel before the seniors — often bowing is observed instead, especially by those who have been abroad for higher education. Whatever the formalities, the primary object is veneration, and the keynote is sincerity. Where the senior member is rich, valuable *ang pau* gifts are distributed, especially to his favourites, married or unmarried.

This *ang pau* gesture resembles the gesture of Santa Claus who distributes gifts of toys to children at Christmas. Token sums are often extended to beggars. New Year *ang pau* gifts are annually distributed to the poor and aged by such Chinese organisations as the Haw Par Brothers and the Shaw Brothers prior to New Year's Day. Bands of musicians, usually Indians and Filipinos, also seize the occasion to travel from house to house to enliven the atmosphere and are tipped with an *ang pau* for their unsolicited services.

There are cogent reasons for the custom of making red packet gifts. The red packet is a symbol of luck — luck for the giver as well as for the recipient. If it is blessed to give, how much more blessed it is to do so during the New Year season! Red is believed to exorcise evil, for it is the colour dreaded by the mysterious monster which, according to an ancient legend, pounced upon innocent human victims and destroyed their property on New Year's Eve.

New Year Taboos To make the New Year blessings doubly sure, the Chinese impose upon themselves certain taboos. On New Year's Day, everyone refrains from using foul language or unlucky words, everyone wears new or clean clothes and new hats, and there is no sweeping of the floor. According to a correspondent in an English newspaper, knives, scissors and other sharp instruments that may "cut the thread of good fortune" are tucked away. He goes on to say that mothers always warn their children on New Year's Eve that in the morning they must take great care in what they say lest unlucky words may bring misfortune to the family.[12]

These Malaysian taboos are the modified survivals of mediaeval traditions of China, which enjoined the wearing of new dresses, the use of lucky words and taboos on floor-sweeping, on drawing water from the well, on borrowing fire from others, and on applying the needle and the scissors. The Amoy Chinese explained that if needle-work were done on New Year's Day, then the maidens' fingers were liable to be pricked in future; and that if

12. SM, "Chinese New Year Special Feature", 12th February, 1961.

children were thrashed, then they were inclined to fight throughout the year. The people from Tiechiu (潮州) insisted that the pair of chopsticks used should be of the same length; if one was shorter than the other, then they would miss the boat whenever they (the people) wanted to travel.[13]

There was an old belief in China, not later than 220 BC, that the 1st day of the 1st Moon was the birthday of chickens; the 2nd day, dogs; the 3rd day, pigs; the 4th day, sheep; the 5th day, cows; the 6th day, horses; the 7th day, human beings; the 8th day, cereals. Accordingly, the killing of chickens was forbidden on New Year's Day, of dogs on the 2nd day, of pigs on the 3rd day, of sheep on the 4th day, of cows on the 5th day and of horses on the 6th day. On the 7th day, no execution was carried out.[14]

This age-old belief is modified in Malaysia, where all butchers stop the slaughtering of pigs from New Year's Eve to New Year's Day. Most Chinese homes reserve a surplus of cooked food on New Year's Eve for consumption on New Year's Day. The reason is twofold: slaughtering is tabooed on New Year's Day, and the "left-over" from the previous year is a sign of super-abundance of material wealth. In nearly all cases vegetarian food, with or without the "left-over", is consumed, especially at breakfast.[15] On the birthday of human beings, many people eat uncooked lettuce, called *sang choy* (生菜 — Cantonese), and raw fish, called *sang yee* (生鱼 — Cantonese), especially the carp or freshwater fish, which are sold at fabulous prices on this occasion. For to consume *sang choy* (literally, "live" vegetable) and *sang yee* (literally, "live" fish) is symbolic of keeping alive forever, because a "live" vegetable is still called "live" vegetable whether it is cooked or left to rot. Similarly, a "live" fish is still called "live" fish even after its expiration. As the Cantonese maxim has it, "the 'live' fish never dies" (生鱼无死日).

13. 新年，*op. cit.*, pp. 55, 110.
14. 董勋问礼俗 in 玉函山房辑佚 series, under 问礼俗 Section, vol. xxviii, p. 72.
15. See p. 185 below.

CHAPTER 6:
These Flowers Are Symbolic

I t is the fashion to decorate the house with flowers in the New Year season, for their fragrance augments the hilarity of the atmosphere and their presence has a symbolic significance. In China "flowers are all the rage",[1] and there is always a wide range to select from, for many varieties bloom in the spring.

In Malaysia orchids are the popular choice. These flowers are so well cultivated in Chinese gardens that some varieties have received international recognition. In Singapore, there is the much appreciated orchid "Tan Chay Yan" (陈聚贤), named after Malaysia's first rubber pioneer of Bukit Asahan Estate (Malacca) fame, who died in 1916; in Penang, species include *Vanda* "Heah Joo Seang" (连裕祥), named after a multi-millionaire rubber magnate, *Dendrobium* "Cheah Seng Khim" (谢成金), named after a Malaysian senator, and the famous *Vanda* "Saw Seng Kew" (苏承球), named after one of Malaysia's most prominent Chinese, a past-president of the Penang Branch of the Malayan Chinese Association.

The floral display in pre-war Malaya so impressed a European writer that he described it in these glowing terms:

"Outside each house there are quaint decorations showing that the old year is finished and that a new time of hope is coming . . . . Each householder tries to make his own house a different pattern, and one was very much reminded of the flower feasts in Belgium, when the fronts at Heyst and Blankerberg are made beautiful with garlands and flowers. Here the householders put large trellis frames outside their houses or shops . . . and these frames are decorated with creepers and flowers. Frequently these flowers are artificial, and they are of every shade which it is possible to conceive. Very often wreaths of fresh flowers are put up . . . and give off a splendid scent during their early freshness. At

A little girl and her grandmother take a trishaw ride to the temple, with traditional offerings of flowers and food.

1. Ball, p. 244.

nighttime the whole of this erection is lighted up with lanterns —inside which are fixed electric lights or candles — festooned amidst the flowered trellis-work. The effect is a very distinct . . . brightening of the street."[2]

To the Chinese, flowers and plants are not merely botanical products, soft to touch, pretty to watch, fragrant to smell: many of them have a special significance or symbolic meaning. As we have shown in a previous chapter, at about midnight on New Year's Eve flowers are also offered to the deities and the ancestors. These flowers are placed at the altar and are not removed until the end of the New Year season on the 15th day of the 1st Moon. The most significant item is the pink pineapple flower, called in Hokkien *ong lai hua* (黄 (凤) 梨花), which rhymes with an expression meaning "the flower that brings luck" (旺来花). Equally significant is the orchid, known as the "Prince of all that are fragrant" (兰为王者香), which is symbolic of numerous progeny.[3] Whilst in Greek mythology the narcissus is said to be the transformation of a youth who had pined away for love of his own image, flower-lovers in China euphemistically call it the "Water-Fairy Blossom" (水仙花). In South China, it is *par excellence* the New Year's flower, and if the first bud opens on New Year's Day it is construed as a lucky sign.[4]

Symbol of Spring   The choice of flowers, like the choice of many other lovely things in this world, is a matter of individual taste. Is your favourite a plain rose, which Shakespeare thinks would smell as sweet by any other name? Traditionally, the Chinese have popularized through their literature some flowers and plants by associating them with the four seasons.

The peony, which bears the title of "King of Flowers" (牡丹花王), is the symbol of spring. It is also regarded universally as a symbol of riches, honour and nobility.

On a wintry day, in the reign of T'ai Tsung of the T'ang (唐太宗) dynasty (AD 627–649), Empress Wu Tse-T'ien (武则天) once took a stroll in the imperial park at Hsi An Fu (西安府) to inspect the flowers. As it was the season for only a few species to bloom, Her Majesty was rather displeased with what she saw. In a whimsical moment, she declared: "Let all blossoms open to greet me. Don't wait for the spring rains or the summer sunshine. Let all hearken and obey without fail." In response to this imperial command, all flowers unfurled their petals without hesitation. The peony, however, proudly declined, and was prepared to accept the consequence rather than blossom in the wrong season.

Furious at this *lèse-majesté*, the Empress ordered that the peony be exiled to Lo Yang.[5] At that time the flowers of Lo Yang, in Hunan Province, were famous all over the world, and, as the peony surpassed all others, it was labelled the "Lo Yang Flower" (洛阳花). Au-Yang Hsiu (欧阳修), a famous poet and calligraphist of the Sung,[6] described it as "the only true flower in the world" (天下真花独牡丹).

Symbol of Summer   The lotus represents summer, and is sacred both to the Buddhist and the Taoist, who regard it as an emblem of holiness. All Buddhas you see at the temple are enthroned each upon a lotus seat; whilst the Taoist Ho Hsien-Ku (何仙姑), the only female member of the Eight Immortals of Taoism, invariably carries a lotus-stem.

2. Sidney, pp. 59–60.
3. This epithet came from Confucius. After wandering from state to state, Confucius failed to obtain notice from any of the rulers of his time. On his way back to the state of Lu (his birthplace) from the state of Wei, Confucius was attracted by the fragrance of the orchid in a valley and remarked with a sigh, "The orchid should be the prince of all that are fragrant. But it has to remain in the company of grasses." Confucius was likening the orchid to himself; for like the "Prince of Fragrance", he had to rub shoulders with the common people instead of serving as counsellor to a ruler or prince. (See 家语 cited in 故事 , 仿宋子版 , 香港广智书局 , ch. 4, p. 241.)
4. Skinner, p. 191; and Ball, p. 244.
5. 纪原 , 高承 , 商务 , June 1937, vol. iv, ch. 10, pp. 394–395. This account has been dramatized in our translation.
6. 欧阳修牡丹记 in 格致 , *op. cit.*, vol. xiii, ch. 71, p. 1.

When Wang Tzu-Mou (王子懋) of the Tsin dynasty (AD 265–313) was seven years old, his mother was afflicted with a serious sickness. Bonzes were engaged to pray for her recovery, and amongst the offerings to the Buddhas was a lotus flower. To prevent the lotus from withering, the bonzes placed it in a brass pot.

Whereupon Tzu-Mou addressed the Buddhas in tears: "If this would make my mother recover, why not command the flower not to wilt at the end of the seven-day vegetarian ceremony?" The lotus was so touched by the child's filial piety that it grew fresher when the observance was over.[7]

Confucian scholars were profuse in their eulogies.[8] Because it "grows out of the mud without being tarnished," it was called the "Gentleman of Blossoms" (花之君子). Chang Min-Shu (张敏叔) labelled it the "Silent Guest" (静客); whilst Li Chun-Yu (李群玉) likened its roots to "Jades in the Mud" (泥中玉) and its seeds to "Pearls beneath the Dew" (露下珠).

Towards the end of the Tsin dynasty (*circa* AD 313), Huang Tsu (黃祖), after securing two medicated pills from an old man for the treatment of his sickly mother, subsequently visited a lotus pond, as directed. What greeted him at the entrance were three characters, *shan fu men* (善福门 , the Door to Goodness and Happiness), thereby implying the attributes of the lotus blossom.[9]

Symbol of Autumn   The chrysanthemum, which represents autumn, is popularly known as the "Flower of the Recluse" (隐君子 or 隐逸者) after T'ao Yuan-Ming (陶渊明), the famous hermit and poet[10] who resigned from the governorship of P'eng-Tse (彭泽) district because of his refusal to bow to a senior official "for the sake of five bushels of rice" (不为五斗米折腰).

Yuan-Ming did not aspire to riches, honour or rank; nor did he expect to become a ruler. So he retired to live in a cottage in front of which were planted five willow trees, which inspired him to call himself Wu Liu Hsien Sheng (五柳先生). Contented with few worldly possessions, he loved to read, but not too deeply, indulging in writing and wine whenever opportunity arose. The chrysanthemum was his favourite, because, like him, the flower does not compete with other varieties to bloom in the spring but blossoms alone in the frosty autumn.[11]

On the 9th day of the 9th Moon when scholars and government officials scaled the mountains to observe the *Teng Kao* custom, they invariably drank the chrysanthemum wine[12] which was believed to "confer long life" (饮菊花酒令人长命). In the precious collection of ancient paintings on silk paper by Lung Hsien-Sheng (龙先生 , Mr Dragon), in the book entitled *Pictures on Festivals and Customs*, there is an exquisite portrayal of three Chinese beauties,[13] each holding chrysanthemum blossoms in her hand on the 9th day of the 9th Moon "in expectation of long life" (以期永年). This was perhaps wishful thinking, but it was the prevalent belief.

According to the scholar Li Shih (李适), whenever Emperor Kao Tsung of T'ang (唐高宗 , AD 650–683) went up to the Tz'u En Monastery (慈恩寺塔) in autumn, he offered chrysanthemum wine to ask for longevity.[14] And it is stated in the *Legend of Immortals* that K'ang Feng-Tzu (康风子), who had eaten the chrysanthemum flower and the cypress seed on a moonlight night, eventually became an immortal.[15]

7.   南史 in 群芳 ··圣祖敕 ·in 万有 · 商务 · March 1935, vol. vii, ch, 29, p. 487.

8.   宋周惇颐 in 格致 · *op. cit.*, vol. xiii, ch. 72, p. 5; and 三余赘笔 and 李群玉莲叶 in 群芳 *op. cit.*, vol. vii, p. 692 & vol. viii, ch. 31, p. 731. But note that the lotus is called "a friend of purity" 净友 in 三余赘笔 in 图书 · *op. cit.*, vol. 531, ch. 11, p. 57.

9.   幽明录 in 群芳 ·*op. cit.*, vol. vii, ch. 29, p. 688.

10.   事类 *op. cit.*, vol. xi, ch. 78, p. 28; and 陶渊明 · 梁启超 · in 万有 · 商务 · 1929, pp. 64–65.

11.   陶渊明 · *ibid.* For many years we wrote a column on "Matters Chinese" under the pen-name Wu Liu, a pseudonym inspired by T'ao Yuan-Ming's *Wu Liu Hsien Sheng*, meaning "Mr Five Willows", and his way of life.

12.   干宝 in 子史 · *op. cit.*, vol. vii, ch. 151, p. 4.

13.   节令风俗图 compiled by 龙先生 (date and publisher not stated), in the Archives of the National Library, Singapore.

14.   李适传 in 月粹 · 秦嘉谟 · 琳琅仙馆 ·vol. iv, ch. 14, p. 6.

15.   格致 *op. cit.*, vol. xiii, ch. 73, p. 2.

Flowers for sale outside a temple dedicated to Kuan Yin in Waterloo Street, Singapore.

16. 事词类奇in 群芳·*op. cit.*, vol. vi, ch. 22 p. 520.
17. 万花谷·*ibid.*, p. 518.
18. 宋史隐逸传in 事类·*op. cit.*, vol. xi, ch. 78, p. 20; and 图书·*op. cit.*, vol. 548, ch. 212, p. 16.

Symbol of Winter As the plum-blossom radiates more beauty and fragrance in the winter months, it is regarded as an emblem of winter.

The 10th Moon is the prelude to winter in China, and since plum-trees begin to blossom in that period of the year it is called the Plum Month (梅月) in Chinese literature. Hence a scholar observed: "There are many flowers on land and water, whose fragrance is adorable, but only the plum-blossoms are the first in the world to bloom before the arrival of spring.[16] Another scholar, Tseng Tuan-Po (曾端伯), likened this flower[17] to a "friend of purity and honesty" (梅花为清友).

Lin P'u (林逋), a recluse who retired to live in the Western Lakes, found solace in his bachelor life in the cultivation of the plum and the rearing of storks, and in cruising the lake in a boat. His guests were presented with storks.[18] "The plum is my spouse," he said, "and the storks are my children" (妻梅子鹤).

Above all, the plum is said to have four noble characteristics (四贵：贵稀不贵繁，贵老不贵嫩，贵瘦不贵肥，贵合不贵开). It prefers quality to quantity, mellowness to immaturity, slimness to

plumpness, and privacy to publicity.[19]

In China, the plum, the bamboo and the pine figure prominently in Chinese homes during the New Year season, because the trio is metaphorically regarded as "Three Winter Friends" (岁寒三友) who remain constant and true to each other in wintry days, that is to say, in time of adversity.

The Bamboo Both the bamboo and the pine are upright, the virtue of a gentleman. The bamboo is important in the New Year, because the Chinese believe that it is the harbinger of peace to the household and also confers the threefold blessings, san to (三多：多福，多寿，多男子。), i.e. abundance of luck, abundance of years and abundance of male offspring.

Many and varied are its other virtues. It has strength of character, for the firmness of its roots and nodes are not thwarted by the snow or ice. It has a tender heart, for its leaves remain eternally green. The inside is hollow but its outside is straight, frank and unconcealed, showing staunch loyalty. It does not grow singly but in clusters, indicating chivalry.[20]

19. 及之潜确类书 in 群芳，*op. cit.*, p. 520.
20. 事类，*op. cit.*, vol. xi, ch. 82, p. 66.

A story was told of Meng Tsung (孟宗), a filial son, whose moribund mother expressed a desire to eat the bamboo shoots in winter. Meng Tsung entered the bamboo groves and wept bitterly. The shoots sprouted in response, thereby demonstrating the compassionate nature of the bamboo plant.[21]

The Duke of Li Lou (离娄公) is believed to have become an immortal after consuming the bamboo juice.[22]

The Pine   The pine is a "winter friend" because, as Chuang Tzu (莊子), the great philosopher, once observed, "When the cold weather has come and the frost and snow have fallen, then only would I know that the pine and cypress are at their best."[23]

And likening the pine and cypress to a *chuan tzu* (gentleman), Hsun Tzu (荀子), another great philosopher, remarked, "As the pine and the cypress prove their worth only in the cold season, so a person proves himself a gentleman only in time of adversity."[24]

The sprigs and the needles of the pine remain green in all the four seasons, indicating stamina and endurance. Because it lives to several hundred years, it signifies longevity.

It is recorded that when Shih Huang Ti of Ts'in (秦始皇帝), builder of the Great Wall of China, was on an excursion to the sacred mountain T'ai Shan (泰山), he was caught in a violent storm,[25] and was saved by holding fast to a pine tree, which he later ennobled as the "Fifth Minister of State" (五大夫).

An interesting anecdote is told of the strict disciplinary virtue of the pine tree. When Hsuan Tsang (玄奘), famous monk, traveller and philosopher of T'ang, was on his way to India to secure the Buddhist canon for China, he touched the branch of a pine tree at a monastery, commanding it to face the west during the monk's westward mission. In obedience to this, the branch pointed to the west year after year. Upon the monk's return, the branch changed its direction to the east.[26]

Deification of Flowers   Whilst flower-lovers weaved verses and wrote maxims about the blossoms and plants, Chinese myth-makers went a step further to deify them and associate some of them with the months of the lunar year. In the T'ang dynasty, the flowers were accorded a national birthday festival, originally on the 15th and subsequently on the 12th of the 2nd Moon. Besides creating the "Goddess of All Flowers", there was in each month of the year a flower-god or flower-goddess. For example, Hsi Shih (西施), a famous beauty of China, was made goddess of the lotus for the 4th Moon; T'ao Yuan-Ming, god of the chrysanthemum for the 9th Moon; and Po Chu-I (白居易), god of the camellia for the 11th Moon. These human beings were deified, after their death, to identify with the particular flower they had loved during their lifetime.[27]

The Flower Nymphs   More fascinating than the flower-gods and flower-goddesses was the creation of flower-nymph stories. One such story was translated by Prof. Herbert A. Giles. It relates to a Mr Huang of Chiao-Chow (胶州黄生), who built a house for his studies at the lower temple on Mount Lao (劳山) where camellias and peonies of gargantuan dimensions flourished. One day, and for some days in succession, Huang saw a beautiful young lady in white, a peony nymph, named Hsiang-Yu (香玉). Pursued and courted, the nymph eventually consorted with Huang

21. 楚国先贤传 in 事类 , *ibid.*
22. 神仙传 *ibid.*, p. 65.
23. 庄子 in 事类 , *ibid.*, ch. 81, p. 54.
24. 荀子集解, 王子谦 in 诸子 , *op. cit.*, vol. ii, ch. 19, p. 333.
25. 汉官仪 in 事类 , *op. cit.*, vol. xi, ch. 81, p. 54.
26. 神僧传 in 逸史 series, 吴琯 , 涵芬 , vol. 53, ch. 6, pp. 3–5.
27. Chiang Yee, pp. 33; 吴越风土录 , p. 1 in 小方 , *op. cit.*, vol. vi; and 事类 *op. cit.*, vol. xii, ch. 5, p. 42.

as man and wife. The happy mood of Hsiang-Yu was reflected in a
song sung by her:

> In pleasant company the hours fly fast,
> And through the window daybreak peeps at last.
> Ah, would that, like the swallow and his mate,
> To live together were our happy fate.

A pretty camellia nymph in red, named Chiang-Hsueh
(绛雪), half-sister of Hsiang-Yu, became the couple's constant
friend, and for some time the trio enjoyed each other's company.
One day, however, the peony was removed by a visitor and
planted in a new place, where it died a few days later. The
disappearance of Hsiang-Yu thereafter made Mr Huang realize that
his mate was a flower nymph. So both Huang and Chiang-Hsueh
wept bitterly for the missing peony, but the persistent and copious
tears shed by Huang every night so touched the Flower-Goddess
that Hsiang-Yu was permitted to return to life. There were initial
obstacles, followed by a series of incidents, one of which concerned
Chiang-Hsueh's timely rescue by Huang, but soon things turned
out well for the trio, who resumed their happy company as before.
One day as they were chatting gaily in the garden, Huang
expressed the wish that his spirit be always by the ladies' side. A
decade after, Huang was seriously ill. He told the priests of the
temple that he would be reborn "a red shoot with five leaves
alongside the peony", and requested them to take good care of it.
A year after Huang's death, a shoot did come up on the precise
spot; and the priests nurtured it as promised. "In three years it was
a tall plant, and a good span in circumference, but without
flowers. When the old priest died, the others took no care of it;
and as it did not flower, they cut it down. The white peony then
faded and died, and before the next Feast of Lanterns the camellia
was dead too."[28]

Another wishful story relates to a retired scholar of the T'ang
dynasty, who had rendered service to the flower nymphs.
Accordingly these nymphs came to offer their gratitude. "We
know," said one of them, "that we cannot make you any adequate
return, but we have brought you these blossoms, which, if you will
eat, will confer upon you the gift of everlasting youth . . . . ." So
the aged philosopher partook of the blossoms when suddenly his
face grew young again, the wrinkles disappeared from his brow, his
complexion became fair and delicate, and he felt a new strong
current of energy coursing through his veins . . . . "[29]

In short, if we may reiterate, a flower or plant is not just a
botanical product, exquisite and aromatic to the Chinese. It has its
physical appeal as well as spiritual import. It attracts the eye of the
common man; excites the ingenuity of the poet; and stirs up the
imagination of the myth-maker. And what imparts to the wishful
Chinese more sentimental value in the New Year season than an
imposing array of such virtues as are attributed to the flowers and
plants?

28. Hsiao Ch'ien, pp. 504–510 (The Flower
Nymphs). The original story is entitled *Hsiang Yu*
香玉 in 聊斋 , *op. cit.*, vol. i, ch. 3, pp. 137–138.
29. Balfour, pp. 176–186.

CHAPTER 7:
Yam Seng to You!

I n the New Year season, the sound of *yam seng* (饮胜) resounds everywhere, for, like all national carnivals, it is the time for gaiety, merriment and indulgence. And if we may add, wine merchants are amongst the traders who cash in enormously a week or so before the New Year, when appreciative clients send costly New Year gifts, including intoxicating drinks, to their patrons and friends, European and Asian.[1] Such gifts are one of the tangible expressions of the season's goodwill, kind thoughts and proverbial Chinese hospitality towards their fellow men, though in some rare cases an ulterior motive is not entirely absent. When gifts are received by the Chinese, they invariably make a return gift, or at least a token one such as some oranges as symbols of luck.

Yam seng (Cantonese) is often interpreted in English as "bottoms up". Though the English version gives you an idea of quantum, it fails to convey the deeper significance implied in the Chinese phrase. *Yam* means to drink; and *seng* means victory. The whole expression means "to drink to one's victory or success". In other words, *yam seng* is essentially a Malaysian form of toast — a toast to your health as well as your success in any undertaking. Unfortunately, because of its misinterpretation as "bottoms up", many an uninitiated, especially the European guest, gets scared of the phrase *yam seng*.

The correct Chinese equivalent to "bottoms up" is *kan pei* (乾杯). According to an authority, since the T'ang dynasty the etiquette in wine-drinking was *chiu hsun* (酒巡), "to drink by rotation", and it was the tradition to "order drinks after food" (食讫命酒), unlike the tendency of the present day, probably influenced by Western practice, which is to drink on an empty stomach, long before dinner is served.[2]

An aged Singapore carpenter pours a full glass of brandy for the photographer so the two can yam seng.

1. [The sending of "gifts" to business clients at the New Year has been actively discouraged by the Singapore government since the late 1970s.]
2. 博异记,摭异记,段成诸桌记,许汉阳传 cited in 历俗,*op. cit.*, ch. 7, pp. 109–119.

It is the empty-stomach drinking that sends many an amateur under the table. When the belly is filled with food, the alcohol loses its intoxicating effect, and a drinker may consume a larger quantity without a "black-out". At any rate, if you are liable to get drunk, with or without an empty belly, then you may find consolation in an ancient Chinese maxim,[3] which says "Wine-drinking is like soldiery" (酒猶兵也). In a thousand days, a soldier may not be called up, thus the maxim explains, but once he is in battle he should fight with absolute courage. A drinker may abstain for a thousand days, but once he starts drinking, he should drink till he is drunk. (兵可千日而不用 , 不可一用而不勇。 酒可千日而不饮 , 不可一饮而不醉。).

The Generous Host   In the New Year and on other occasions, your Chinese host is usually generous when he beckons you to drink. He pours a *stengah* into his glass, perhaps a little below measure; then he pours a *stengah* into each of the guests' glasses, usually more than the measure; and insists on your *yam seng*. The process of *yam seng* goes on, almost infinitely; for the magnanimous host is not happy until some of the guests literally go under the table. Sometimes when the genial host invites you to a *yam seng*, another *yam seng*, and yet another *yam seng*, he remains unaccountably sober, whilst your head begins to swirl. Your friend at the next table also invites you to a *yam seng*, another *yam seng*, and yet another *yam seng*. He too remains mysteriously sober; whilst your head keeps on swirling.

Then, to your astonishment, you realize that your host has been sipping Chinese tea, and your friend, ginger ale! To prevent such possible "ragging", the veteran drinker often suggests an exchange of drinks, or insists on mixing all the contents together and dividing them up proportionately. The process of "mixing the contents together" is sometimes deplored; but we see no serious harm in this practice. When you were in the midst of the jovial gathering, shouting yourself hoarse, roaring to the infectious laughter, and repeatedly vociferating *yam seng*, *yam seng*, you would be a prig indeed if you thought of the inhibitions of "hygiene" and the host of "hygienic principles" which you had learnt in the class room.

Famous Drinkers   Perhaps it is your misfortune that the liberal supply of drinks incapacitates rather than stimulates you; for there are many drinkers who show more brilliance and perform better intellectual work after drinking.

There was, for instance, Chang Hsü-Shan (张旭善) of the T'ang dynasty, a skilful calligraphist, who was excessively fond of wine.[4] When he became intoxicated, he usually created a lot of noise, with beads of perspiration dripping from his forehead into the ink. It was in this state of exhilaration that he invariably grabbed the Chinese brush to scribble the most beautiful Chinese characters in endless patterns, "as if guided by divine help" (若有神助). Thus he earned for himself the epithet "The Drunken Ink" (醉墨). In an earlier era, there was K'ung I (孔颐), a government official, who remained drunk most of the time, but whose decisions on state affairs never went wrong even once. The unanimous opinion was: "Duke K'ung may be drunk twenty-nine days in a month, but he is more discerning than other people who remain sober twenty-nine days a month."[5]

3. 费补之 cited in 茶余客话 , 阮葵生 in 明清笔记丛刊 series, 中华 · May 1959, vol. ii, ch. 20, p. 605.
4. 国史补 in 事类 · *op. cit.*, vol. vii, ch. 48, p. 52; and 太平 · *op. cit.*, vol. xvii, ch. 208, p. 8.
5. 南史孔颐传 in 月粹 · *op. cit.*, vol. i, ch. 2, p. 3.

A parallel in the West was Sir Toby Butler, a famous lawyer of his day. A client, gravely concerned about the success of his case, begged of Sir Toby to refrain from drinking his customary bottle before going to court. Sir Toby promised. The case was won after an eloquent pleading. As Sir Toby left the court, the client thanked him for having abstained; when to the client's surprise, Sir Toby said that if he had NOT taken the bottle, he would have lost the case.

"But your promise, Sir Toby?" inquired the client, somewhat bewildered.

"I kept it honourably," replied Sir Toby. "I did not DRINK a drop. I poured the contents of the bottle into a wheaten loaf and ATE it."[6]

Li Po and Omar   One of the most famous drinkers of all times is the Chinese poet Li Po, who could compose one hundred stanzas after drinking a *tou* (斗), or almost six litres, of wine. A story was told that he had never made a single error in his compositions whilst in a state of intoxication, and nobody was his match in controversy either.[7] The people of his time dubbed him "The Drunken Sage" (醉圣). Many of his gems were written extemporaneously, and some of the finest dwelt on the subject of drinking. The following is one of Li Po's famous poems, translated by James Lee Zee-Min in *Chinese Potpourri*:[8]

SPRING DAY AWAKENING

After all, life is but a dream,
And why should so much fuss be made?
Drink heartily like me and beam,
I sleep all winter in the shade.

At the courtyard, I look when I awake,
Amidst the flowers a bird sings,
I ask; "Tell me what day is today?"
The gentle breeze answers; "Tis Spring."

How time flies, I deeply sigh,
Another full cup I slowly pour,
I'll wait till the moon rises high,
Then happily I'll sing as of yore.

This view of life finds a kindred soul in Omar Khayyam, another of the world's most famous drinkers. Omar expressed the same thought, even more tersely, in another form:[9]

Ah, fill the cup: what boots it to repeat
How time is slipping underneath our Feet:
Unborn To-morrow and dead Yesterday,
Why fret about them if To-day be sweet!

Immortal Drinkers   The life of abandon advocated by brilliant poets and scholars is not without valid reason. In every age, there are ambitious men — and women, for that matter — who, taking advantage of their position and authority, throw the country or the world into chaos to attain their own selfish ends. Genial souls, who really have the welfare of the people at heart, despairing of

6. This anecdote is from one of the English books on humour, probably *Humour in Parliament*, which has been mislaid or lost.
7. 开元 p. 15, 王仁裕 in 说库，上海文明书局，January 1915, vol. viii.
8. James Lee, p. 189. The Chinese title of the poem is 春日醉起言志．(See 李白，in 作家与作品丛书 series, Shanghai Book Co., Hong Kong, July 1962, p. 240.)
9. Arberry, p. 176.

"Yam seng to you!" cry this group of young Singaporeans.

such nefarious policies, become recluses to escape the sordidness of man. Such was the case of the "Seven Sages of the Bamboo Grove" (竹林七贤), famous drinkers in Chinese history, who lived in the third century AD when China was torn asunder by warlords.

The leader of the group was Juan Chi (阮籍), a profound scholar steeped in the philosophy of Lao Tzu and Chuang Tzu, who defied the convention of his day. On one occasion when a matrimonial alliance was proposed from high quarters, which necessitated a tactful answer, he primed himself in drinks for a succession of sixty days, thus evading the issue. Many a civil and military appointment was offered to him — all this he declined, for he preferred intoxicating drinks to dirty politics.[10]

The best known of these sages was Liu Ling (刘伶), an ugly looking man with an insatiable thirst for alcohol. Once his wife remonstrated with him, saying that inordinate drinking would ruin his health. Whereupon Liu Ling knelt on the ground and declared, "Heaven gave life to Liu Ling and bestowed upon him the name of wine. Liu Ling drinks one *tan* (石 , fifty-seven litres) at

10. 文学・文史出版社・Hong Kong, October 1961, pp. 89, 96, 97.

a stretch and gets over his dipsomania after five *tou* (twenty-eight litres)." He is best remembered as the drunk who frequently travelled in a deer-cart with a jug of wine, followed by a servant with a shovel. "When death overtakes me," said he to the serf, "bury me on the spot."[11]

Chi K'ang (嵇康), a close friend of Liu Ling and another member of the group, was born a genius. He was an erudite scholar, a great musician, a versatile poet and an incorrigible drunk. Nevertheless, he was recommended for service with the government. This he politely refused,[12] and his refusal was embodied in the famous paper called *Severance of Relationship* (绝交书).

A few centuries later, during the T'ang dynasty, there arose another group of drinkers who were called "Eight Immortals of the Wine-Cup" (饮中八仙歌), made famous by the *Odes* of Tu Fu (杜甫). The eight immortals alluded to in the *Odes* are Li Po, the most celebrated of the band; Ho Chi-Chang (贺知章), an inordinate drinker; the Prince of Ju-Yang (汝阳), who used to hold court after three *tou* (eighteen litres) of wine; Li Shih-Chih

11. 晋书刘伶传 in 子史 *op. cit.*, vol. viii, ch. 151, p.1; 太平 *op. cit.*, vol. xix, ch. 233, p. 3; and 文学 , *op. cit.*, 96. In rendering the Chinese measures used in mediaeval China, we have adopted the rendition given by E-Tu Zen Sun & de Francis, p. xix, [in which the unit *sheng* is equivalent to 31.6 cubic inches English measure or 0.9118 Imperial pints:

Chinese Measures		Pints		Litres
	1 sheng (升) =	0.9118	=	0.5179
10 sheng	= 1 tou (斗) =	9.118	=	5.179
5 tou	= 1 hu (斛) =	45.59	=	25.895
2 hu	= 1 tan (石) =	91.18	=	51.79

In round figures, the *tou* can be regarded as five litres, the *hu* as twenty-five litres and the *tan* as fifty litres.]

12. 文学 , *op. cit.*, p. 97.

(李适之), an imperial clansman; Ts'ui Tsung-Chih (崔宗之), a noble who was Li Po's constant partner in "wine, song and poetry"; Su-Chin (苏晋), a famous scholar; Chang Hsü (张旭), the calligraphist; and Chiao Sui (焦遂), the stammerer.

Ho Chi-Chang used to ride on a horse when he became tipsy, fancying himself in a rocking boat. Sometimes he became so dizzy that he toppled into the bottom of a well where he lay asleep. But the wonderful effect that wine produced on Chiao Sui, the stammerer, astounded all those present at the feast. After five *tou* (twenty-eight litres), he became exceptionally eloquent, talking eruditely and debating with tremendous force.[13] The same wonderful effect, it is said, was produced on R.B. Sheridan. According to Samuel Rogers, Sheridan did not display his wonderful powers in company till he had been warmed by wine. During the earlier part of a dinner, he was generally heavy and silent. After dinner, when he had had a tolerable quantity of wine, he became brilliant.[14]

Alcohol and Vice   Almost every nation has its alcohol discoverer, perhaps with pride; but the first wine-maker of China was disgraced for his discovery. He was Ti-Yi (狄仪), who created wine from fermented rice and wheat, a mixture with five different flavours. Overjoyed with his discovery, he presented the mixture through his daughter to the Great Yu (大禹 , 2205 BC), founder of the Hsia dynasty. After tasting the beverage, which gave him a stimulating sensation, the Great Yu proscribed the mixture and ordered the discoverer to be exiled to a distant province.[15]

But the wine did not vanish with the unfortunate exile. For the alcohol vice reared its ugly head toward the end of the Hsia dynasty when its last ruler Chieh (夏桀 , 1818 BC), infatuated with his concubine Mei-Hsi (妹喜), revelled in debauchery and orgies until his downfall.[16] The new dynasty was the Shang, whose last ruler, Chou Hsin (纣辛 , 1154 BC), created the most notorious case in wine-drinking history. To pander to the whims of his favourite Ta Chi (妲己), heavy taxations were levied to build the famous deer terrace (鹿台), occupying a space of three Chinese miles with a height of two thousand one hundred metres, taking seven years to complete. In this terrace was a wine-pond and a "meat forest" with viands of every description hanging on the trees nearby. Men and women who attended the orgies were all in a state of nature, and, at the signal of the droning drum, "more than three thousand ministers and courtiers had to drink like bulls from the pond" at a time. This bacchanalian gusto lasted till dawn. When eventually Chou Hsin lost the throne, the founders of the Chou dynasty (1122 BC), who regarded alcohol as "evil", prohibited the Chou people from wine-drinking with the death penalty.[17]

However, the laws were modified or changed with every new dynasty according to the whims and fancies of the emperor, or the political, social and economic order of the day. An interesting story relates to Yang Kuei-Fei (杨贵妃), the favourite concubine of Ming Huang, Emperor of T'ang (AD 713–755). One night when Ming Huang had broken his promise and gone to another apartment to spend the night with her rival, Kuei-Fei became so jealous that she sought solace in the "rose dew" wine (玫瑰露), drinking one jug after another. When she became inebriated, she capered and danced and, losing control of herself, tried to flirt with her eunuch-attendant. This episode is known as *Kuei-Fei Gets*

13. 杜甫诗 compiled by 傅东华 , 商务 , 3rd ed., October 1949, p. 5. In the commentaries, the compiler questions the correctness of Tu Fu's inclusion of Su-Chin in the celebrated band. Su-Chin is believed to have died in 开元二十二年 (AD 733–734), and to include him as one of the Eight Immortals of the Wine-Cup is obviously an anachronism. It is suggested that 裴周南 should be one of the group, proof of which is the engraving of his name on the new tombstone of Li Po as one of the eight immortals. On this tombstone the name of 苏晋 does not exist.

14. Rogers, p. 71.

15. 吕氏春秋 and 战国策 in 纪原 , *op. cit.*, vol. iv, p. 329. Another discoverer of alcohol was Tu K'ang (杜康), who made wine from rice (世本 in 事类 , *op. cit.*, vol. x, ch. 67, p. 3). In Malaysia, Tu K'ang is generally accepted as the first discoverer, and as such is popularly known as the patron saint of wine dealers and restaurants.

16. 史记 , 司马迁 , 涵芬 , 1916 ed., vol. ii, ch, 3, p. 4. According to another source, Chieh of Hsia was an unprincipled ruler. He created a "hill of meat" and a "pond of wine" and built a luxurious palace and a jade terrace. (See 通鉴 in 故事 *op. cit.*, ch. 3, p. 167.)

17. 史记 , *ibid.*, pp. 10–11; and Creel, *Birth of China*, p. 328.

Drunk, (贵妃醉酒), made famous in modern times by the Peking Opera, with actor Mei Lan-Fang (梅兰芳), the world-renowned female impersonator, playing the title role.[18]

Drinking Games   A sumptuous Chinese dinner is incomplete without the traditional drinking games. One of these games in China is the poetry game in which any number of people could take part. The leader, usually the host, gives a number of words to be used as rhymes, or the first words of the lines. The leader begins by coining a line containing the first key word in the stipulated place. The next man on his right coins another line containing the second key word, keeping in rhyme with the first line — and so on, until all the key words are used and the poetry completed. If a line is well coined, all join in drinking the author's health. The author has to drink a cup alone if he commits a blunder. There are many patterns of poetry forming, but the principles are the same.[19]

Another game is known as "Beating the drum to hasten the blooming of blossoms", in which any number of players could take part. A man, concealed behind a screen, is beating a drum whilst the participants at the table pass a filled cup of wine from one to the other. The movement of passing the cup has to quicken or slow down to keep time with the beat of the drum. If one spills the cup or happens to hold the cup when the drum stops all of a sudden, he drinks the cup, and the same process is repeated.[20]

Then there are the finger-guessing games, which are occasionally seen at Malaysian banquets or functions. One is called *ts'ai-mei* (猜枚), *morra* in Italy, or the *micare digitus* of the old Romans.[21] It is an amusing and witty game, played by two contestants, who stick out their fingers, simultaneously calling out a number to indicate the sum of the combined fingers. The loser drinks the cup. We had occasion to witness an expert who won or lost as he pleased, because he seemed to have read the mind of his opponent like an open book. When the expert wanted a drink, he relaxed to allow victory; and when he wanted his opponent to drink in succession, he guessed the sum correctly in almost every game.

Another finger-guessing game is played by using the thumb, the index finger and the little finger. The thumb is the husband, the index finger is the wife, and the little finger is the concubine. The husband "beats" the wife; the wife "beats" the concubine; and the concubine "beats" the husband.[22] We have seen this amusing game played in Malaysia, and laughter is invariably provoked when the concubine keeps up her victory over the crestfallen husband again and again.

18.   James Lee p. 87; and 贵妃醉酒，许原来，
(梅兰芳主演)，新美术出版社 Shanghai, 3rd reprint,
June 1955.
19.   (Anon.), p. 11.
20.   (Anon.), p. 11.
21.   Townley, p. 198; and S.W. Williams, vol. i, p. 808.
22.   Wilhelm, *Soul of China*, p. 334.

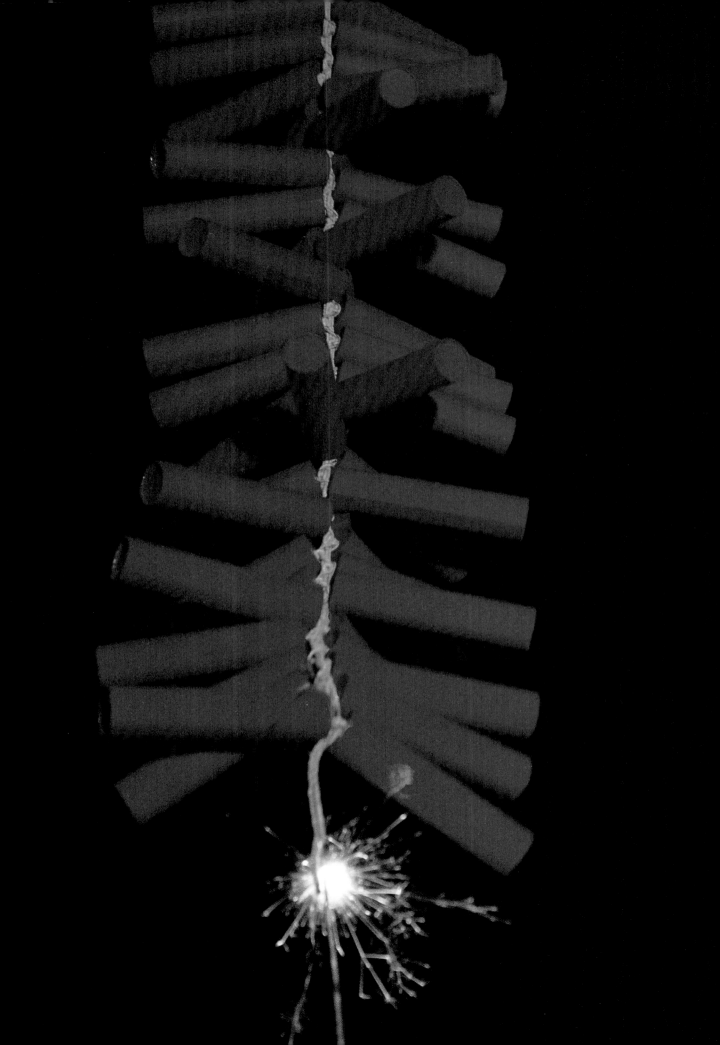

CHAPTER 8:
In Defence of Fire-crackers

Way back in the period between 740 and 330 before Christ there existed an ill-smelling giant more than three metres high in the deep forests on the western side of the village. Because of the stench radiating from his body, he was named Shan Sao (山臊) of the mountains. Human beings who offended him, intentionally or unintentionally, were afflicted with fever and cold, resembling what is known today as malaria. One day, someone had a brilliant idea: he suggested that a din be created to scare the monster away from human society. Accordingly, the people constructed a heap of bamboo stems and set them on fire, and as the burning stems resulted in a series of explosions, the monster scooted off in fright and was never seen in the vicinity again.[1]

Later, another legend told of the use of the detonating bamboo stems on a New Year's Eve. Li T'ien (李畋) had a neighbour, named Chung-Sou (仲叟), who was frequently set upon by malignant spirits of the hills. On the advice of Li T'ien, detonating bamboo stems were suspended from dozens of poles. On a New Year's Eve these stems were burnt, and at the fusillade of the scorched bamboo stems, the evil spirits vanished into thin air.[2]

From that time onwards, the creation of a din either by bamboo-stem burning or beating the drums, supplanted in about the fifth century BC by gunpowder explosives, became a national ritual in the observance of New Year's Eve and other important festivals in the lunar calendar. As may be inferred from the two early legends, the function of the din was originally of a religious or quasi-religious nature, and as the universe was believed to be infested with benevolent spirits (shen, 神) as well as malevolent spirits (kuei, 鬼),[3] it became an established practice to discharge

The use of fire-crackers has been banned in Malaysia since 1969, and in Singapore since 1972.

1. 荆楚 · 宗懔 in 说郛 series, 明抄本 · 涵芬 · vol. xiv, ch. 25, p. 9. A description of the Shan Sao is given by de Groot, *Religious System*, vol. 5, p. 498, which says they existed in Fu-Yang (about present Hangchou), and "have a human countenance and an ape-like body, and can speak."
2. 异闻录 in 格致 · *op. cit.*, vol. ix, ch. 51, p. 30.
3. 管子 in 子史 *op. cit.*, vol. vi, ch. 111, p. 4. See also 订鬼论 in 论衡 by 王充 in 诸子 · Shanghai 中华 · pp. 219–222. Whereas the belief in evil spirits exists in the East as well as the West, as is simply shown in Frazer, *Golden Bough*, ch. LV, pp. 544–551, in China fire-crackers constitute the chief agency in the expulsion of these spirits. (See also *CJSA*, Sowerby, p. 56.)

fire-crackers to drive away the malignant spirits which tended to lurk around to molest human beings.

The Cracker's Riddle   This practice was so interwoven with the life of the people down through the ages that by the seventeenth century AD the riddle of a fire-cracker was identified with the cracker's main function. It read:

> So great is my power that all demons and sprites, I control —
> Like thunder my voice, though my form, 'tis a mere shapeless roll!
> Men tremble in sudden affright at my terrible sound,
> Yet I'm ashes and dust ere the startl'd one turns him around.[4]

But though fire-crackers hold demons of every description in fear, it is paradoxical that demons, on the other hand, also hold rulers and men — creators of the small detonators — in awe. This was so, at least in monarchical China, as is attested by an anecdote relating to a powerful Manchu ruler. He was Emperor Ch'ien Lung (乾隆皇), who held sway over the then mighty Chinese empire in the period between 1736 and 1795. His Majesty was reported to have the uncanny habit of discharging bamboo crackers every night — between the day of the departure of the Kitchen God to Heaven on the 23rd of the 12th Moon and his return to earth on New Year's Eve — on the corridor of the palace suites to avert the (possible) molestation of malignant spirits.[5]

Multifarious Functions   Since then the functions of the fire-cracker have become manifold, and not necessarily connected with the expulsion of evil spirits. In Malaysia they are used in joyous events like marriages, processions and festivals, and on sad occasions like a funeral, with the dominant motive of exorcising evil. In a funeral procession, when the newly departed soul is being escorted to Western Paradise through the chanting of liturgies by bonzes and Taoist priests, there is a tendency for stray ghosts to try to hinder the soul. Detonators are therefore discharged *en route*. On the same theory, at the cemetery during the *Ch'ing Ming* festival, crackers are let off to prevent hungry spirits from trying to molest the ancestors and grab at the food-offering. Fire-crackers are let off at a theatrical performance of the traditional type before the curtain is up, and in a pugilistic exhibition, especially in the fast-moving sword-and-spear duels, to avoid possible accidents — accidents believed to be engineered by mischievous spooks.

Specific cases were aplenty demonstrating the multifarious parts played by fire-crackers. In about October, 1911, the Manchus were overthrown by the Chinese Revolutionaries headed by Dr Sun Yat-Sen (孙逸仙 (中山)), who was then in London. When the news of the fall of Peking reached Singapore in about November, the Chinese all over Singapore were jubilant and the principal streets of the Chinese quarter were "scenes of excitement, animation and rejoicing." These scenes were enlivened by the incessant firing of crackers with debris lying "ankle-deep in the Market Street" and covering "the long line of North and South Bridge Roads like a carpet."[6] In 1921, Chung Thye-Pin (郑大平), a worthy son of Kapitan Chung Keng-Kwee alias Ah Quee (郑景贵 (亚贵)), was appointed the Kapitan China of Perak and the installation ceremony took place on 28th March in the royal town

4. 红楼梦 · 曹雪芹 or 曹沾 · cited and translated in *JNCBRAS*, Mayers, p. 79.
5. 清史 · 中华 ·1 5th ed. September 1930, vol. i, pp. 38–39.
6. Song Ong-Siang, pp. 471–472.

of Kuala Kangsar. "In the afternoon, a Chinese procession went round the town amidst the Chinese drum-and-cymbal music and the profuse firing of crackers to usher in the installation of Chung Thye-Pin. Thye-Pin and his wife rode in a lavishly decorated car, led by Chinese towkays in their resplendent Mandarin garments." There was another memorable event on that historic day. In the morning, a ceremony was held in honour of the Sultan, who became the·proud recipient of the insignia of a Knight Commander of the most distinguished order of St Michael and St George (KCMG). These events marked the crowning success of the harmonious co-operation and combined efforts of the Malays, Chinese, Indians, Europeans and others, who, like their forebears before them, played a role in the building of a peaceful and prosperous state under a British-guided stable government.[7]

Some Recent Cases Generally speaking, there are two main types of crackers used by the Chinese in China and abroad. They are the single-packet type and the long-streamer type. The single-packet type, which detonates for a short duration, is euphemistically called *i pen wan li* (一本万利), which means anyone who spends money on this packet of crackers will be awarded gains ten thousand times. The streamer type, which suspends from the top storey of a building to the ground below, is euphemistically called *p'ao wang pien* (炮旺鞭) meaning the "explosive whip announces prosperity."

Perhaps local history was made in September, 1964, when the rich and influential Chinese Chamber of Commerce of Singapore (新加坡中华总商会) held the inaugural opening of its magnificent ten-storey building at Hill Street. The unveiling ceremony was performed by Lee Kuan-Yew (李光耀), the dynamic and statesman-like Prime Minister of Singapore, in the presence of a gathering of thousands of members, guests and interested spectators. Apart from the spectacular dragon and lion — four separate teams — dances, the main attraction, as far as the curious sightseers were concerned, was the lengthy streamer of fire-crackers suspended from a crane more than fifteen metres above the courtyard. When these fire-crackers were let off after the unveiling ceremony, their deafening explosion was heard far and wide for several minutes. As this day coincided with the 15th day of the 8th Moon, four artistic lanterns were hung up atop the streamer, each bearing a character to constitute the meaning "The Moon is round; the flowers fragrant" (月圆花好), to imply a dual celebration: the opening ceremony as well as the Moon Festival.[8]

In good old China, high-ranking Mandarins on tour were greeted with a fusillade of crackers wherever they visited, just as in Western countries distinguished visitors are saluted with the booming gun. Following the China tradition, when Lee Kuan-Yew and his dedicated PAP (People's Action Party, 人民行动党) colleagues were elected to hold the reins of the state government in 1959 and 1963, they were afterwards greeted by the voters with the popping and spluttering detonators on various occasions. On the evening of 22nd September, 1963, Kuan-Yew, his colleagues and supporters went round the main streets in the Chinese quarter of the city to thank the voters, and crackers were lavishly let off in their honour. A Chinese reporter who covered the news described the crackers as "detonating incessantly, with flashes of red glow, and roaring like the thunder."[9]

7. Wong, *Gallery*, pp. 85–86. (See *SET*, 31st March, 1921, for full coverage of the ceremonies.)
8. 南洋 ·21st September, 1964.
9. 星洲 ·23rd September, 1963.

An old Chinese print demonstrating the
traditional use of fire-crackers.

Upon entering into occupation of new premises, some
Chinese deem it an important ritual to initiate the entry with a
discharge of the spluttering crackers, which also play a role at the
inaugural ceremony of a newly established business. Not long ago,
when the $60,000 air-conditioned office of the Tourist Promotion
Board, Singapore, was opened in John Little's building, with Dr
Goh Keng-Swee (吴庆瑞博士), the Minister of Finance, popularly
known as the "financial wizard" of Singapore, performing the
unveiling ceremony, crackers popped and spluttered amidst the
jubilant crowds.[10] The theory, like that in the New Year, is to
cover the floor with a carpet of pink or red debris from the
crackers' wrappers — to fill the hall with red, *man t'ang hung*
(满堂红), a sign of prosperity.[11]

When a Chinese is assaulted by his fellow man, he does not
prefer, if he had his choice, to air his grievance in court. He
chooses to demand a gift of fire-crackers — the more, the better —
in addition to a pair of red candles and a set of "golden flowers"
(金花) and "red silk threads" (红绸) — a Chinese form of apology.
Where the case is of a more serious nature, a monetary award,

10. *ST*, 21st May, 1964.
11. 仪征岁时说 cited in 全国，胡朴安，广益书局，
Shanghai, October 1923, pt. ii, vol. i, ch. 3, p. 100.

denominated "compensation for medicine", is made as well. A recent assault case involving two Malaysians in Singapore substantiates the fire-crackers theory. After the case had been going on for five and a half hours before a district judge, it was announced that the matter was amicably settled between the parties because the aggressor had offered "a long streamer of crackers" to the aggrieved.[12]

Influence of Fire-crackers   Not many years ago, we witnessed a farewell party at the Penang wharf. A European and his charming wife, who were going home on furlough, were garlanded by their Indian friends, employees of a rubber estate, after the fashion of the Nabobs in former British India. Their Chinese friends, who did not desire to be behind the Indians in formalities, hastily procured some packets of crackers from a nearby shop and began to let them off cheerfully, followed almost instantly by a joint chorus of "For he is a jolly good fellow . . .". Truly this was a unique scene of the East meeting the West or *vice versa* in an atmosphere of amity and genuine brotherhood.

12 *ST*, 4th April, 1964.

In fact, the crackers custom has taken root in Malaysia where citizens of all origins find pleasure in letting them off for fun and merriment and for driving away evil spirits. In celebration of their *Hari Raya Puasa* the Malays, especially boys and girls, discharge fire-crackers as well as home-made bamboo detonators; in observance of their *Deepavali*, the Indians enliven it with the Chinese type of crackers — they even did so on 3rd November, 1964, despite the ban imposed by the government because of the Emergency.[13] Fire-crackers are also let off on Christmas Eve when Christians and non-Christians rejoice themselves with Santa Claus. And there is a recorded case in Kelantan where the British Resident himself was concerned. On 2nd August, 1918, the flagstaff at the Residency was struck by lightning, and this incident was regarded by many as a portent of evil. To repulse this evil, a Buddhist purification ceremony was conducted by a number of Siamese priests. During an almost twenty-four-hour preparation, chanting and praying took place in and about the precincts of the Residency, amidst the letting off of "bombs" and "fire-crackers" as auxiliary evil-expulsion agents.[14]

History of Gunpowder   To sum up, though a mellow race, the Chinese are Peter Pans at heart, irrespective of their age. Grandpa enjoys the detonation as much as the street urchin. Whereas to the imaginative mind of grandpa, this tiny explosive is a miniature pyrotechnic display, as a table on the Chinese stage is a scenic mountain to the imaginative and appreciative audience, the street urchins may find it good sport to fling the exploding missile at any unwary victim, especially of the fair sex. Grandpa's child-like indulgence in the explosives may not be fully appreciated by many non-Chinese. But history shows that the Chinese (in China) have had a proud record of explosives and their application. This is testified by W.F. Mayers, who had made an extensive research into China's use of gunpowder and concluded, in effect, that it was about the 5th or 6th century AD that the invention came from India or Central Asia into China "in connection with the manufacture of fireworks for purposes of diversion", and that this new material supplanted the practice of crackling bamboos as "a charm against evil spirits". There was no evidence of the employment of the explosive for warfare until the use of *p'ao ch'e* (炮车), a projectile carriage, against the Kin Tartars during the twelfth century, nor did a knowledge of its propulsive effects come to the Chinese until about 1407 when the *shen-chi* (神机) methods of spears and guns were acquired — a thousand years after its first employment in fire-crackers.[15]

That should occasion no surprise, because for centuries in the past the old Chinese maxim on soldiery was to the effect that "as good iron was not used for making nails, so good sons did not enlist for the battle fields" (好铁不造钉 , 好仔不当兵). As a matter of fact, the Chinese had not learnt the art of using the explosive for large-scale human massacre until she was brought down to her knees by alien powers in the latter part of the nineteenth century. Yet the Chinese proved themselves to be brave, disciplined soldiers in the famous "Ever-Victorious Army" (常胜军) in the 1860s — and that was formed by an American named Frederick Ward, and later trained and commanded successfully by an English officer, Major Charles Gordon.[16]

Gunpowder was known to the West only as late as 1242.[17]

13. 南洋 , 3rd November, 1964.
14. *JMBRAS*, Farrer, pp. 261–263.
15. *JNCBRAS*, Mayers, pp. 82, 84, 94.
16. Douglas, *Li Hung Chang*, pp. 27–44. See also Allen (no page reference).
17. *The World Book Encyclopaedia*, Chicago, 1963, vol. vii, p. 426.

The record of some Western countries shows that they applied the explosives again and again for mutual massive slaughtering. The discovery of dynamite by Alfred B. Nobel, the Swedish inventor, in the nineteenth century, is a case in point. Nobel became a multi-millionaire and ought to have been a proud and happy inventor, but instead was a wretched man in the evening of his life, brooding over his guilt at having created a substance that was largely responsible for blasting South Africans to smithereens in the Boer War. His remorse at the massacre of South Africans was reflected in his bequest of a fund of $9,000,000 (US currency) for the formation of the internationally famous Nobel (Peace) Prize.[18]

Complaints and Abuses   It is conceded that the din created by the fire-crackers does give cause for complaint, especially to a small number of intolerant residents perhaps suffering from nerves. There was George Bilainkin, a former North Malayan newspaper European editor, who considered the crackers a torture. "I planned to sleep on the first night of a Chinese New Year celebration in the rest-house at Taiping," he wrote. "I stopped there late in the evening because I was too tired to drive on to the next rest-house on the road to Singapore. Throughout the night with intervals of fifteen or twenty minutes crackers were fired by young people and old people, by Europeans and by Chinese." Poor George probably did not sleep a wink and was naturally annoyed and prejudiced. On the next morning, he was surprised to find out that Singh, his driver, "had slept soundly through the night in the back of the car."[19] In view of Singh's sound slumber in the discomfort of a vehicle, was it not possible that George's sleeplessness in the cosy bed was due primarily to his nerves?

The complaint from another European in pre-war Malaya was as exaggerated as it was naive when he said, "My first feelings, indeed, were that I had gone back to the war and was coming into a town under bombardment! Quite near my house . . . a deafening noise of machine-gun fire and intermittent rifle fire could be heard. I was quite at a loss to understand this until my friend told me that it was merely Chinese crackers which were being fired."[20]

It is also conceded that there were cases of abuse, which were recorded as early as the second half of the last century, when on New Year's Eve unruly Chinese youths found sadistic pleasure in throwing lighted crackers under the noses of horses ridden by Europeans, setting the animals off helter skelter down the streets.[21] In recent years we have seen cracker-enthusiasts strutting around the streets with cigarettes between their lips, tossing odd crackers at gaily dressed maidens driving by. The radio patrol did a good job in nabbing a couple or so of them on the spot. But the fact that some hooligans and thugs did misuse crackers is no reason for condemning the legitimate and innocuous use of crackers as a whole.[22]

Noise to the Chinese is a national characteristic and assuredly not a vice; for noise is the articulate sign of life in the universe — anywhere, any time. When a babe comes into the world, he starts crying: the louder, the healthier. If the babe makes no noise, the knowledgeable doctor and the experienced nurse are alarmed, and prompt action is taken to make the baby squeal; for the hearty scream of the newly born is a signal of human triumph — the triumph of procreation. Noise is life and, as J.J.M. de Groot has observed, noise-making is a "work of merit" to the Chinese.[23]

18. *The World Book Encyclopaedia*, Chicago, 1963, vol. xiii, p. 339. Cf. *The Encyclopaedia Americana* re South African (Boer) War, 1899–1902.
19. Bilainkin, pp. 166–167.
20. Sidney, p. 58.
21. Vaughan, p. 34. According to the *Pinang Gazette* of 27th January, 1849 (microfilm, National Library, Singapore), the Chinese New Year of that year was ushered in by the "noisy accompaniment of discharges from great and small guns, crackers, etc. and the beating of gongs".
22. For a number of years, the government had imposed a ban on crackers since the Emergency (1948) in the Federation of Malaya and lifted it, whenever circumstances permitted, on Chinese festival days and on the festival days of other races. Such measures were taken in the public interest and for security reasons, with which we agree *in toto*. Our views apply only in normal times, and on no account should be construed as innuendo. The nation-wide ban on fire-crackers on Malaysia Day on 31st August, 1964, testifies unequivocally to the fact that the tolerant and democratic Malaysian government makes no discrimination against any creed, colour or race in its imposition (*ST*, 28th August, 1964). [A ban on the use of fire-crackers had in fact existed in Peninsular Malaya and Singapore from 1923 onwards, the ban occasionally being waived on specifically gazetted festival days. A total ban on the use of fire-crackers was imposed in Malaysia following communal riots on 13th May, 1969, and the use of both fire-crackers and fireworks was banned in Singapore from 1st August, 1972; the bans are still in force in both countries.]
23. de Groot, *Religion*, p. 39.

CHAPTER 9:
Night of Moonlight Romance

The New Year celebrations wind up in a grand finale in the first full moon of the year (called *yuan hsiao,* 元宵), known locally as the *Chap Goh Meh* (a Hokkien term for "fifteenth night"). On this night, many houses are illuminated and lanterns are hung over the five-foot way; and feasts and dance parties are held on a lavish scale.

When the enchanting full moon is visible, festive makers sally forth in their cars and motor-cycles, which form a mammoth procession in such favourite resorts as the old Esplanade, Gurney Drive and the Botanical Gardens. It is the tradition for every newly wedded couple to join in the vehicular parade on this glamorous night.[1] Youths and maidens put on their best attire, and vehicle owners seize the occasion to display their latest limousines. Highlights of the procession are the eagerly awaited *kronchong* parties, which regale the spectators with their music, *lagus* and *pantuns* (songs and improvised verse in the National Language) and modern English hits. Often the sweet, melodious soprano, which resounds through the air, is that of a man impersonating a woman, which makes the music and song even more intriguing.

Thus everyone, young and old, looks forward to this enchanting moonlight when the moon shines in all her glory and splendour.

The Good Old Days   Some decades ago, when the fair sex was sequestered, the *Chap Goh Meh* was a unique occasion for blushing maidens to parade in pony carriages and gharries and rickshas. Their routes invariably included the crossing of bridges — seven bridges being the ideal — at such places as Bridge Street, Sungei Pinang Road, Perak Road, Dato Kramat Road, Ayer Itam

A young Chinese girl and boy dressed in traditional Nonya *costume at New Year.*

1.   This appears to be an evolution of the "Seeing the Bride" custom of Changchou in Fukien Province, when on the 15th night of the 1st Moon any woman or girl might enter the house of a newly wedded couple to see the bride. Such a house was indicated by a lighted lantern hung up outside the doorway. On the lantern were written four characters *T'ien Kuan Tz'u Fu,* "May the Lord of Heaven confer Blessings" (新年 *op. cit.,* p. 60). Instead of remaining in the house, the newlyweds in Penang parade themselves in the car procession for public notice.

Road, and back to Scotland Road, Western Road, Waterfall Road and the Botanical Gardens; for crossing bridges was symbolic of changing one's luck for the better.[2]

Those were colourful days. Dressed in the Malayan *kebaya* and gorgeous sarong, the *Nonya* (Malayan Chinese ladies of the former Straits Settlements) wore a peculiar coiffure jutting out like a rudder from the back of the head. A coil of hair crested the crown, and diamond hair-pins, each about the size of your little finger, were used to hold the coil in place, which, in turn, was encircled by a slim garland of fragrant flowers.

The front of the *kebaya* was held together by a set of gold and brilliant brooches. To match these brooches, a costly necklace was worn round the neck. And from the necklace a set of brilliant pendants dangled in resplendency. A pair of brilliant earrings flashed from the ears; whilst the wrists and fingers dazzled with equally resplendent bracelets and rings. Sizeable anklets of gold glittered from the ankles and gold-and-silver embroidered slippers afforded cover for the dainty toes. Verily, it was a night for jewellery exhibition, and in 1905 the estimated value of the jewels was recorded in the *Straits Chinese Magazine* of September, 1905, as "no less than $30,000,000".

The evening was first heralded by the inordinate explosion of thousands of crackers, big and small — the terrific din being created to exorcise lurking monsters or evil spirits. In certain residential and commercial areas, the more affluent members of the community and the bigger business firms rivalled one another in discharging the streamer type of crackers, hanging menacingly from the eaves to the ground. Over and above this, there were innumerable packets of the smaller detonators being thrown onto, and often across, the streets, which caused what the police today describe as "fire-cracker skirmishes".

Lighted lanterns swayed merrily from the ceilings over the five-foot way hung by householders and shopkeepers living in areas through which the spectacular parade of the *Nonya* passed. Rows of chairs were placed in front of the buildings at vantage points for the admiring male spectators to watch the beauty parade, for it was really an exciting experience to feast your eyes on the vast number of demure maidens who seldom ventured out of doors. Cases occurred of love at first sight; and thereafter professional matchmakers got busy; for it was not decorous in those days for boys and girls to have direct marriage negotiations.

Pious Wishes   It was also a night for making wishes by youths and maidens who threw oranges, apples, dragon's eyes, red dates and pebbles into the water at the Esplanade or the Sungei Pinang and muttered a simple colloquial couplet.[3] If a maiden desired to have the good things of life, she quoted this couplet whilst throwing some dragon's eyes into the water:

> *Tim leng-geng* (投龙眼 ,),   Dragon's eyes I throw,
> *Ho boay keng* (好尾景).   A good life to follow.

If she wished to be blessed with an ideal bridegroom, perhaps tall, handsome and rich, the couplet she muttered would take the following form:

> *Tim ho kam* (投好柑 ,),   Good oranges I throw,
> *T'an ho ang* (得好婿).   Good spouse will follow.

Nor were the youths unequal to the occasion. If a young man wanted to be married to a charming and sweet-natured

2. This tradition is traceable to Fukien Province, where it was customary for women and maidens to walk across a few bridges on the 15th of the 1st Moon, called 转三桥 , to turn "wheel of luck" at three bridges. (See 福建总志 in 全国，胡朴安，上海广益书局， 2nd ed., October 1923, pt. i, ch. 4, p. 39; and 吴趋风土录 , p. 2 in 小方 , *op. cit.*, vol. vi, wherein it is stated that women and maidens walked over three bridges on the 15th night of the 1st Moon to avoid sickness.)

3. This seems to have been adapted from the prefecture of Ch'ao-chou in Kwangtung Province, where on the 26th day of the 1st Moon the God of Human Destiny was believed to ascend to Heaven and to pass through bridges. On this evening, small Tiechiu boys go to the bridges to throw pebbles into the water, uttering wishes to be blessed with the good things of life, riches, honours and longevity (新年 , *op. cit.*, p. 113). See also the *SET*, 24th February, 1905, which makes this observation: "A strange superstition about Chap Goh Meh is that any wish made known to the Goddess of the Sea on that night will very likely be granted, hence pretty maidens may be detected here and there on the sea-beach casting stones into the water and praying for a rich husband and all kinds of good luck."

companion, he too muttered an appropriate couplet:

Tim p'ing ko (投苹果，),   Apples here I throw,
T'an ho bo (得好妻).   A good wife will follow.

If he was more ambitious and wanted to own a mansion or two for his bride-to-be, he recited another formula:

Tim chioh thau
(投石头，),   These stones I throw,
Khi ang-moh lau
(起洋(红毛)楼)!   Bungalows galore!

And if a boy and his girl friend jointly made a wish, they would repeat some words like this:

Tim ang cho (投红枣，),   These dates we cast away,
Ban soo ho (万事好).   All good things come our way.

Night of Freedom   In China, the 15th night was originally called *fang yeh* (放夜), the "night of freedom", which goes back to the Han period (first century AD) when the city gates were kept closed at all times and a curfew was imposed at night, so that the Son of Heaven was at ease to move about without fear of foul play. It was only on the 15th evening, and on the eve before and the eve after, that Chin Wu (金吾), the chief police officer in charge of security, was ordered to lift the curfew for the people to rejoice out of doors.[4] A few centuries later the Freedom Night was celebrated with fireworks. The origin of the display of fireworks is attributed to Emperor Yang of the Sui period (隋炀帝, AD 608–616), who on New Year's Eve had some tens of lofty beacons built in front of the palace buildings. Each beacon consisted mainly of fragrant woods, and when it was lighted at night the fire rose scores of feet skywards and its fragrance spread miles around. An observer of that time likened the beacons[5] to "fire-trees" (火树). Subsequently when the art of pyrotechnics was improved, fireworks were let off in the firmament at the "Chin Ya Pleasance" (金衙园), and in the words of a poet, "golden snakes" were traced in fire floating in the air, whilst on the ground the sound of "explosives assailed the ears".[6] Another poem revealed there were "numerous flowers blossoming in the moon", whilst "five-coloured auspicious clouds hovered over the terrace", with tracings of more than a hundred varieties of blossoms, human beings and other creatures afloat in the air.[7]

Feast of Lanterns   It was only during the time of T'ang that the festival became the *Teng Chieh* (灯节, Lantern Festival), known to the West as the Feast of Lanterns.[8] Taking the lead in the celebration was Ming Huang, an Emperor of T'ang (AD 713–755), who had the loveliest and loftiest lantern-towers constructed in commemoration of the 15th night of the 1st Moon. In all, thirty lantern-towers were built by Mao Shun (毛顺), the skilful craftsman, each about five hundred metres from the ground. Each lantern-tower was adorned with pearls, jades, gold and silver, which gave forth musical rhythms when swayed by the gentle breeze. The lanterns took the form of dragons, phoenixes, tigers and leopards, dangling and prancing in mid-air, so skilfully created that they appeared to be real.[9]

The people followed suit, and lanterns were hung up in great numbers, both inside and outside their private dwelling houses. Made of transparent paper on thin silk, the illuminations were of varied colours and in diverse shapes, representing phoenixes,

4. 西京记 in 月粹，琳琅仙馆编刻，1812, vol. i, ch. 4, p. 18; 汉志 in 事类，*op. cit.*, vol. xii, ch. 5, p. 42; and 荆楚 in 图书，*op. cit.*, vol. xvii, ch. 26, p. 22.

5. 纪闻 in 事类，*op. cit.*, vol. xii, ch. 7, p. 58; and 纪原 cited in 清录，*op. cit.*, p. 17.

6. 范来宗金衙园观烟火诗 cited in 清录，*ibid.*, p. 17.

7. 瞿宗土烟火戏诗 cited, *ibid.*

8. The Taoists call this festival the *Shang Yuan Chieh* (see pp. 60–67 above).

9. 明皇杂录，郑处海 in 格致，*op. cit.*, vol. ix, ch. 50, p. 8.

A young Nonya *bride receives advice on the elaborate wedding ritual from an experienced "auntie".*

tortoises, dragons and other creatures. Impressed by the lively artificial creations, Wang Kuei (王珪), a T'ang poet, portrayed a couple of phoenixes as "descending side by side from the clouds" and six tortoises as "rising from the seas to mount the hills".[10] Amongst the hosts of celebrants was Madam Han Kuo (韩国夫人), who established a record by making one hundred multi-coloured lantern trees, each almost two hundred and fifty metres in height. When the trees were lighted up at night, their glow was brighter than the moon and could be seen at a great distance.[11]

To commemorate the 15th night, Ming Huang also held a grand dance party on the terrace in front of the palace pavilion, in which palace courtesans put on their best performance to entertain His Majesty and his nobles and ministers.[12]

During the Ts'ing dynasty, the Manchu rulers celebrated the 15th night on an even more lavish scale. As soon as night fell, a lantern parade was held in front of the "Hall of Light", participated in by three thousand people in formation, each carrying a lighted azure lantern. At a given signal, the three thousand participants took their place to form the character *t'ai* (太 , supreme), followed instantly by the formation of another character, *p'ing* (平 , peace). Almost in a twinkle, two more characters took shape as *wan sui* (万岁 , eternal). Thus the combined four characters indicated "Eternal Supreme Peace". In the midst of this spectacular exercise, elegant dances were exhibited and fireworks were shot into the sky with thunderous claps. When the fireworks were halfway up, thousands of fishes were traced in the illuminated firmament, merrily diving in and out of the clouds, as if disporting themselves in water — presenting a marvellous scene.[13]

10. 王珪 cited in 清录 , *op. cit.*, p. 17.
11. 开元 · 王仁裕 · p. 15 in 说库 series, vol. viii.
12. 旧唐书音乐志 in 月粹 , *op. cit.*, vol. i, ch. 4, p. 17; and 明唐杂录 in 岁时 , *op. cit.*, vol. i, ch. 2, pp. 114–115.
13. 清史 , *op. cit.*, vol. ii, p. 15.

Evolution in Malaya In the Penang State of Malaysia, the *Chap Goh Meh* celebrations have had their evolution too. In the early years of the nineteenth century, if we may infer from the recorded writings of a European official, the traditional pyrotechnic display was in vogue. In 1836, there was a splendid show in honour of Ma-Chor P'o (妈祖婆) on 8th May (23rd day of the 3rd Moon), and this was described by the European official thus:

"One of the best of fireworks is a box from two to three or four feet square, within which are tiers of fireworks of almost every description. At the expiration of each separate tier, a small platform or frame, drops about a foot below the box, on which are exhibited in fire, puppets of men and animals, and Chinese characters traced in fire."[14]

Besides fireworks, there was also a grand display of lanterns — survivals of the Sui and T'ang traditions. And the impressions of another European eye-witness were that at the beginning of the Chinese year the lanterns reached their glorious height: "There were then lighted lanterns here, there, and everywhere. Lanterns of paper, and silk, and horn, and mica, and glass. Lanterns square, round, oblong, lozenge-shaped, octagonal. Lanterns in the form of birds, horses, tigers, fishes, snakes and crocodiles. Lanterns white, blue, green, red, and yellow. Lanterns in the fashion of jewels of gold and vessels of silver. Huge solitary lanterns, and strings of tiny and many-coloured lanterns. Lanterns stationary, and lanterns peripatetic. Lanterns of wheels circling within wheels, and lanterns of men galloping on horses, and lanterns of men fighting with spears and swords."[15]

The "lanterns of wheels circling within wheels" are called in Chinese *chou ma teng* (走马灯), the "galloping-horse lanterns", which are occasionally revived in postwar years, on a small scale, by such groups as members of the Penang Rubber Trade Association, Anson Road. There are also commercialised lantern processions promoted by and held in various parks. But such revivals are trifles in comparison with those held in the last century. A European writer said in the 1870s there were thousands of lanterns of every conceivable shape and size "with moveable figures of men, birds and beasts revolving within", suspended in the verandahs of the houses running along the side of the streets with picturesque effect.[16] Besides this, it was customary for Chinese children to make the round of Chinese houses in town with lighted lanterns and they were rewarded, in turn, with *ang pau* or candles in red.[17]

At the turn of the century, the colourful lanterns gradually disappeared, and the celebration took the form of a sort of beauty parade in exquisite gharries with the important ritual of throwing oranges, apples, dragon's eyes, pebbles and stones into the water.[18] In about 1930, local Chinese writers already noted the conspicuous absence of lanterns in the *Chap Goh Meh* and their complete transference to the Moon Festival, during which lanterns came into vogue in addition to the traditional moon cakes.[19]

An Anti-Mongol Legend The 15th night of the 1st Moon again became a liberation or freedom night in the fourteenth century, this time from an alien yoke, according to a later legend. In the last year of the Mongol rule, the government was corrupt and decadent and the nation was in chaos. Groups of patriotic

A Nonya lady sports her jewellery, in the traditional set of three clasps known as krosang, *at a New Year dinner in Singapore.*

14. Low, p. 305.
15. Beighton, pp. 168–169.
16. Vaughan, p. 44.
17. *SET*, 24th February, 1905.
18. *SET*, 24th February, 1905.
19. 星洲十年 ed. 关楚璞，星洲日报社，January 1940, Section V, ch. 5, pp. 1069, 1074. (See "The Moon Festival", pp. 173–179 below.)

Chinese were plotting against the Mongols on a nation-wide scale. At about this time, an epidemic broke out, causing more hardship to the people.

Amongst the patriots was Chu Yuan-Chang (朱元璋), who went about, disguised as a Taoist priest, selling and distributing pills for treatment of the pestilence. As the pills were efficacious, Yuan-Chang went about the second time to sell and distribute the pills to forestall another epidemic said to be the worst of its kind. To each possessor of the pills, Yuan-Chang said the box of pills should be opened only on the 15th night of the 1st Moon, otherwise their efficacy would be lost. When the day was due, the owners opened their boxes and were astounded to find a slip of red paper containing these words:

"This night, the Mongols should be overthrown. Arise altogether and attack them."

Since the people had resented the Mongol rule, they arose as one man to massacre the Mongols. Yuan-Chang, the would-be founder-emperor of the Ming dynasty, was already on the spot with his secret army, and, with the uprising, succeeded in ousting the Mongols.[20]

According to Wolfram Eberhard, the aforesaid is one of the numerous typical examples of folklore originating with the rise of nationalism among the Chinese in the last decades of Manchu rule over China (1644–1911), and were deliberately directed upon the Mongols of the fourteenth century as a camouflage to avoid vengeance from the Manchus.[21]

Malaysian Celebrations The Manchus were overthrown in 1911, and, as far as Malaya is concerned, it is a singular coincidence of history that from about that time onwards, the main celebration of the *Chap Goh Meh* had begun to evolve from pony carriages to a motorcade or vehicular procession — a revival of the "night of freedom" of the first century AD and indirectly in commemoration of the liberation from the Manchu yoke. The festive spirit is so infectious in recent years that many citizens of other races also join in the mammoth car procession and shout a hearty "hallo" to their Chinese friends and acquaintances — a truly cosmopolitan gala.

Maidens were chaperoned in the days of the gharries; whereas nowadays girls invite (perhaps "inveigle" is the right word) their boy friends to join in the motorcade, not as escorts, but as companions. More and more youths take to evening dress or tuxedo (the Yankee boys with their tight-fitting trousers excepted); whilst the modern girls beam in their flowing *cheong-sam* or bare-backed gowns of Western origin.

In many cases, Chinese dinners are served and wine flows liberally in parties where Western-style dances are held, reminiscent of the gaiety of the Ming Huang era when courtesans stole the show.

In other words, what was originally the Freedom Night has become a Night of Moonlight Romance in Penang, when girls meet their boy friends in favourite rendezvous. Perhaps it is no mere coincidence that the Malaysians have chosen this glorious moonlight night for romance and for eventual matrimony; for, as a Chinese legend has it, Yueh Lao Yeh (月老爷, the "Venerable Old Man of the Moon"), the divine matchmaker, is on eternal watch.

20. 传记，严殊炎，国光，2nd ed., November 1948, pp. 14, 15; and Eberhard, pp. 64–66. However, another popular legend of similar nature, but different in details, in circulation amongst the Malaysians relates to Liu Po-Wen (刘伯温), who impersonated a Taoist priest to distribute moon cakes to the people of Hsu-Chou city (滁州城). In each of the moon cakes an anti-epidemic amulet was supposed to be hidden. The people were told to cut open the cakes on the Moon Festival day, which they did. To their astonishment, they found a note urging them to kill the Tartars (Mongols) and the uprising started. (See 中国节令掌故，孟寻，香港中华，1954, pp. 27–33. But see our comment on another moon-cake legend in p. 175 mn.8.)
21.2 Eberhard, pp. 64–66.

Moon and Marriages   In Western mythology, Cupid wounds the heart of a lover with the arrow, and the heart only heals when the parties end up at the Hymeneal Altar. Therein lies the snare. For when the heart heals up after matrimony, it may direct its attention elsewhere, and divorce possibly follows.

But the Chinese Venerable Old Man of the Moon is more thorough. He has with him a book in which are recorded all the marriages that shall take place on earth (天下婚牒). He also carries a bag of "red cords" (赤绳子) and ties up the prospective bride and the groom with a red cord, and, even if they come from embittered families or alien countries, their marriage shall be permanent and their conjugal life happy and constant.[22]

From the T'ang dynasty came the story of Yueh Lao Yeh and a military officer (Wei Ku, 韦固), who once lost his way amongst the mountains. On one of the peaks he saw a monolith upon which were inscribed three words: "Summit of Marriage" (婚姻岭). As he roamed about the hills, he discovered a pavilion in which was an old man poring diligently over a huge book.

"What book are you reading?" inquired the officer politely.

"It contains the marriage fate of those on earth," explained the Venerable Old Man of the Moon. "If you wish to know your own fate, walk in the westerly direction. There you'll meet a girl and she it is who is destined to be your life partner."

True to the prediction, the officer came upon a small immature girl, whose plain look rather enraged him. In a moment of anger, he unsheathed his sword and lunged at the girl, wounding her on the brow.

Years later, the military officer was promoted to high office and many proposed marriages were offered to him. Fascinated by the portrait of a very charming girl, he selected her to be his wife. After the wedding ceremony, when the bridal veil was lifted, the groom saw a scar over the bride's eyebrow — the scar on the little girl whom he had tried to slay![23]

Thus it is not inapposite that the *Chap Goh Meh* has become a Night of Moonlight Romance. No wonder it makes old hearts eternally young, and young hearts throb with anticipatory excitement.

If the Chinese New Year begins well, it also ends well in the first fascinating moonlight night — the memorable *Chap Goh Meh* (十五夜（ 晚 ））!

22. 故事(仿宋字版)，广智书局，Hong Kong, (n.d.), ch. 3, pp. 80–81 under 韦固与月老论婚 · Ayscough, p. 59, points out that this legend is probably "the earliest embodiment of the Chinese belief in the existence of an invisible link (typified by the red cord) between bride and bridegroom, and expressed in the saying that 'Matches are made in Heaven and the bond of fate is forecast from the Moon'."
23. 民新，正气书局，Shanghai, (n.d.), ch. 1, pp. 4–5. A similar story in Burkhardt, vol. i, p. 48, tells of the predestined marriage of Wei Ku with a vegetable-vendor's daughter. A longer, more interesting and highly embellished account is told in Birch, pp. 43–47.

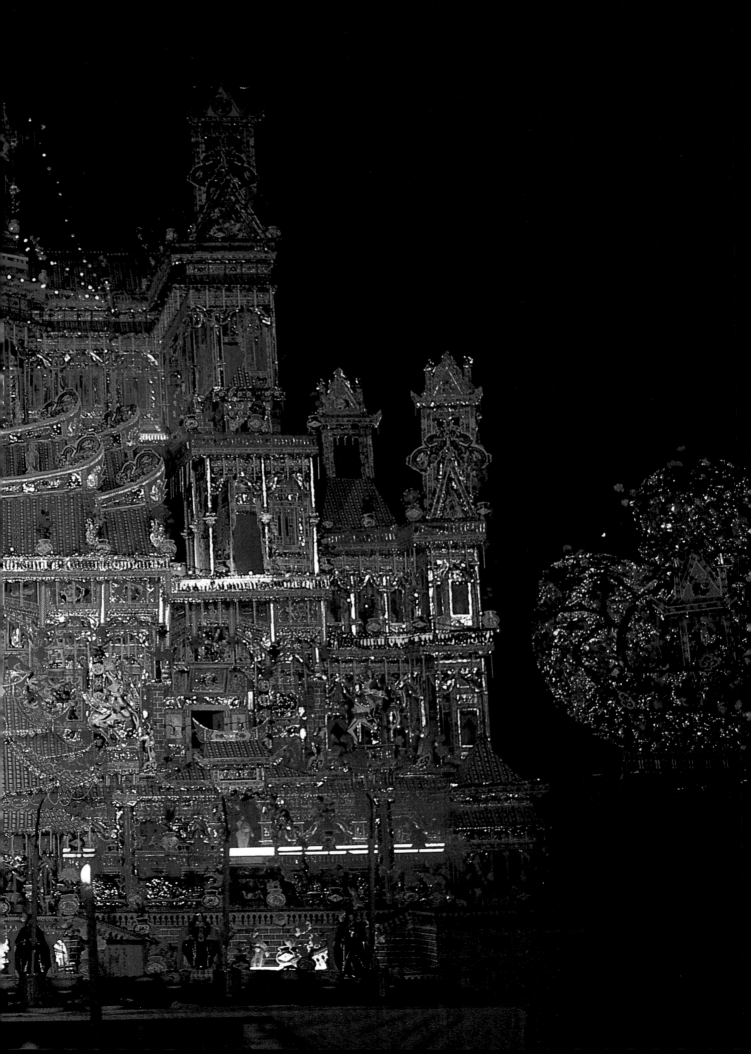

(Preceding pages) This glittering paper house is about to be burned and so transferred to the spirit world, where it is required by ancestral family members. It is often a dream that initiates the process of convening a family "action" committee to discuss such a project.

PART III:
The Traditional Festivals

CHAPTER 10:
Homage to the Ancestors

Many a Chinese regards the *Ch'ing Ming* (literally, "pure and bright") festival, known to Westerners as the "Feast of the Dead", the "Cult of Ancestral Worship", or "All Souls' Day", as an important festival, which normally falls on 5th April of the solar year. On this day, or a week or two before and after, the Malaysians make a pilgrimage to the cemeteries to pay homage to the ancestral tombs, called *chi mu* (祭墓).

At the graveyard, the tomb of one's ancestor is tidied up, and renovated if need be; the weeds in the vicinity are uprooted;

B

A. Door gods, or men shen, in civil attire at the Heah Kongsi in Penang. B. A wide-angle view of the Heah Kongsi.

the granite altar is wiped clean; and, where necessary, the inscription on the tombstone is repainted to facilitate identification — this process being called *chi sao* (祭扫).

Food offerings, including pork, chicken, roast duck, cakes, fruits, and cups of wine and tea, are made. Candles and joss-sticks are lighted and stuck into the improvised urn or sockets. When all arrangements are set, the devotees take turn to *kowtow* (磕头), genuflect or bow to pay obeisance, AS IF the dead were present. After a while, a libation of wine and tea is poured onto the ground and incense-papers are consigned to the flames. Some unfolded sheets (which are not for burning) are strewn all over the surroundings of the tombstone. Towards the end of the ritual, a few sheets of the smaller variety of mock money or incense-paper are placed atop the tombstone. Until the ban on fire-crackers, the ceremony always included the discharge of the popping and crackling small explosives. There are a number of peregrinating flageolet-players who, upon an agreed fee, are ready to pipe a dirge or two appropriate to the occasion. There are also a few professional wailers who wail and scream on the spot by proxy whenever their services are required. This, in brief, is the Chinese observance of the *Ch'ing Ming* festival at the graveyard.

In the case of families, which, due to unavoidable circumstances, are unable to go to the cemeteries, a deputy is despatched beforehand — sometimes a few days ahead — to deposit atop the tombstone some incense-paper to "invite" the ancestors home where a similar type of offering is made to the "spiritual (ancestral) tablet". In opulent conservative homes there are special shrines where many such tablets, purporting to represent several generations of ancestors, are systematically arranged in rows. In the clan associations there is a formidable array of such tablets to represent the deceased clansmen, to whom an offering is also made in general. And in some temples, like the Temple of Paradise, Penang, there is a special sanctuary for the display of tablets of prominent citizens — a sort of Memorial Hall.

Early Tombstones   The history of *Ch'ing Ming* needs a short explanatory introduction. In the ancient days, homage to the ancestors was paid in the ancestral temples and not at the graveyard. The first recorded individual to make a food offering in the open was the son of the Great Yu, who was transferred by Emperor Shao K'ang (少康 , 2079 BC), on promotion, to the state of Yueh (越), where he did homage to the ancestral tombs at K'uei Chi (会稽) in Chekiang Province.[1] This practice was followed in the Chou period. There was, for instance, the case of Hsiao Tsung-Po (小宗伯), to whom homage was done at his tomb. To pay homage at the tomb, says the *Chou Li Ti Kuan* (周礼地官), is equivalent to doing homage to one's ancestor.[2]

At the beginning the dead were buried without identification marks on the tombs. Tomb identification began in the Western Han period (AD 1–23) with Tu Tzu-Hsia (杜子夏). When Tzu-Hsia was about to die, he made a written instruction that a tombstone with an inscription of his name be erected by the side of his grave and that a cluster of five pine and cypress trees be cultivated in front.[3] Following the precedent created by Tzu-Hsia, the practice of tomb inscriptions began to spread, resulting in more families doing homage to their ancestors at the cemeteries.

However, there was no fixed date or season for the open-air

1. 吴越春秋 cited in 清录 , *op. cit.*, p. 31. But de Groot, *Religious System*, vol. ii, p. 388, cites 汉官仪 , which says "In ancient times there was no sacrifice on the tombs, but Shí Hwang of the House of Ts'in (221–208 BC) erected a temple at the side of his tomb and this was initiated by the Han dynasty and has not since been abolished," and seems to accept this as the origin of tomb visits. In the *Original Records of Things* (事物纪原), Shih Huang-Ti is also cited, but the origin is attributed to Confucius' period (*circa* 551–479 BC), when the sage approved the sons of concubines, who had no ancestral temple, to do homage to the ancestors in accordance with the seasons in the open air, facing the directions of the tombs. (庶子无庙，孔子许望墓以时祭祀 ,vol. iii, p. 305).

2. 清录 , *ibid*.

3. 西京杂记 cited in 历俗 ,*op. cit.*, ch. 22, p. 279.

offering. A recorded case discloses that Hsing Ch'ang-An (幸长安) personally visited eleven mausoleums to pay homage in the 8th Moon in the tenth year of Chien Wu (建武 , AD 39);[4] whilst in the *Remaining Writings of the Two Ch'engs* (程氏遗书 (程颢 , 程颐)) it is stated "homage at the tomb took place on the 1st day of the 10th Moon: bitter cold from frost and snow."[5]

Han Shih Festival　To trace the origin of the *Ch'ing Ming*, we have to start with the story of Chieh Chi-T'ui (350 BC), who had perished in a forest fire and to whom we have traced the origin of "spiritual tablets" in a previous chapter. Another legend says his name was Wang Kuang (王光), who, after serving abroad for the Marquis of Tsin for more than ten years, declined to accept any reward and retired to the hills. After thirty years in the hills, he was once seen on the coast of the Eastern Sea selling fans. Thereafter, his whereabouts were unknown.[6] The implication is that he had become an immortal.

Acting on the belief that Chieh Chi-T'ui was burnt to death on the 5th day of the 3rd Moon, the people observed a period of "fire prohibition", called *chin yen* (禁烟), on the anniversary.[7] To make the prohibition effective, a theory was advanced that any violation would result in the damage of crops by rain and hail.[8] As there was "no fire", the people had to observe what was called *Han Shih* (寒食), to eat food uncooked or raw.

At the beginning, and for many centuries, the *Han Shih* practice was observed for a period of one month. This was a severe strain on the people, old and young; and widespread privation resulted. By the middle of the Later Han (*circa* 100 BC), the number of days was reduced to three. But as this shortened period still caused hardship, it was finally reduced to one day and it fell on the 105th day from the winter solstice.[9]

As late as the first year of Yuan Feng of the Sung period (元丰初 , AD 1078), the "fire prohibition" was still strictly enforced in the district of Chen Yang (镇阳). If anyone violated the tradition, his name would be recorded, and if there was any sudden damage to crops by wind and hail, he would be called upon to pay compensation to the victims.[10]

Meanwhile, *Han Shih* had become an important festival for out-door games in the T'ang period (AD 618–906). Amongst these games was football, said to have been introduced by the legendary Emperor Huang Ti, and employed for the physical and tactical training of soldiers in the Warring States (战国 , 481–221 BC).[11] Another game was the swing, called *ch'iu ch'ien* (鞦韆). It originated from the performance staged by the Shan Yung (山戎), mountain barbarians from the north. The Chinese learnt the game and played it at the *Han Shih* festival.[12] A board was tied to two lengths of multi-coloured rope suspended from the branch of a tree. The participant sat on the board and propelled it with the movement of his body until the swing gained momentum and swung rhythmically in the air, forward and backward. The swing was novel at the time, and in the reign of T'ien Pao (天宝 , AD 742–755), Ming Huang held swing competitions in the palace annually on the *Han Shih*, and charming courtesans were delighted to take part in them, after which feasting and rejoicing followed.[13] The Emperor, who enjoyed himself thoroughly, likened it to a "demi-fairies show" (半仙戏), and the swing game thereafter became ever more popular with the populace.

4. 后汉光武纪 cited in 纪原 , *op. cit.*, vol. iii, p. 305.
5. 程氏遗书　cited in 清录 , *op. cit.*, p. 31.
6. 神仙传 in 逸史 , *op. cit.*, vol. 49, pp. 8, 9.
7. The phrase 禁烟 literally means "smoke prohibition", but to save undue explanation, we have given its implied meaning by a direct reference to "fire".
8. 岁时记 in 事类 , *op. cit.*, vol. i, ch. 5, p. 45.
9. 移书 *ibid*; 邺中记 and 荆楚 cited in 岁时 , *op. cit.*, vol. ii, ch. 15, pp. 115, 159; and 历俗 *op. cit.*, ch. 29, p. 440.
10. 岁时杂记 in 岁时 *ibid.*, p. 160.
11. 刘向别录 *ibid.*, p. 175; also 图书 , *op. cit.*, vol. 18, ch. 18, p. 29.
12. 古今艺术团 in 岁时 *ibid.*, p. 174; and 图书 *ibid*.
13. 开元 p. 10, in 说库 *op. cit.*, vol. viii.

A. Ch'ing Ming, *in an early print.* **B.** *It is not only paper houses that are burned and so transferred to the spirit world — but also temples! This extremely rare ceremony occured in Ang Mo Kio, Singapore, during the inauguration of a new clan temple and was intended to encourage the ancestral spirits to assist their earthbound relatives in their daily lives.* **C.** *Mock money for burning.*

Ch'ing Ming Celebrations   The *Han Shih* was followed by the *Ch'ing Ming* festival on the ensuing day — 106th day after the winter solstice. From the T'ang period onwards the *Han Shih*, which had been observed for tomb offering as well, began to decline, whilst the *Ch'ing Ming* rose to supplant it as the festival for homage to ancestors.[14]

An important factor contributed to the widespread popularity of the *Ch'ing Ming*. Until the end of the Sui period (AD 617), genuine articles had been offered as sacrifices. A legend of the Sui period attributes the use of paper for mock articles to Jen Ch'ien (仁蒨) of Chihli, a teacher of Wen Pen (文本), the son of a district officer. One day Ch'eng Ching, a Mandarin from the world of shades (冥官成景), happened to pass through the district. As he was an old friend of Jen Ch'ien, the latter entertained him, and later made him a gift through his student Wen Pen. "What's this?" Wen Pen inquired, puzzled at the queer article. "This is paper impressed with yellow tinfoil — a substitute for genuine silk fabrics. Men and ghosts are not the same. For the ghosts, counterfeits are preferable to genuine articles."[15]

14. 历俗 '*op. cit.*, pp. 441, 448. Wilhelm, *Soul of China*, p. 315, says that the *Ch'ing Ming* "has maintained itself under the Republic (in the 1920s). It is celebrated as the feast of trees in all the schools, and it has developed the custom that the pupils make an excursion and plant trees in an open place." This is palpably a revival of the *T'a Ch'ing* tradition of the T'ang period.
15. 广陈鸿睦仁蒨传 cited, *ibid.*, ch. 27, p. 332.

From the T'ang onwards (AD 618–906), mock money or incense-paper became the vogue for offering to the shades, as is amply substantiated by textual evidence. A story relates to Wang P'o (王勃), the famous prodigy of T'ang who had started literary composition at the age of six. When he was fourteen, he attended a party given by Governor Yen Kung (都督阎公), in which the prodigy excelled every guest in a literary competition. On his homeward voyage, at the Ma Tang Hill (马当山), the prodigy again met the old man who had earlier given him a hint about the Governor's party, and, kneeling before the old man, thanked him profusely. The old man told Wang P'o that he owed the Ch'ang Lu Spirit (长芦神) $10,000 as a gambling debt, and urged the boy to repay that debt when his boat passed the Spirit's temple. When the vessel reached the temple, Wang P'o forgot about his promise, and suddenly a flock of crows formed a wall to prevent the craft from advancing. Then Wang P'o remembered the old man and caused mock money to be burnt at the temple.[16]

And there was the story of Mrs Wang Lun (王抡妻), who dreamt that her husband had perished and that he had appeared to demand thirty strings of cash. To meet the demand, the poor woman took out reams of paper and, scissors in hand, cut them into the size of mock money. Having done this, she requested a witch to burn it.[17]

In the T'ang period, the *Ch'ing Ming* also became a festival for picnics or excursions, called *T'a Ch'ing* (踏青). On this day, willow twigs or leaves were hung atop the front door to ensure "clear eyesight" or "sharp eyes" (明眼) for the occupants of the house. Farmers did so to forecast "rain or drought" (占水旱). If it rained, then there was to be plenty of water for the crops. City dwellers went out of doors to hold picnics. And to prevent possible interference from evil spirits, picnickers invariably wore a bouquet of willow twigs or leaves.[18] A further reason is given in a maxim: "If you don't wear the willow on the *Ch'ing Ming* festive day, your ruddy complexion will turn from pink to ashen grey" (清明不戴柳红颜成皓首).

The cock-fighting season also occurred during the *Ch'ing Ming*. A story relates again to the famous Ming Huang, who was captivated by cock-fighting when he was a child. Upon accession to the throne, Ming Huang caused an imperial farm to be established for the rearing of the finest species of cockerels in the realm. He put the farm in the charge of five hundred children under the leadership of Kia Ch'ang (贾昌), aged thirteen years, whose services were so satisfactory that valuable gifts were sent to his home regularly.[19]

Observance in Malaysia To-day, the *Han Shih* is dying out in China and is practically unknown in Malaysia except for allusions to it in print. On the other hand, *Ch'ing Ming* festival has remained to this day and is widely observed in Malaysia mainly because it has its roots in the Confucian cult of filial piety. In our view, so long as this cult flourishes — and flourish it shall even in this era of space craft — so long will homage to ancestors (call it "ancestral worship" if you like) be continued. As we have shown in the foregoing pages,[20] it was Confucius who inculcated that homage should be done to the ancestors.

According to the code of filial piety,[21] "filial sons cannot bear to neglect for one day their duty to serve their parents; therefore

16. 摭言，王保定，p. 5 in 说库 series, vol. viii.
17. 再生记 cited in 历俗，*op. cit.*, ch. 27, p. 332.
18. 清录 *op. cit.*, p. 29; 历俗 *op. cit.*, pp. 442–443.
19. 岁时 *op. cit.*, vol. ii, ch. 17, p. 184.
20. See pp. 00–00 above.
21. de Groot, *Religious System*, vol. i, p. 120.

every day they set out the articles in the lower chamber as if the deceased were still abiding with them alive" (孝子不忍一日废其事亲之礼，於下室日设之，如生存也). It is further enjoined to "serve the dead as they were served when alive, and those who have passed away as if they were still abiding amongst us, this is the summit of filial conduct" (事死如事生，事亡如事存，孝之至也).

In compliance with this code, honour is paid to ancestors in some important festivals other than the Ch'ing Ming. For instance, the 5th Moon Festival, during which homage is done to the ancestors at home with the symbolic triangular pulut-rice cakes as the chief item of food offerings, as if inviting the ancestors to partake of the special cakes with the living members of the family. On 15th of the 6th Moon (being the middle of the year or half of an annual cycle), ancestors are honoured with marble-shaped rice balls as the principal offering (Hokkien custom). Again on the 14th and 15th of the 7th Moon, the Ghosts' Month, offerings are made to the ancestors (Buddhist origin), which is to be dealt with an detail in another chapter. For reasons of coherence, there are two other festivals which we deem appropriate for incorporation in this chapter.

One of these festivals falls on the 9th day of the 9th Moon, otherwise known as the Ch'ung Yang Chieh (重阳节), after the theory of the Yang (male) principle in Chinese cosmology.[22] On this occasion, members of the family (Cantonese custom) make a pilgrimage to the cemeteries to do homage at the old tombs, i.e. tombs over three years. This is carried out on a less elaborate scale and there is a much smaller crowd. An interesting feature of this festival is the hunt for the dilapidated tombs, especially the tombs of the lower income group which are not so easy to locate when the inscriptions thereon are worn out. If the tombs are too dilapidated for recognition, and if the devout searchers are exhausted, they often do the next best thing: they go back to the chapel of the cemetery and burn the incense materials in the open by the side, or in front of, that building, AS IF the ancestors were present[23] — a practice quite in accord with Confucius' teaching (祭如在).

The Winter Solstice   The other festival is the Tung Chih (冬至, the winter solstice on 22nd December), which was once "as important as the New Year" (冬大如年) because it was the turning point of the season in China. During the time of Prince Huai-Nan (淮南子, died in 122 BC), the Son of Heaven led a party of "three dukes, nine ministers and twenty-seven high court officials" to the northern suburb to "welcome the year" in the winter solstice. Upon their return, the Son of Heaven ordered largesse to be bestowed on the descendants of deceased loyal subjects and orphans and widows (in the belief that nature would be similarly generous in its gifts to mankind) . . . . . During the month, there were grand banquets and the Son of Heaven prayed for the next year's blessings. Sacrificial offerings were made in the temple, followed by homage to the ancestors.[24]

Some centuries later, it was essential for the court officials to offer felicitations to the emperor who wore the (black) ceremonial robe, and there were banquets and rejoicings for a stretch of five days to observe the "Welcome to the Arrival-of-the-Sun Ritual" (迎日至之礼). In the metropolis, even the poorest of the poor put on new clothes, prepared feasts, and paid homage to the ancestors.

22. In South China, the Ch'ung Yang is a kite-flying season and people make a pilgrimage to the cemeteries as they do in Ch'ing Ming. (See 全国，op. cit., pt. i, vol. i, ch. 4, p. 43 and vol. ii, ch. 8, p. 6. See also 重阳节别，a well-documented article in the Supplement of the 南洋，5th October, 1962.)
23. 论语，ch. 3, p. 53 in 十四经新疏 series, vol. i, 世界，Formosa, 1956.
24. 淮南子 (时则训) in 诸子，op. cit., vol. vii, pp. 80–81, and 通历及高氏小史 in 岁时，op. cit., vol. iii, ch. 36, p. 409. See also Soothill, Hall of Light, p. 26, in which it is stated that in spring the Son of Heaven wore "green" robes and ornaments; in summer, "red"; in autumn, "white" (unbleached); and in winter, "black".

A and B. *Traditional New Year rice cakes made for altars in the home and the temple.* **C.** *A young girl meditates on the question she is about to ask the gods as she clutches two kidney-shaped divining blocks* (seng puay).

Greetings were exchanged as if it were a New Year festival.[25] A special red-bean broth (赤豆粥) was served, the tradition being derived from a legend that once upon a time the son of Kung-Kung (共工) died in the winter solstice and became the devil of pestilence. The devil, however, was scared of red beans, and the people cooked "red-bean broth" to offer to him to avert pestilence.[26]

During the T'ang dynasty, in AD 838, the Winter Solstice became a three-day festival when everyone remained awake on the night before, and when the customary greetings were to wish one another "a myriad of blessings". Its observance in imperial China was so important that even in the present century, when Hsuan T'ung (宣统) — better known as Henry P'u Yi (溥仪) — was put on the throne in Manchuria (changed into Manchukuo by the Japanese usurpers), he tried to induce popular response by reviving the ancient ritual of the Winter Solstice in 1935, which was propagated to the world by radio through "his thin sharp voice".[27]

25. 唐礼乐志，东京梦华录，易通卜验 in 岁时，*ibid.*, pp. 412–414.
26. 荆楚 in 玉烛宝典，杜台卿 in 丛书 series, 商务，Changsha, December 1939, vol. ii, ch. 11, p. 380.
27. Reischauer, *Ennin's Travels*, pp. 126–129; and Soothill, *Hall of Light*, p. 189.

Survival in Malaysia   What has survived of the Winter Solstice Festival in Malaysia is mainly the tradition of homage to ancestors at home, usually in the morning, and in the clan temples in the daytime, followed by a dinner participated in by the clansmen and their children. The chief item of food in the morning offering is the marble-shaped rice balls (汤丸) — emblem of family reunion. In conservative well-to-do homes, some decades ago, the head of the family used to put on the traditional Mandarin robe to make obeisance to the spiritual tablets.

In some clan temples, a *lu chu* (炉主 , literally the "master in charge of the urn", and metaphorically the chairman of sacrificial offerings) is appointed. He is nominated annually, by rotation, from the committee, subject to approval by casting the two kidney-shaped divining blocks before the shrine. It is his duty to have rice balls, denominated by some English writers as "dough cakes", prepared and sent to the clan temple for the purpose of offering to the spiritual tablets (Hokkien custom) on the festival day. Made of pulut-rice powder, the ball cakes for sacrificial offering are, strictly speaking, white (bigger size) and pink in colour; pink, because they are probably founded on the "red-bean broth" theory to expel sickness.[28] For fanciful reasons they are also coloured green or yellow, which are for consumption generally. In other temples, different arrangements may be made. In the Cheah Kongsi, for instance, the duty of making rice-ball offerings falls on the most senior member, according to the Cheah genealogy. In the Chew Kongsi of Kimberley Street, in addition to the rice balls, there were in 1964 offerings of a roast pig, *mi ku* (面龟 — Hokkien: wheat-flour tortoise-shaped cakes, tinged in pink on top), bananas, and other dishes of Malaysian-style food (symbolic of wealth, long life and numerous descendants), which were later distributed to the clansmen who attended the Winter Solstice ritual.

It is little known that the rice-ball custom originates from Fukien Province. Formerly, a wood-cutter who had gone up to the mountain, accidentally fell into a torrent, and remained therein for more than ten years, eating nothing but a species of ginger for sustenance. As a result, his weight became so light that he contrived to spring up from the torrent, a strange creature, with long hairs sprouting from his body. When he returned home in this condition, members of the family treated him with pulut-rice-ball cakes. In due course he recovered, and a family reunion feast took place.[29] From that time onward rice balls were used to signify happy reunion.

Penang Celebrations   In Penang, an elaborate dinner is given, each on a selected day in the 11th Moon, not necessarily on the actual festival day (22nd December), by the various territorial and clan associations (Hokkien, Tiechiu and Cantonese); and members, as a rule, make it their duty to take part in the dinner on a subscription basis in order to enjoy themselves in the convivial spirit of a large family reunion. On 4th December (1st day of the 11th Moon), 1964, we were privileged to witness, in the forenoon, a series of significant rituals performed at the famous Leong San Tong Khoo Kongsi (龙山堂邱公司 — Hokkien), the most opulent clan association or temple in Southeast Asia. The president and trustees, who were to perform the rituals, were dressed in black ceremonial suits made of light woollen fabric — reminiscent of the black robe worn by the emperor on the day of

28. At an interview in January 1965, Ong Sek-Pek of Heeren Street (now Jalan Tan Cheng Lock), Malacca, said members of his family had been using the white and pink rice balls for generations. As the eldest member of the fifth generation, it was his duty, now passed on to his younger brother, to offer these two types of rice balls to his ancestors during the annual Winter Solstice. In addition, he had to climb up every door in the house to stick two white and two pink rice balls to the top of the door. (These balls are for the Door Gods, outside our scope.)

29. 全国 ·*op. cit.*, pt. ii, vol. iv, ch. 5, p. 61.

the winter solstice.

The programme of the morning rituals consisted of four parts, two of which related to the (i) installation of nine new spiritual tablets and (ii) homage to the ancestors. These two rituals were held in the "Shrine of the Spiritual Tablets" (诒谷堂), occupying the left wing of the Kongsi's magnificent building. Food offerings were placed on the altar before this shrine and they consisted of a roast pig, roast ducks, fried crabs, cooked chicken, pork, duck and bowls of palatable Malayanized *Nonya* dishes, in addition to an array of fruits such as grapes, oranges, apples, pineapples and bananas.

Each of the nine new tablets for installation was carried by the chief mourner, who first walked round the spacious courtyard of the Kongsi, and then marched in single file into the "Shrine of the Spiritual Tablets", preceded by two members, one beating the drum and the gong, and the other playing the flageolet. When the nine mourners were assembled at the shrine, they stood in two rows, awaiting the "Dotting the *Chu*" ceremony to be performed by a master of ceremonies. Each mourner placed the tablet behind his back, holding it with two upturned hands in pick-a-back fashion. The master of ceremonies dipped a Chinese brush into the vermilion ink on the altar. He then dangled the brush over the mouth of a mourner, who was to exhale a breath of air to the brush — emblematic of imparting life to the vermilion ink. Immediately after this, the master of ceremonies applied the brush and ink to the tablet, first on the top section (symbolic of calling Heaven to witness); then on the base of the tablet (symbolic of calling Earth to witness); and finally on the dot of the character *chu* to spiritualize the tablet. When this "dotting" ritual was over, the spiritualized tablet was installed in the shrine. This same process of "Dotting the *Chu*" was repeated until all nine new tablets were spiritualized and installed in their proper places in the shrine.

After this installation, the ritual of homage to the ancestors, past and present, began. The ritual was heralded by an ablution ceremony. Outside the shrine was a basin filled with water, and in it was a new face towel. The principal devotee cleansed his hands and face by means of the towel — an emblematic act of purification through the process of ablution. This purification ceremony was then performed by other members. Then, preceded by the drum-and-gong and the flageolet, about a dozen members trooped in single file into the shrine, where they assembled in two or three rows to do homage to the spiritual tablets. A series of orderly rituals was drawn up and was performed, by rotation, by each and every member — offering of lighted incense-sticks, kneeling and kowtowing, pouring out a libation, and offering food to the ancestors. This was followed immediately by another set of rituals performed by representatives of the members, who knelt and kowtowed, sipped the "lucky" wine and sampled the food, as if inviting the ancestors to partake actively of the wine and food together with the living descendants — a veritable family reunion feast.

In the meantime, a Tiechiu *wayang*, which was performing on a concrete stage facing the Kongsi's building, enacted the well-known story of *Lu Kuo Ta Feng Hsiang* (六国大封相), the "Appointment of a Premier by the Six States" of the Ts'in period, purporting to offer felicitations to the ancestors and confer luck,

A. A leading lady of the Sin Yong Hua Heng Tiechiu opera troupe in the role of a xiao sheng (young nobleman). **B.** Tung Yung and his fairy wife pay homage at the altar. **C.** Chuang Yuan, a highest graduate of the Hanlin Academy, and his bride. **D.** The toy baby that symbolizes everlasting progeny.

success and long life to the living descendants.

Whilst the homage rituals were in progress in the "Shrine of Spiritual Tablets" and at the juncture when the ancestors were supposed to be feasting with the living members, two troupers, impersonating the celebrated Tung Yung (董永) and his fairy wife of the "Seven Fairies" (七仙女) fame, entered the shrine with four armed escorts in T'ang costumes, and deposited a toy baby on the altar. They bowed and did homage to the spiritual tablets, as if to endow them with everlasting progeny symbolized by the toy baby. A few minutes after their exit, another couple of troupers, representing a highest graduate of the Hanlin Academy, called Chuang Yuan (状元), and his bride, also accompanied by four armed escorts, entered and offered a gift of two red candles to the ancestors — an emblem of extending luck, success, longevity and the good things of life to the living members of the Khoo clansmen.

At the conclusion of the rituals, a heap of joss-paper piled up like a mound on the courtyard facing the shrine was set ablaze. Whilst the joss-paper was being lighted, the black-suited members stood in a circle around the bonfire. A member in charge of a metal decanter went round the bonfire, pouring out a libation to trace a circle of alcohol around the burning heap. This ritual was repeated twice, and three distinct alcoholic circles were formed, perhaps indicating that there were at least three living generations gathered at this impressive Winter Solstice celebration.

In the evening, more than a thousand members of the Khoo clan, hailing from all parts of Malaysia, took part in the gay atmosphere of the Winter Solstice reunion dinner. At this imposing gathering, consisting of members of all walks of life, Khoo Ewe-Aik (邱有益), president of the Kongsi, delivered a stirring speech reminding the Khoo descendants of the laudable aims and objects of the association and finally the duty of every member to give full support to the government in the defence of Malaysia against Indonesian aggression.[30] Announcing that the Kongsi had taken the lead to donate a token sum of $2,000, the president urged all members to contribute generously to the National Defence Fund as a tangible sign of their absolute allegiance and undivided loyalty to the new nation.[31]

Observations and Commentaries   Since the coming of Westerners to China, the tradition of homage to ancestors has been a subject of severe criticism by some Western writers and sinologues. One of them is Herbert A. Giles, one-time Professor of Chinese in the University of Cambridge and compiler of the authoritative Chinese-English dictionary, who writes, "These offerings are made for the special purpose of conciliating the spirit and of obtaining in return a liberal share of the blessings and good things of this life. This is the essential feature of the rite, and this it is which makes the rite an act of worship pure and simple."[32]

This criticism is unfair and misleading, because the primary purpose of homage to ancestors, as J.J.M. de Groot has authoritatively interpreted it, is to "serve the dead as they were served when alive".[33] It is true that, in addition to serving the dead, many unsophisticated Chinese do expect to be blessed with the good things of this life. But this is a subsidiary motive and, as a corollary, of secondary importance. It is analogous to charging Alfred Nobel with seeking world fame and cheap publicity with his

30. [Following the formation of the Federation of Malaysia in 1963, President Sukarno of Indonesia of launched armed attacks agains the new Federation, which he accused of being in the hands of "NEKOLIM" or "neo-colonial imperialists". *Konfrontasi*, as the aggression was termed, waned with Sukarno's overthrow in 1965 and had been completely abandoned as Indonesian policy by the end of 1966.]

31. See also 星槟，5th & 24th December, 1964. Among other associations, the two Lee (surname) clan temples of Penang donated $1,000 to the National Defence Fund when the Lee clansmen celebrated the Winter Solstice Festival.

32. Giles, pp. 65–66.

33. de Groot, *Religious System*, vol. i, p. 120.

Nobel Prize, which primarily aims at promoting peace and humane service to mankind.

On the other hand, there are also some sinologues who appreciate the true spirit and the fundamental significance of the Confucian cult. One such sinologue is Professor Reginald F. Johnston, one-time Professor of Chinese in the University of London, who writes, "Very closely associated with *Hsiao* (孝) or Filial Piety is the Cult of ancestors . . . . What is not sufficiently understood by those whose knowledge is derived from books or hostile critics rather than from personal observation and sympathetic insight is that 'ancestor worship' has a practical and utilitarian as well as a religious or spiritual aspect, and is consciously and deliberately maintained as a method whereby a Chinese family not only shows its reverence or respect for its departed forefathers but also maintains the continuity of its traditions, strengthens its ties with its scattered members and collateral branches, and safeguards the material interests of its descendants. In actual practice the cult is not so much a cult of ancestors as a cult of the family."[34]

And what is the purpose of the family cult and why is it so precious? To this Liang Ch'i-Ch'ao (梁启超), a famous modern thinker, once said, "The family group underlies the whole fabric of society. Each smaller group is gathered up into a larger group, so that all trace their relationship to the prime ancestor . . . . The logical result of such concepts is the recognition that all mankind is but one large family."[35]

34. Johnston, *Confucianism*, p. 54. Professor Johnston remarks, *ibid.*, that "worship" is far too strong a word. In our text, we have consistently employed the word "homage" and other synonyms in the sense of "respect or reverential regard . . . especially respect paid by external action" (Webster's *Collegiate Dictionary*).
35. Liang Ch'i-Ch'ao, pp. 153–154.

CHAPTER 11:
Festival of the Patriotic Poet

The 5th Moon Festival falls on the 5th day of the 5th Moon (about June), and its symbol is the triangular pulut-rice cake, wrapped in bamboo leaves, called *tsung tzu* (粽子). This cake is on sale throughout the year in the Chinese quarter of towns all over Malaysia, but a few days before the 5th Moon Festival, street vendors decorate their stalls with flamboyant posters and exhibit a larger quantity and a wider variety of cakes to meet the season's demand. Many private homes too prepare this special cake in celebration of the festival.

There are generally three main varieties: the meat variety, the bean variety and the lye variety. The meat variety, consisting mainly of pulut-rice, pork, and chestnut, is the largest in dimension. Second in size comes the bean variety, comprising the main ingredients of beans and pulut-rice. The lye variety is, as a rule, smallest in size. Yellowish-green in colour, the cake is made of pulut-rice preserved in a kind of strong caustic alkaline solution called *chien shui* (枧水). In the contents is a tincture of pink caused by a tiny slip of *su mu* (苏木条 , sapanwood), an evil-dispelling agent. The *chien shui* solution was formerly imported principally from China, either in liquid form or in dry-powdered balls known in Malaysian official parlance as the "lye". As this solution may also be lixiviated from the ashes of the skin of the local durian fruits, from the Japanese occupation onwards, this lixivium (lye) has begun to supplant, to some extent, the China-imported stuff.

According to a prevalent belief in pre-Communist China, the lye pulut-rice cake had certain medicinal properties; and the longer the cake was preserved, the higher was its medicinal value. Some cakes which had been kept for several months became so dried and hardened that they were almost as solid as granite. If a person was afflicted with dysentery, an efficacious medicine was this type

A dragon-boat race.

of hardened pulut-rice. The rice was ground into powder, which was dissolved with the juice or liquid extracted from pomegranate flowers; to this mixture, honey was added with a little water and the whole concoction was then administered to the patient.

Suicide of Ch'u Yuan   The story of the triangular cake is generally ascribed to Ch'u Yuan (屈原 , *circa* 287 BC), who is honoured annually on the 5th Moon Festival,[1] often called the "Patriotic Poet's Festival" (爱国诗人节). Ch'u Yuan was a loyal minister of the state of Ch'u (楚国) and was a court favourite until his replacement by a rival through court intrigues. He was banished. When General Pai Ch'i of the Ts'in state (秦国白起将军) launched the second attack on the capital of Ch'u in the spring of 278 BC, Ch'u Yuan knew all hope to save the state was lost. Smitten with grief, he wrote the two famous odes, *Ai Ying* (哀郢) and then the *Huai Sha* (怀沙), the latter disclosing his suicide design. Then with sallow cheeks and dishevelled hair, he went to the shore of the Mi-Lo (汨罗) — an affluent of the Tung-T'ing Lake (洞庭湖) in Hunan (湖南) — with the intention of ending his life. A fisherman who met him, said, "Are you not the minister? Why should you seek a watery grave?" To which Ch'u Yuan replied, "The whole country is corrupt, except me. The people are inebriated, except me. So it's better that way." "But in that case wouldn't it be better for you to move with the trend and rise in power?" Ch'u Yuan replied that he preferred a death of honour and to be interred in the bellies of the fishes of the river. So saying he clasped a huge stone with both hands and jumped into the Mi-Lo and drowned himself.[2]

Traditional history adds that as soon as he jumped into the water, the fishermen instantly rowed out in their boats to try to save him, but in vain. This was later followed by the throwing of rice into the river for the spirit of the heroic minister. This incident happened on the 5th day of the 5th Moon and annually the people rowed out in their boats and scattered rice into the water.[3]

The Triangular Rice Cakes   In about 40 BC, according to a legend, a man who called himself a minister appeared on the shores and told the fishermen that it was a good thing that they did homage to Ch'u Yuan, but as the rice was eaten up by the dragon of the river, future offerings should be inserted into bamboo stems. The end of the stem should be closed up with *lien* (楝叶 , "Pride of India") leaves and tied up with five-coloured threads. These *lien* leaves and five-coloured threads were dreaded by the dragon monster. Then the food would remain intact for Ch'u Yuan's spirit to consume.[4]

It is generally believed that the triangular cakes, with which we are now familiar, were thrown into the river not long after this complaint against the river-dragon. However, a Chinese source says that historically the triangular cakes were first used in the Tsin dynasty (晋朝 , AD 265–419) in celebration of the turning point of the year at the Summer Solstice by the peasantry. In North China, millet was cultivated extensively and the first harvest of millet took place in the 5th Moon, the summer month. So these cakes were originally made of millet, with tortoise meat as the chief ingredient, wrapped with bamboo leaves in triangular shape. The underlying theory was to conform to the Yin and

1. 爱国诗人 , in 恨事 , 严殊炎 , 国光 , 1949, pp. 1–5.
2. Abridged from 屈原贾生列传 , in 史记 , *op. cit.*, vol. xix, ch. 84, pp. 1–14; and in 屈原 , 陆侃如 , 亚东图书馆 , Hong Kong, July 1962, pp. 1–6. See also Shanghai, 6th ed., May 1933; and *JNCBRAS*, Billas.
3. 郑振铎 , *ibid.*
4. 续斋谐记 , 吴均 in 逸史 , vol. 55, pp. 6, 7.

Yang principles which have an important bearing on the seasons. The tortoise within represented the Yin and the bamboo leaves outside represented the Yang. It was about this time that triangular cakes were used jointly for the Summer Solstice and the 5th Moon Festival in commemoration of Ch'u Yuan.[5] In course of time, the 5th Moon Festival ousted the Summer Solstice, which remained a season of agricultural importance.

The Dragon-Boat Races   It was about the Tsin period that the now famous dragon-boat race first took place.[6] A twentieth-century account throws light on the dragon boats in Amoy, Foochow and Canton, where "the water festival is particularly brilliant, and the races sometimes last several days."[7]

Everywhere there is the bustle of thickly thronged life, says this account, a kaleidoscope of colour and sound, of lights and shadows, of moving boats and people, an ever-changing grouping on land and water in the tawny sunshine with its fierce, prowling splendour . . . . They are a fine sight, these huge boats resembling dragons, each over [thirty metres] long and so gracefully slim that two men are crowded as they sit side by side. High sterns with long steering-paddles rise [high] above the gunwales, high prows are shaped like a dragon's head with open mouth and cruel fangs, and the long body between is gaily painted to represent scales, and touched up with brilliant gilding. One man stands in each bow, as if looking for the corpse of Ch'u Yuan, and throws his arms about as though casting rice upon the waters. Others, interspersed among the rowers, wave brilliant flags or beat gongs and cymbals, so that the deafening clamour may frighten away the monster that Ch'u Yuan feared.

Generally speaking, in Malaysia the dragon-boat race did not come into vogue, though it is known such races were held at intervals in Penang in the earlier years of the last century. The dragon boats, resembling canoes, were narrow and gilded like snakes, each with about fifty paddlers. On one occasion, a commander of one of the British frigates challenged Penang to race against his ship's boats. Amongst others, the Chinese entered the contest with a "gilded snake-boat". As soon as the signal was given, the snake-boat dashed off from the starting-post "with a shuttle-like velocity" and would have out-distanced every other boat, had it not unfortunately met a strong gale in the harbour. In consequence, the boat capsized and sank. In 1836, a dragon-boat race, probably the first on record, was held on the 5th day of the 5th Moon. Prizes were awarded in the form of gold articles and dresses, worth less than $100, which were affixed to the winning post, stuck in the mud. The owner of the boat which reached the winning post first secured the entire prize. There was also side-betting, which became the chief attraction of the spectators.[8]

But in the twentieth century, such dragon-boat races do not seem to have continued. The latest race took place after Merdeka on the 5th day of the 5th Moon in 1958 under the name of "Water Festival". This was a mixed event, including competitors from the English and the Chinese schools. The participants were divided into two groups: (a) the professional boatmen from Weld Quay, the youths of the Malayan Chinese Association and members of the Chinese Swimming Club; and (b) boys from the Chung Ling (Chinese) High School (钟灵中学校) and boys from other secondary (English) schools. The race of the first group

5. 端午・黃石・Hong Kong 泰兴书局・April 1963, pp. 17–19.
6. *Ibid.*, p. 104.
7. Bredon & Mitrophanow, pp. 304–305.
8. Low, pp. 306–307.

A clan association dinner at North Boat Quay, on the banks of the Singapore river. Note the wayang *stage, left.*

started at 4.00 p.m. from Weld Quay to Gurney Drive, and the second group at 5.05 p.m. In this gala programme were also sampan races and swimming contests for boys and girls above and under seventeen years of age. Prizes were given away by His Excellency, Raja Sir Uda, the Governor of Penang. Except for its varied scope, the races lacked the skill, glamour and splendour of those held annually in Hong Kong where this event is a big affair.[9]

Observance in Malaysia Though the absence of the dragon-boat race is conspicuous, the celebration of the 5th Moon Festival is by no means unimportant in Malaysia where Chinese newspapers publish annual supplements or special features in commemoration of the patriotic poet. On this festival day, triangular cakes are exchanged as gifts between relatives and friends to mark the death anniversary of Ch'u Yuan. In China, the 5th Moon was considered as an "evil month" (恶月), and in Malaysia, much stress is laid on this aspect of the festival, to judge by the host of subsidiary observances by the less sophisticated section of the public.

Early in the morning, conservative housewives buy a bunch of greens from the markets for hanging over the lintels of their doors to drive away evil. A bouquet consists of four kinds of green leaves and a nosegay of tropical flowers. The numeral "5" is obviously symbolic of the month and the day of the festival. The tropical flowers perhaps convey no special meaning; but the four kinds of greens — pomelo leaves, mugwort, rush and willow leaves — are believed to possess powers of exorcising malignant influence and averting sickness and disease.

The willow leaves need more amplification: for in China willows are as popular as chestnuts in England. During the *Ch'ing Ming* festival, willow twigs are torn off from the tree and taken home to hang over the gates or doors to ward off evil spirits. Lunacy, as believed by some people, is caused by malicious spirits,

9. 星槟 20th June, 1958 and 光华 21st June, 1958.

and to dispel these spirits, the patients are thrashed or beaten with willow leaves or twigs. In Balik Pulau, Penang, there is a Kuan Yin temple. For many years the nun in charge gave successful treatment to a number of patients afflicted with mental derangement and one of the treatments was the gentle thrashing of the patient with willow leaves and twigs.[10]

This "greens" practice has its origin in mediaeval China, where the extreme summer heat was liable to cause an outbreak of epidemic diseases and the people resorted to wearing talismans and seasonal herbs and hanging up mugwort flags, rushes and other greens to avert these diseases. An even more cogent reason[11] was that "the mugwort-flag brings a hundred (all kinds of) blessings" (艾旗迎百福) and "the rush-sword kills thousands of evils" (蒲剑斩千邪). A legend says that the tradition of mugwort and rush originated in the ninth century from the time of Huang Ch'ao (黄巢), the notorious rebel, who slaughtered the people at sight. In the course of the massacre, Huang Ch'ao saw a middle-aged man carrying pick-a-back a teenage youth, whilst dragging with one hand a boy about six years old. When challenged, the fugitive knelt down begging that his nephew be spared. "Which one is your nephew?" "The teenage . . ." replied the fugitive in earnest. "What nonsense!" Huang Ch'ao interrupted, "Do you mean to tell me that the boy you're carrying is your nephew and that the younger one is your own son?" "I'm telling the truth, your Highness," explained the fugitive. "I carry my nephew to ensure his escape, because he's an orphan. If my own son be lost, then so long as I'm alive, I could re-marry and have other children. But should anything happen to my orphan-nephew, then the line of descendants from my deceased brother would terminate abruptly." Touched by the appeal of his victim, Huang Ch'ao spared the lot of them, saying, "Exhibit mugwort-and-rush at the door of your house and no harm will come to the inmates." This was done and the family escaped death.[12]

10. SG, Wu Liu, 27th April, 1952. See also Latourette, p. 641, wherein it is stated that "insane persons are controlled by *kuei* (devils)".
11. 荆楚・抱朴子 and 风土记 in 图书・*op. cit.*, vol. 19, ch. 51, p. 48. Our research shows that the use of mugwort was — and still is — widespread in some parts of Europe where mugwort is believed to possess "wondrous virtue" if it is gathered on the Eve of the Day of St John. In France, it is called the herb of St John; and in Germany and Bohemia it is worn round the waist, called St John's girdle, to protect the wearer against ghosts, misfortune, magic and sickness. (See Frazer, *Balder*, pp. 58–60.)
12. 端午・*op. cit.*, p. 193, and 传说・*op. cit.*, pp. 3 & 4.

Rituals and Beliefs In the forenoon, every family in Malaysia pays homage to the ancestors to whom the usual food offering, with the triangular cakes as the main item, is made. In some cases, tropical flowers are also proffered. After this, members of the family rejoice themselves over the sumptuous food, as if in the company of their ancestors.

A special ritual is held at the noon. Offerings are made in the open to what is locally denominated the "Mid-day Deities" (午时神). The offering consists of a plate of triangular cakes, a plate of seven varieties of flowers, a slab of vermilion ink and a basin of water containing seven kinds of flowers, which are laid out on a table used as a temporary altar. The so-called "Mid-day Deities" are obviously evolved from the "Five Anti-epidemic Deities" (五瘟司) of the Sui (隋) era during the reign of Emperor K'ai Huang (开皇 , AD 581–600). Originally, the five deities were charitable physicians, who specialized in treating epidemic diseases. After their death, they were deified as the deities for protection against pestilence.[13]

When the offering is over, children take a bath using the water or a portion thereof from the basin on the theory that this water is a powerful evil-expelling agent. In some Cantonese homes, the thick, absorbent rind of the pomelo is put into the bath-tub on the same theory. A few of the triangular cakes of the lye variety are retained and exposed to the sun for drying. These are afterwards kept for future emergency use. Locally, such dried-up cakes are believed to be efficacious in the treatment of stomach ailments (Hokkien custom). When a person suffers from stomach-ache, the lye cake is cut up into slices, which are mixed with brown sugar syrup. The mixture is then orally administered to a patient. Many patients have attested to the efficacy of this treatment. Some adults wash their hair at noon on this day in the belief that the ritual may drive away bad luck. A sulphuric substance is also ignited in mid-day to fumigate every nook and corner of the house against possible poisonous or evil agents lurking in the building — a custom derived from the famous story of the "White-Snake-Spirit" (白蛇精) and the "Black-Snake-Spirit" (黑蛇精) popularized by the Chinese *wayang* and the highly dramatized Chinese talkies. In this tender story of snake-and-man romance, Hsu Hsien (许仙), the husband of the White-Snake-Spirit, was counselled to burn sulphur on the 5th day of the 5th Moon to avert his impending doom. This he did most reluctantly — and presto! His beautiful spouse was transformed back to her original state, an ugly snake!

In the territorial associations and clan temples, where the spiritual tablets of the ancestors are set up, similar offerings are made on this festival day. Some years ago, the Khoo Kongsi at Penang was reported to have observed the festival with offerings of the triangular cakes, fruits and vegetarian food to the ancestors of the Khoo clan. The ritual was highlighted by the reciting of liturgies by Buddhist adherents, led by the recorded chanting of five nuns.[14]

The "Evil" Theory There is also a vague belief in Malaysia that children born on the 5th day of the 5th Moon are likely to cause the premature death of their parents — a belief originated in China in the period of the Warring States (战国 , 403–211 BC), when Chi-Mai (起迈), whose birth took place on the 5th day of

13. 端午 *ibid.*, p. 61.
14. SG, Wu Liu, 27th April, 1952.

the 5th Moon, was abandoned by his parents. From this time onwards, people looked askance on such births, and infanticide came into practice until its decline in the T'ang period.[15]

However, there are a good many historical cases to explode such a belief. There was the case of Prince Meng Ch'ang (孟尝君), born on the 5th day of the 5th Moon, who rose to serve the state of Ch'i (齐国) with distinction. At the time of his birth his father did not want him. But his mother clandestinely brought him up. When he was grown up, his father explained, "Sons born in the 5th Moon reach the height of the door and bring bad luck to their parents." To which the boy replied, "Is the life of a human being dependent on Heaven or is it dependent on the door? If it depends on Heaven, why did you worry? If it depends on the door, then raise the height of the door and who could reach it?"[16]

And there was in the Han period a brilliant administrator who held three ministerial posts concurrently. Originally, he was born of the Huang (黄) family on the 5th day of the 5th Moon. As the parents abhorred his birth, they thrust the babe into a gourd and cast it into a stream. Somebody picked it up and brought up the child. When he grew up and became famous, he gave himself the name of Hu Kuang (胡广) indicating that he owed his life to the gourd, without being unfilial to his natural parents, who claimed him, and without being ungrateful to the foster parents who had reared him.[17]

In the Tsin era, there was Wang Feng (王凤), born on the 5th day of the 5th Moon, whose father wanted to abandon him but for the intercession of his paternal uncle. He grew up to be a war minister. And there was Wang Chen-O (王镇恶), born on the 5th day of the 5th Moon in the Tsin period, whose abandonment was prevented by his grandfather. He became famous and rich. Some centuries later — in the T'ang period — there was born on this supposed evil day Ts'ui Hsin-Ming (崔信明), who made a name in the literary world. He was lucky, for his parents did not try to discard him at birth.[18] So deep-rooted was the prejudice of that time that Emperor Chen-Tsung (宋真宗 , AD 998–1022), third ruler of the Sung dynasty, who was born on the 5th day of the 5th Moon, had his date of birth altered to the 10th day of the 10th Moon.[19]

Even as late as the Manchu dynasty (1644–1911), the scholar P'ing Pu-Ch'ing (平步青), who tried to court popularity on the prevalent "evil" theory, made an attempt to run down the historical 5th-day-born celebrities. He labelled Prince Meng Ch'ang as "crafty", Wang Feng as "presumptuous", Hu Kuang as "fawning", and Wang Chen-O as "avaricious". He added that no case had come to light where a person born on the "evil" day had acquired fame for moral conduct.[20] Pu-Ch'ing's *non sequitur* reasoning is too puerile to merit more consideration than pointing out that there are men and women born any time, anywhere, with the same human failings as those attributed to the four historical celebrities. As to "moral conduct", it is a highly debatable issue, depending on a strict definition of the term and on one's cherished values. It also applies to anyone born any time, anywhere.

Though the "evil" theory is still held in Malaysia, it is with pride that we note there are no serious attempts at infanticide, though cases of secretive child-abandonment are not unheard of in our midst, perhaps due more to the stricken poverty of the parents than to the influence of the unproven "evil" theory.

15. 历俗 *op. cit.*, ch. 27, p. 321.
16. 孟尝君传 in 图书 , *op. cit.*, vol. 19, ch. 52, p. 53.
17. 汉书 cited in 端午 , *op. cit.*, p. 212. In 世说 , 许慎 , it is narrated that Hu Kuang was put into a jar and was picked up by a Mr Hu. Hence his adoption of Hu as his surname instead of Huang.
18. 晋书 and 唐书 cited in 端午 , *op. cit.*, pp. 212, 213. See also 西京杂记 and 宋书 in 图书 , *op. cit.*, vol. 19, ch. 52, p. 53.
19. 霞外攟屑 , 平步青 in 明清笔记丛刊 , Shanghai 历俗 , November 1959, vol. i, ch. 8, p. 581. (Cf. 中华 , *op. cit.*, ch. 27, p. 321, which says it was Emperor Huei Tsung (徽宗) of the Sung dynasty who was born on the 5th day of the 5th Moon and had it changed to the 10th day of the 10th Moon.)
20. 霞外攟屑 , *ibid.*

CHAPTER 12:
China's Two Immortal Lovers

Every nation has its Romeo and Juliet, and the Chinese have the immortal love story of the Cowherd and the Weaving Lady (牛郎织女). The Chinese story is doubly fascinating, because of its astrological origin, and because from it a festival has evolved and been observed by millions of devout believers, Chinese, Japanese and others. Early Chinese star-watchers had discovered that the circumpolar stars, revolving round the pole star (fixed position), would return to the same place in about 27.33 days, thus forming a sidereal month.

In relation to this discovery, the Chinese devised the twenty-eight Hsiu (二十八宿 , lunar mansions) system as early as the middle of the Shang period (*circa* fourteenth century BC).[1] These lunar mansions are equatorial divisions, or segments of the celestial sphere bounded by hour-circles. For each of these twenty-eight mansions a name was given. The ninth lunar mansion (Altair or Vega) was called Ch'ien Niu (牵牛 , Cowherd), and the tenth lunar mansion (Acuilae or Lyrae) was called Chih Nu (织女 , Weaving Lady).

As the Altair and the Lyrae are in close proximity to one another, it was easy to tempt the imaginative myth-makers to draw inspiration from their sexes to create the boy-meets-girl romance in Heaven. One of the early stories goes back to the state of Ch'u (荆楚 , 740–330 BC). It tells of the marriage between the Cowherd and the Weaving Lady, a grand-daughter of Heaven. To pay the dowry, the Cowherd secured a loan of twenty thousand strings of cash from T'ien Ti (天帝 , King of Heaven). As, for a long time, the Cowherd was unable to repay the loan, the couple was separated — the Cowherd to the west and the Weaving Lady to the east of the Milky Way (天河) and was permitted to meet only once a year on the 7th night of the 7th Moon.[2]

A. *An actor of the Ki Meng Tiechiu* wayang *troupe in the role of Tzu-Yi: on his scroll are the characters* wan shih ju i, *i.e. everything shall be as you desire it. This ritual is actually performed at the beginning and end of each "season in the village", and is intended to bring luck to pious devotees in the audience.* **B.** *The Sago Lane Cantonese Sisters' Association, Singapore.*

1. Needham, vol. iii, p. 242.
2. 荆楚 in 岁时 '*op. cit.*, vol. ii, ch. 26, p. 293; and 历俗 '*op. cit.*, ch. 39, p. 446.

Another Chinese allusion to these lovers came from a story of the Ch'i period (齐, AD 479–501). There was once an immortal, named Ch'eng Wu-Ting (成武丁), living in the district of Kuei Yang (桂阳), who fraternized freely with human beings. One day, he suddenly told his brother, "On the 7th day of the 7th Moon, the Weaving Lady travels across the Milky Way and all immortals have to return to the Celestial Palace. I myself have been summoned and cannot tarry any more on earth. I must bid you farewell now and meet you again in three years' time." "Why has the Weaving Lady to cross the Milky Way?" the younger brother inquired. "The Weaving Lady has to meet the Cowherd in temporary reunion," came the explanation. On the next day, there was no trace of Wu-Ting anywhere.[3]

Poets and Myth-Makers In those early days, poets, now and again, made isolated allusions to these two stars, which tended to excite the curiosity of the people, and stimulate their interest. One ancient poem read:[4]

> Yonder's the Cowherd pining, far, far away,
> The Weaving Lady brightens the Milky Way.
> Keeping them asunder, the water rises high,
> Great was their love: silently they stare and sigh.
> （古诗：迢迢牵牛星，皎皎河织女，盈盈一水间，脉脉不得语）

Meanwhile, myth-makers did not remain idle; for they began to expand and adorn the original stories with many interesting and romantic features. One of these delectable myths comes from Japan, which, influenced by China about twelve hundred years ago, has since been holding the Feast of Tanabata (the Weaving Lady) annually.

"A great god of the firmament had a lovely daughter Tanabatatsume," says the Japanese myth of Chinese origin, "who passed her days in weaving garments for her august parent. She rejoiced in her work, and thought that there was no greater pleasure than the pleasure of weaving. But one day, as she sat before her loom at the door of her heavenly dwelling, she saw a handsome peasant lad pass by, leading an ox, and she fell in love with him. Her august father, divining her secret wish, gave her the youth for a husband. But the wedded lovers became fond of each other, and neglected their duty to the god of the firmament, the sound of the shuttle was no longer heard, and the ox wandered, unheeded, over the plains of heaven.

"Therefore the great god was displeased and separated the pair. They were sentenced to live thereafter apart, with the Celestial River between them, but it was permitted them to see other once a year on the 7th night of the 7th Moon. On that night — providing the skies be clear — the birds of heaven (magpies) make, with their bodies and wings, a bridge over the stream; and by means of that bridge, the lovers can meet. But if there be rain, the River of Heaven rises, and becomes so wide that the bridge cannot be formed.

"So the husband and wife cannot always meet, even on the 7th night of the 7th Moon; it may happen, by reason of bad weather, they cannot meet three or four years at a time. But their love remains immortally young and eternally patient; and they continue to fulfil their respective duties each day without fault and are happy in the hope of being able to meet on the 7th night of the next 7th Moon."[5]

3. 续斋谐记 in 逸史 *op. cit.*, vol. 55, pp. 6, 7.
4. 历俗，*op. cit.*, ch. 39, p. 446.
5. "The Romance of the Milky Way", in Hearn, pp. 480–481. See also Granet, p. 239 and fn.1 & fn.2; and 七夕在日本 in supplement of 南洋，15th August, 1964.

Tradition in China A few customs originated from the imperial palace, which took the lead in their observance. The tradition of "airing clothings" (曝衣) on the 7th day of the 7th Moon was started by Emperor Wu of the Han period (140–88 BC). Emperor Wu had a special terrace constructed for the courtesans to air the Queen's robe.[6] This practice was copied by the people, who exposed canonical books and clothes to the sun on the 7th day to get immunization from insects.[7] So prevalent was the practice in later years that Hao Lung (郝隆 , about AD 305), a scholar of high standing, took part in it in good humour. Lying supine in the courtyard, he exposed his naked trunk to the solar heat.[8] Asked what he was doing that for, he curtly replied that he was "airing the books in his belly."

From the T'ang period onwards, celebrations in relation to the Cowherd and the Weaving Lady were held in a variety of forms by both men and women, for the mystery of the Milky Way and the legends of the two immortal lovers had by then been interwoven with the life of the people.

On the 7th night of the 7th Moon, Emperor Ming and his favourite concubine, Kuei Fei, took a stroll in the courtyard to watch a number of courtesans who had laid out fruit, flowers and wine of all varieties on a table to make offering to the Cowherd and the Weaving Lady to invoke their blessings. There was also a "spider-web" contest (蜘蛛含丝乞巧). Each courtesan caught a spider and put it into a small golden case. The cases were exhibited on the laid-out table and allowed to remain till dawn. Then each case was opened for the contents to be examined. The owner of the case, which showed the largest quantity of webs, was the winner.[9]

In another instance, Ming Huang caused a pavilion of variegated colour to be constructed in the palace. Towering more than thirty metres above the city, the topmost terrace had accommodation for scores of people. On the 7th night, the courtesans gathered at the terrace to make offerings to the Cowherd and the Weaving Lady. In the course of the celebration, a needle-threading competition called *ch'i ch'iao* (乞巧) took place. Each courtesan held up a nine-eyed needle and tried to put a five-coloured thread through the eyes in the moonlight (以九孔针 五色线向月穿之). Those who succeeded were winners and acclaimed skilful in needle-work. After this, feasting and rejoicing followed and lasted till dawn.[10]

These imperial celebrations were copied by the people. In the needle-threading competition, the commoners used seven-eyed (七孔针) instead of the nine-eyed needles to test their skill.[11] In addition, there were other subsidiary observances. On the 7th night, if anyone was fortunate enough to see a five-coloured illumination in the sky, he was eligible for three different wishes: riches, longevity, and the begetting of male descendants, from the Cowherd and the Weaving Lady. But he might ask for only one thing, not three blessings, at a time. Furthermore, he should not whisper a word to anybody, until a lapse of three years.[12]

On the eve of the 7th day, according to another popular practice, ladies filled the cups with water and exposed them to dew. On the next day, the cups were exposed to the sun until a thin membrane was formed on the surface of the water. Then a needle was lightly dropped onto the membrane and its reflection at the bottom was scrutinized. In this scrutiny the skill of a maiden

6. 西京杂记in 事类，*op. cit.*, vol. i, ch. 6, p. 52.
7. 四民月令in 月粹，*op. cit.*, vol. iii, ch. 12, p. 6.
8. 世说新语，刘义庆，ch. 6, p. 211 in 诸子，*op. cit.*, vol. viii.
9. 开元in 小史，*op. cit.*, vol. viii, ch. 18, p. 12.
10. 开元 in 说库，*op. cit.*, vol. viii, p. 13.
11. 荆楚 in 子史，*op. cit.*, vol. ii, ch. 26, p. 26.
12. 玉烛宝典，*op. cit.*, vol. ii, ch. 7, p. 295.

was assessed by the formation of the shadow at the bottom of the cup — did it spread out like a blossom, did it move like the clouds, or was it as thin as a thread or as bulky as a mallet?[13]

There was also the *Hua Sheng* (化生 , birth by transformation) custom. On the 7th night, newly wedded women prepared and made wax dolls and frolicked with them on the surface of the water — an auspicious omen for begetting male issue.[14] And there was the custom of watching the clearness or obscurity of the Milky Way on the 7th night to divine the price of rice. If the Milky Way was obscure, the price would be high; if clear, the price would be low.[15] Furthermore, a belief was in circulation that if the weather on the 7th day was inclement and the Weaver was thus prevented from crossing the crow-and-magpie bridge, the rain drops were the tears of the Cowherd and his sweetheart — tears of the unhappy lovers.[16]

A Solemn Wish Wishes for lasting conjugal happiness were also made before the star-lovers. A story was told that Ming Huang and Kuei Fei once stayed at their holiday palace up the hill. It was midnight on the 7th, and Ming Huang and Kuei Fei, whilst gazing at the starlit firmament, were inspired by the two celestial lovers. "Isn't it a shame that the Cowherd is permitted to meet the Weaving Lady only once a year?" Ming Huang remarked. "Yes, it makes me nervous, I hope we shall never be torn apart like them," answered Kuei Fei, clutching the Emperor's hand. Emperor Ming turned to face his beloved and their eyes gleamed.

"We shall always be together," they said in solemnity, "and

13. 清录，*op. cit.*, p. 75.
14. 岁时记事 in 月粹，*op. cit.*, vol. iii, ch. 12, p. 9.
15. 清录 *op. cit.*, p. 75.
16. 岁时杂记 in 岁时，*op. cit.*, vol. ii, ch. 26, p. 293; and Bredon & Mitrophanow, p. 373.

let it be our earnest wish — in our future reincarnations, may we always be reunited as man and wife."[17]

This episode of romance was immortalized by Po Chu-I (白居易 , AD 722–824), who alludes to it in the famous *Ch'ang Hen Ko* (长恨歌), the "Ballad of Endless Woe":

> The seventh moon, the seventh day
> We stood in Chang-sheng Hall,
> 'Twas night, and none beside us;
> We two were all in all.
> We swore that in the heaven above
> We never would dispart:
> One tomb on earth enclose of us
> The frail and mortal part.[18]

Thus with a host of such glamorous tales and pleasant beliefs as background, the 7th night of the 7th Moon became an important festival.[19] But down through the centuries, some of the subsidiary customs began to wane, and by the time of the Manchu period, only the main feature, the sacrificial offering, and one or two subsidiary customs continued to be observed.[20]

Survival in Malaysia Similarly, in Malaysia today such traditions as spider-web competitions and needle-shadow contests are almost unheard of. What has survived is mainly the offering on the 6th night of the 7th Moon to the Weaving Lady by maidens, followed, in some cases, by a formal homage to the Cowherd by boys and adolescents on the morning of the 7th.

In pre-war Malaya there were, in addition to the individual celebrations, some groups of maidens of marriageable age, headed

A. *A Hainanese lady medium in a trance.* **B.** *A devotee at a Sisters' Association altar.* **C.** *A young female medium possessed by one of the Seven Sisters.*

17. 唐乐史·段成式 in 说郛 series, *op. cit.*, vol. xix, ch. 38, p. 15. Our rendition is slightly dramatized. A touching and concise account of this love scene is portrayed in English by Shu-Chiung (Mrs Wu Lien-Teh) in her book *Yang Kuei-Fei* under the chapter "A Midnight Vow" (pp. 71–72), wherein she captures the entire atmosphere of tender romance and the solemnity of the oath.
18. Fletcher, p. 130.
19. According to de Groot (cited in Bredon & Mitrophanow, p. 500), in the olden days the Cowherd and Weaver stars used to reach their zenith simultaneously about the winter solstice (11th Moon). This is also stated in 淮南子 (天文训) ·p. 83 in 诸子·, *op. cit.*, vol. vii. But owing to the precession of the equinoxes down through the millenia, de Groot goes on to say, "they now reach the highest point in the Seventh Moon when their festival is celebrated." The Cowherd became patron of cattle and the Weaver patroness of female dressmakers. They were also guardians of the sexes and particularly of lovers. Our account is not at variance with de Groot's, for we are writing about the festival, not the stellar evolution.
20. 历俗 ·*op. cit.*, ch. 39, p. 448.

by senior female vegetarians and their sympathizers, who held exhibitions in the vegetarian homes. In these exhibitions embroidery and needle-work, designs of sesame seeds and of dragon's eyes, and valuable curios, were on display — a survival of the needle-craft skill competition, coupled with the invocation of blessings from the stellar lovers. The best-known group celebrations in Singapore were held by the so-called Sisters' Associations, organized principally by and for Cantonese female labourers and domestic servants. Members of these associations put on their best attire and gathered at their associations to make offerings to the Weaving Lady. There was no needle-work or other forms of competition. The participants rejoiced themselves with feasting and diverse forms of traditional merriment till late at night.[21] Such associations still operate in postwar years; and similar associations, on a lesser scale, also operate in Penang.

Communication in Trance   On this night there was also a unique practice (Cantonese) in private homes "to communicate with the Seven Sisters" through the chanting of incantations by a female medium. This is little publicised, because the practice was confined strictly to maidens (virgins). A number of maidens, the ideal number being seven, sat around the temporary altar — usually a round table. On the table were arrayed offerings to the Seven Sisters: seven kinds of flowers; seven varieties of fruits; seven dishes of *tau-geh* (豆芽 , bean sprouts); seven cups of tea; hair-binding threads of seven colours; tinted peanuts, pink green and yellow; a few plates of *padi*-shoots; a bowl of special soup made from red prunes, preserved pumpkin, edible wicks, and sesame seeds; and cosmetics. Incense-sticks and candles were lighted. Whilst joss-paper with gold imprint was being burnt, a few sheets at a time, the participating maidens bent over the table with their eyes shut and rested their heads face downward upon their crooked hands, and the medium began to recite a series of incantations to entrance herself. Halfway through the recitation, the participants became unconscious and, in this state, usually cried aloud with their bodies and limbs trembling and quivering, as if entering into a trance. The trance lasted a few minutes, after which the participants woke up, without knowing what they had gone through. According to our Penang informants, only those born with "fairy-bones" (仙骨) are able to effect communication with the Seven Sisters. In doing so, they first travel down to Purgatory and then ascend to Heaven to meet the Weaving Lady or the Seven Sisters. During this process, the hands and feet of the participants become icy cold, and they hum some strange and meaningful songs to describe the scenes. As those we have contrived to interview were failures, we have to accept the informants' explanation, which remains neither proven nor unproven. Nor are we able to trace the origin, except that the practice came from immigrants of certain prefectures, such as Toi-Shan (台山) in Canton.

Celebration in Progress   Some years ago, we explored the Chinese (Cantonese) quarter of the city of George Town, Penang, during this festival. On the pavement of dwelling houses in Cintra Street, we noticed suspended from the pillars or wooden boards several sets of paper contrivances, each consisting of seven suits of full-sized garments of the same pattern but of different hues. By

21.   星洲十年 , *op. cit.*, Section V, p. 1072. The Sisters' Associations are well-organized mutual help societies, to which a member makes a monthly contribution. Usually, a room is rented for this purpose. When a member is out of employment or sick, she may occupy the room free of rental. Members are loyal and help one another in time of need. In the colonial days before the introduction of a fairer set of labour legislations and trade unionism, such simple mutual-aid organizations were useful in affording protection for female wage-earners against exploitation and untoward mishaps. See also CSA, Homer Cheng Hui-Ming, pp. 21–26.

the side of the main door of each house was a gigantic basin-shaped paper tray. Upon the tray were affixed sets of paper paraphernalia, representing powder, rouge, mirrors, combs, shoes (for stunted feet), bracelets and necklaces, each set containing seven articles of the same kind.

In the front hall there was a long oblong table, arrayed with a miniature bridge (for the lovers to meet across the Milky Way), bowls and plates of fruits, flowers and cakes of diverse categories. Flanking the central incense-vessel were two pots, one on each side. The pot on the left contained bean sprouts and the pot on the right, *padi*-shoots — symbolic of prosperity and good harvests. On display were also perfumes, lipsticks, rouge and powder, belonging to the female devotees who invoked the blessing of the Weaving Lady, so that when they later applied these cosmetics, they would look doubly attractive to their loved ones and, under the divine guidance of the celestial lovers, live in happy wedlock.

One of the most conspicuous articles in the exhibition was a bottle of water, which was to be sealed up later, and stored away for general and emergency use. This water, known as the "Seven Sisters' Water" (七姐水), is believed to possess certain curative properties. In a conservative home, this water is kept in readiness, just as a first-aid kit of Western medicaments is kept in a modern household.[22] This practice has its root in Canton, where it was the tradition to draw water from the well or stream on the morning of the 7th day of the 7th Moon and preserve it in a hermetically sealed jar. The water was believed to be immune from putrefaction, and if medicinal powder was dissolved with a few drops of this water, the mixture would become very efficacious in the treatment of sores and abscesses. It was recorded in the seventeenth century that the water should be drawn after the first cock's crow, and such water, called the "Holy Water" (圣水) or "Water from the Grand-daughter of Heaven" (天孙水), besides possessing curative properties, would weigh heavier than other water. However, if the water was drawn after the second crow, then all its attributes would disappear.[23]

Meeting the Fairy   Whether you make offerings to the Weaving Lady and the Cowherd or not, there is the well-known Kuo Tzu-Yi (郭子仪) story to cheer you up — you may have a lucky encounter like him, who knows? Once on the 7th night of the 7th Moon, Kuo Tzu-Yi was travelling towards the "silver town" (银州). Suddenly he saw a decorated carriage descending from Heaven. From it emerged a beautiful maiden. Without hesitation he bowed before the lady and did homage to her, asking to be blessed with riches, honours and longevity. "Thy wishes shall be granted," replied the celestial maiden. It may be sheer coincidence, but it is an historical fact that Kuo Tzu-Yi of the Han dynasty was rapidly promoted and honoured in the imperial service, grew rich, and died a nonagenarian.[24] A legend from the Tibetan foothills says Kuo Tzu-Yi was reputed to have had one hundred sons and one thousand grandsons living at the same time, besides having enormous family wealth. It adds that a statue (commonly known in Malaysia as the God of Wealth), representing Tzu-Yi, depicted him as sitting on a chair, with long white beard and white garment, carrying a sceptre as a sign of authority. On the sceptre are engraved four characters, *wan shih ju i* (万事如意), i.e. everything shall be as you desire it.[25]

22. At an interview, a young Penang housewife, now of Singapore, assured the author that she had carried out experiments on the "Seven Sisters' Water" and the ordinary pipe-water, and that her conclusions were that the former was truly efficacious in treatment of sores and abscesses and immune from the pollution of larvae, year in and year out. She had also used such water to make the popular *bedak sejok*, a Malaysian home-prepared face-powder made of rice powder, and discovered that whereas the rice dough normally gave a nasty smell, this smell was absolutely absent when the dough was mixed with the "Seven Sisters' Water". She stressed that some of her friends, who had made similar experiments, were of the same opinion.

23. 广州岁时 cited in 全国 , *op. cit.*, pt. ii, vol. ii, ch. 7, p. 15 and pt. i, vol. ii, ch. 8, p. 28; and 广东新语 , 屈翁山 , 天水阁绣版 , 1680, vol. iii, ch. 4, p. 36.

24. 太平 , *op. cit.*, vol. ii, ch. 20, p. 29.

25. NCR, vol. ii, 1920, pp. 381–382.

CHAPTER 13:
The Hungry Ghosts' Month

Called *Kuei Chieh* (鬼节), the Festival of the (Hungry) Ghosts in the 7th Moon is the most important and most widely observed festival in Malaysia, second only to the New Year.[1] These ghosts fall under the category of neglected shades, who have not been cared for by their living relatives and who are, therefore, prone to be malignant and mischievous.

According to popular belief, the gates of Purgatory are thrown open as from midnight on the last day of the 6th Moon, and the hungry ghosts (*pretas*) are released from incarceration to mingle with human beings for a period of thirty days till the last day of the 7th Moon. To appease these straying destitute ghosts, the Chinese generally make a preliminary offering on the evening of the 1st day of the 7th Moon. Candles and incense-sticks are lighted in a row extended over the frontage of each residence, and incense-papers are burnt. On the last day of the 7th Moon, the same ritual is repeated as an *au revoir* or rather, a "good riddance".

The main sacrificial offering takes place on the evening of the 14th day (Cantonese custom) or the 15th of the 7th Moon (Hokkien, principally). In this offering, the chief items of food are the Malaysian fruits, such as *buah rambai*, *rambutan*, mangosteen and jackfruit, and rice. Candles, incense-sticks, incense-papers, mock money and a special kind of *shao-i-chih* (烧衣纸), "paper dress for burning", are set ablaze by the side of the street. The *shao-i-chih* or mock textile for making clothes is varied in colour, green, yellow, blue and pink, each about 10 cm × 25 cm in dimension, and rolled into cylindrical shape like small lengths of water-pipe. In the course of the offering, a portion of the food and fruits is thrown on to the road, palpably to gratify any straggling ghosts. In recent years, the mock money is often an imitation of the currency note, denominated the "Hell Bank Note" (冥通银行，

A nine-metre-high figure of Kuei Wang, the King of Devils, is consumed by flames at the end of the 7th Moon ceremonies in Penang. Note the small figure of Kuan Yin on the head of the effigy: this demonstrates that the goddess is in control of the demon.

1. The Cantonese call this observance *Shao-i* (烧衣), "the burning of (mock) dresses" for the ghosts; whilst the Hokkien people, who are, on the whole, more enthusiastic in the celebrations, call it *P'u-tu* (普渡), "saving the suffering souls from torment". (See 全国 *op. cit.*, pt. ii, ch. 7, p. 15 and ch. 5, p. 66.)

地府通用) for circulation and use in the nether world. Some believers go a step further by providing the ghosts with passes or passports, as an act of hospitality. They are designated "Permit for the Souls" (神魂执照). These constitute part of the paraphernalia burnt at the sacrificial offering by the roadside where you see bonfires in parts of the Chinese quarter of the city. "It's like Guy Fawkes' Night," exclaimed Katharine Sim, our *Sunday Gazette* fellow-columnist, who had made a tour with us during one of these festal evenings.

Story of Mu-Lien   This evening ritual is preceded in the daytime by doing homage to the ancestors before the spiritual tablets. During the day, there is a sumptuous feast, and the ancestors are invited, as if they were alive, to share the feasting with the living members of the family. The origin of this custom is traceable to the *Canon of the Yu-Lan-P'en* (盂兰盆经), in which the story is told of an attempt by Mu-Lien (目莲 , Maudgalyayana), a favourite disciple of Buddha, to save his mother from torture in Purgatory. Mu-Lien's mother had taken meat-soup without her knowledge and was condemned to Purgatory for having unwittingly denied it.[2]

Mu-Lien saw his deceased mother in the company of hungry ghosts, says the *Canon*.[3] When he offered his mother a bowl of rice, it was transformed into charcoal before she could eat it. Whereupon Mu-Lien screamed in anguish, and hastily reported the incident to Lord Buddha. To which Buddha explained: "Your mother's sin is grave and it is futile for you alone to come to her aid. You should invoke the help of all bonzes and spirits in the ten directions of space, and make offerings on the 15th day of the 7th Moon to the ancestors of seven generations. The offerings should consist of all varieties of food and the five kinds of fruits and be assembled in vessels." Accordingly, Buddha ordered all bonzes to chant the liturgies, and Mu-Lien carried out his directions. Then only was Mu-Lien's mother rescued from the molestation of the hungry ghosts.

After that, Mu-Lien inquired of the Lord Buddha, "Is it all right for filial sons to make similar offerings during the *Yu-Lan-P'en* festival?" "Very good," replied Buddha.

The Magnolia Festival   From this Buddhist story arose the *Yu-Lan-P'en* (Ullambana) festival (盂兰胜会 or 盂兰盆节), said to have begun in the Six Dynasties (六朝 , AD 220–557), and known to the West as the Magnolia Festival. However, it was only during the T'ang and Sung dynasties that it gained popularity in China. *Yu-lan* means "to hang upside down", referring to extreme suffering in Purgatory, and *p'en* signifies a vessel filled with offerings of food. Its meaning is amplified in the *Canon of Mu-Lien* (目莲经) thus: "Build a three-legged scaffold with bamboo stems, ten to sixteen metres high, with lighted lanterns attached to the top. Then hang mock money and mock clothes on to the scaffold for consignment to the flames as offerings to the ancestors."[4] The 15th day of the 7th Moon also coincides with a Chinese tradition that Lord Buddha was conceived on that day[5] and was born on the 8th day of the 4th Moon in the tenth year of King Chou Chuang (周荘王). This adds weight to the Buddhist claim on the Magnolia Festival.

In Penang, an annual celebration on a grand scale is held on

2. See pp. 185–186 below.
3. 大正新修大藏经，日本高楠顺次郎编，Tokyo, 6th Year of Showa, Bk. xvi, 经集部 , p. 779, item no. 685. See also 搜神记，in 续道藏，*op. cit.*, vol. no. 高上·1105, ch. 3, p. 2, in which Mu-Lien is given the alias of Lo Pu (罗卜), with whom most Cantonese are familiar because a play entitled *Lo Pu Rescues His mother* was dramatized in the Cantonese opera and also in the talkies. Lo Pu is also associated with Ti Tsang Wang, though there are a few other versions, one of which claims him to be a prince from Korea bearing the surname Chin (金). See 神僧记·ch. 8 in 逸史·*op. cit.*, vol. 54, p. 1.
4. 历俗，*op. cit.*, ch. 39, pp. 446–447; 清录，*op. cit.*, p. 78; and 岁时，*op. cit.*, vol. iii, ch. 30, p. 341.
5. 后汉书，谢承 in 图书，*op. cit.*, vol. xxi, ch. 68, p. 18.

the 15th at the Pitt Street Chinese Temple. In the courtyard outside the temple a temporary stage is erected for the performance of a Chinese opera of the traditional type for a few days. In lean years, at least a puppet show is put up. A marquee is also erected on the adjacent courtyard outside the Chinese Town Hall. Tables are laid out in one or two long rows for the display of all kinds of viands, such as ducks, chickens, pork, roast pigs, sweetmeats, cakes, pastries, apples, grapes and tropical fruits, contributed by devotees, sometimes with labels of their names tagged to them. The grand exhibition looks even more colourful because of the presence of a number of small triangular paper pennants in multi-colours, blue, pink, yellow and green, which are stuck upright over the plates and bowls of viands. In addition, there are a number of paper boxes, contrivances and effigies, pre-eminently dominated by an awe-inspiring giant figure, called Kuei Wang (鬼王), the King of Devils, which augments the solemnity of the atmosphere. On his crown stands a figurette of Kuan Yin, for, according to current belief, he was at one time Kuan Yin's transformation. This probably explains why the main celebration is generally held at Buddhist temples.

Story of Ananda   This so-called King of Devils leads us to another Buddhist legend relating to Ananda, noted as the most learned disciple of Buddha and famed for hearing and remembering his teaching. He was also the creator of the Chen Yen Cult (真言宗 , Yogacarya), otherwise known as Mi Tsung (密宗), the "Esoteric School" of Buddhism. One night Ananda was confronted by the King of Devils, whose weird appearance was described as "flames darting from his mouth with smoke emitting from the crown of his head and having an ugly and vicious physical form with the joints cracking like the noise of a broken carriage. The intensity of his hunger causes his mouth to burn like torches, whilst his throat is small like the point of a needle." When Ananda asked who he was, he replied, "My name is Mien Jan (面然). In three days' time, you'll be degraded and become my kind." Horrified by this strange encounter, Ananda hastened to report to Buddha and asked to be saved from such a possible degration. Whereupon Buddha said, in effect, that substantial food should be offered to the hungry ghosts and, to enable them to swallow the food through their "needle-point" throats, the kan lu (甘露 , "sweet-dew") method of consuming the food should be inculcated through the recitation of genuine Buddhist sutras.[6] This "sweet-dew" method was effective, and when it became known, it was adopted and has since been followed.

The Buddhist Service   On the 15th night, a Buddhist service is held at the marquee before this King of Devils and in the presence of large crowds of interested devotees. During the service, the bonzes of the temple, led by the abbot, recite the printed words contained in the Yu-Chieh-Yen-K'ou (瑜珈焰口 , Yoga Ulka-Mukha), the "Essentials of Offering Food to the Hungry Ghosts in Accordance with Yogacarya Cult", from the first page to the last. The main object of this service is to enable the hungry ghosts to relish the eatables and to intercede for their final deliverance from Purgatory. To appreciate this service, it is incumbent to acquaint you with some fundamental teachings of the Chen Yen Cult:

6.   瑜珈焰口施食要集，金陵校刊，reprinted by the Yung Ch'uan Monastery, Kusan, Foochow, (n.d.), pp. 11–12. This rare sutra was kindly lent to us by the Venerable Cheng-Kor, one-time Deputy Abbot of the Pitt Street Temple, now Abbot of the Kuan Yin Temple at Burmah Road, Penang.

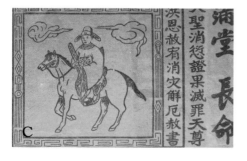

A. A family burn papers as an offering to the ancestral spirits. **B.** A 7th Moon offering of tea leaves and biscuits. **C.** A petition to be burned during the 7th Moon ceremony. **D.** A chalk circle surrounding an offering denotes a specific group of spirits for whom the offering is intended. **E.** The King of Devils prior to burning. **F.** An altar to Hell: note the Ox-Head and Horse-Head Spirits on guard. **G.** A street puppet theatre in progress during the 7th Moon.

"Man is not, like the banana, a fruit without a kernel. His body contains an immortal soul. After death, the soul descends to the hells to be judged there. Pardon of sins, preservation from punishments, so often promised to the devotees, are explained . . . not as derogation from justice, but as the effect of appeal made in favour of the guilty soul, by some transcendent protector. That appeal obtains for the soul a new life, a kind of respite during which it can ransom itself by doing good work, instead of expiation by the torments of hell. The sect believes that the infernal judges prefer the ransom as more fruitful than the expiation, and always willingly grant the appeal of any who solicits that favour . . . . . As to sinners and unbelievers, their relatives and friends, or the bonzes may interject an appeal in their favour, even after death."[7]

At the end of the Buddhist service, the paper paraphernalia are ignited with some of the food and fruits; and spectators, especially beggars and vagabonds, who have been awaiting this moment, scramble for the remaining food offerings.

Kwangtung-Tengchow　　On the evening of the 15th, a similar celebration of the Magnolia Festival is held in the Kwangtung and Tengchow Association (广东暨汀州会馆) at Penang Street, Penang. Within the premises on the ground floor, there is a methodical arrangement of the paper articles and effigies, representing some aspects of Hell, where the Ox-Head Spirit and the Horse-Head Spirit — both are lictors of the court of Purgatory — stand on guard. On one occasion, Katharine Sim, her husband Stuart, and the present writer were there as interested observers, and Katharine Sim later described some of her impressions thus:

"The hall was vibrant with sound, hazy with the smoke of hundreds of incense sticks and blazing with lights. Places were laid for the spirits each with its lamp in oil burning before it, and each with its wine cups, rice bowls, chopsticks and a bottle of wine. Priests were conducting the ceremony, and the drums and gongs throbbed persistently and the flageolet wailed, sounding as it does, like a forlorn bagpipe. Noise, colour, people, incense, smoke, lights and all for the Hungry Ghosts — not a thing was forgotten."

Wu Lien-Teh's Criticism　　Apart from the religious ceremonies held in associations and temples, there are many traders and merchants who hold joint or group celebrations in the 7th Moon on the five-foot way or the side of the public road along such areas as Beach Street. For many decades this has been the practice. Dr Wu Lien-Teh (伍连德博士), who had observed such group celebrations in the first decade of the century, was rather critical of the extent and manner of their celebrations. Condemning them as "wasteful and antiquated customs", he wrote *inter alia*:

"The nineteenth of the seventh moon is a red-letter day for the ghosts of Beach Street, Penang. Along the whole length of this and Bridge Street, and on both sides, there was an almost uninterrupted row of decorated tables covered with the usual paraphernalia for these unseen friends. The two busy streets may for all purposes be looked upon as a huge tent, divided into several compartments, each of which belonged to one or more firms. Wherever one turned one's eye on that day, the same sights met one — neither the white tablecloth, nor the eatables, nor the

7.　Chou Hsiang-Kuang, pp. 154–155. The Penang practice of reciting the *Yoga Ulka-Mukha* at the Magnolia Festival is a bold departure from the tradition of China, where the *Yu-Lan-P'en Ching* (the "Ullambana Scripture") is used. (See Reichelt, pp. 95–96.)

fumes from countless joss-sticks, nor the din arising from the combined voices of the crowd, nor even the unintelligible chantings of the priests varying in the slightest degree from one end to the other.

"After Beach Street comes Campbell Street, the *yoshiwara* of Penang. Here the expenses are borne by the inmates of the brothels, who subscribe large or small sums according to their means. Their celebrations last for four days and nights (25–28), and consist partly of illuminations in their own houses and partly of a general exhibition at the old theatrical hall in Kulim Lane (now demolished) . . . . . Here as elsewhere, the monotonous piles of fruits, cakes, pictures and decorations, and the unending series of paper devils with the fierce-looking 'King' at their head, attract one's attention, and we depart with a heavy sigh that so much trouble has been taken and so much money spent on repeating over and over again for one entire month ceremonies which, even if they are necessary, should have been disposed of in one day . . . . ."[8]

The Spirit of Luck   Dr Wu Lien-Teh, one of Penang's foremost Queen's Scholars, who had then returned from Europe to Malaya after obtaining a string of distinctions and honours for medicine, was naturally annoyed at the traditional way of life still practised by the unsophisticated section of his fellow countrymen in Malaya. There was justification in his angry outbursts, but there was another aspect of the celebration, especially in Beach Street and Bridge Street, which the learned doctor overlooked, or brushed aside.

We allude to the effigy of the Spirit of Luck, called Wu Ch'ang (无常鬼), which the merchants put up in the celebration. This tradition is still followed, and the Spirit of Luck figured prominently at the Kwangtung and Tengchow Association in 1964. Tradition says that this spirit also wanders about in the 7th Moon. He wears a tall cone-shaped hat, like that of a clown in the circus, inscribed with four characters: *i chien ta chi* (一见大吉), "to see me is to be in luck". He holds a palm-leaf fan in his hand and like Santa Claus carries with him innumerable gifts. If he gives you a lump of clay, it will be turned into glittering gold the moment you hold it. If he hands over to your a broken brick, that will be changed into a solid block of gold as soon as you touch it. At the end of each celebration, there is a rush for the fan and other articles in the possession of the Spirit of Luck — a possession highly cherished by every businessman and, for that matter, the man-in-the-street. Who knows?

The belief in the Spirit of Luck is popular with the Hokkien section of the community in Malaysia because in Fukien Province, China, this spirit, called Ch'ang Yeh (长爷), "The Venerable Tall One", was *sine qua non* in the 7th Moon celebrations, which were annually held on a magnificent scale. House to house subscriptions were raised to meet the heavy expenses, to which even the poorest of the poor would devise ways and means to contribute his share.

As a maxim had it, "If you didn't donate to the P'u Tu (普渡) expenses, you would be afflicted with epidemic diseases. If you made no efforts to celebrate the P'u Tu, the 'short devil' (矮爷) would come and get you." After a seven-day celebration, it was followed in the finale[9] by the "putting out to sea ritual" (出海典).

8. Wu Lien-Teh, pp. 589–590. Dr Wu died in Penang, his birthplace, in 1960. He is better remembered in Malaysia for many local reform movements. One of these was his forceful leadership in the anti-opium campaign in the first decade of the century. His activity, which embarrassed the British colonial government, resulted in his departure from Malaya in 1907 for China, where his expert services in the Manchuria plague in about 1910 skyrocketed him to international fame.
9. 全国 ·*op. cit.*, pt. ii, ch. 5, p. 66.

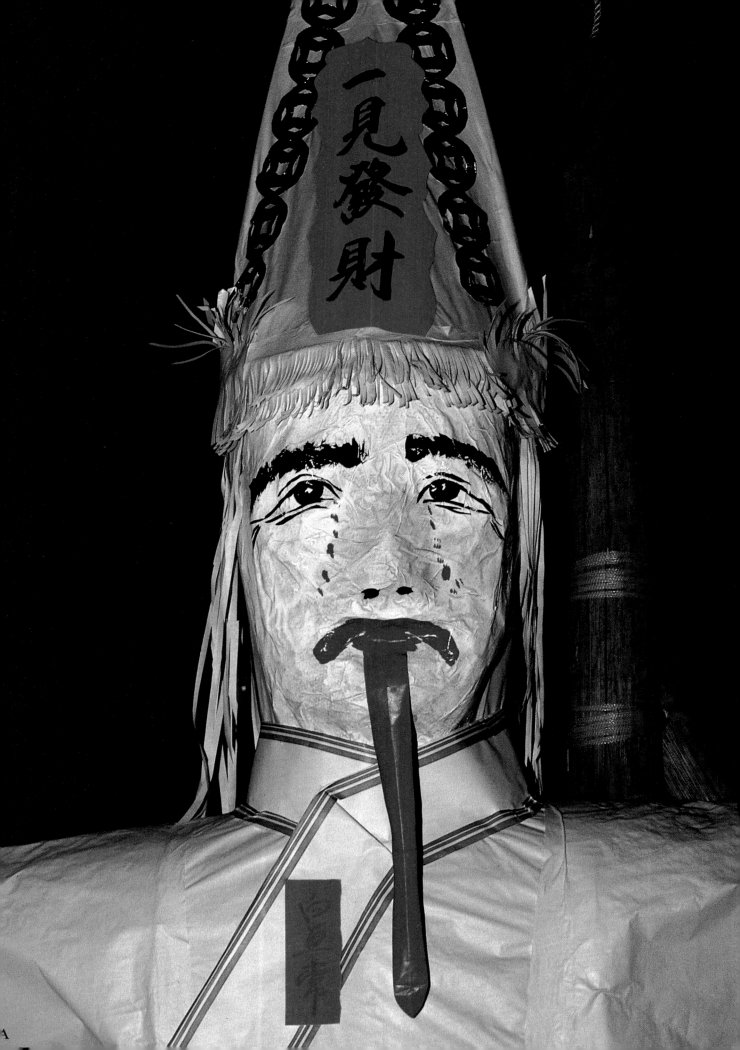

A. Twa Ya Peh, an official who assists the president of the courts of Hell. He can be cajoled with alcohol or opium to grant supernatural favours on behalf of his devotees. **B.** Paper ladies tally the score in a game of mah jong *before being burned as a 7th Moon offering.* **C.** Paper figures depict the tortures of Hell that await those who have sinned on Earth.

Chung Yuan Chieh   The Hungry Ghosts' Festival is also called *Chung Yuan Chieh* (中元节) by those of the Taoist persuasion, because it coincides with the day when the T'ai Shang Lao Chun (太上老君 , Lao Tze) and the Yuan Shih T'ien Tsun (元始天尊 , Primal Celestial Lord) meet to discuss the question of conferring blessings on human beings. On this day, according to the *Taoist Canon* (道经), Ti Kuan (Lord of Earth) goes round to make a survey of the human world to record the merit and demerit of each person, and all Taoist saints are assembled in the Taoist palace to scrutinize the records of men and shades and the registers of hungry ghosts and prisoners in Purgatory. Therefore, a grand offering of vegetarian food, flowers and fruits . . . should be offered to these saints, whilst Taoist priests everywhere should chant the *Canon of Lao Tzu* (老子经) day and night and the Great Saints of the Ten Directions of Space should recite the *Chapter on Souls* (灵篇). Then only would the hungry ghosts and prisoners in Purgatory be fully fed and permitted to return to the human world. If this were not done, redemption would be difficult for them.[10]

Partially because of the Fukien "sea ritual" custom mentioned earlier and mainly because of the *Chung Yuan Chieh* and its link with the *Hsia Yuan Chieh* (on 15th day of 10th Moon, associated with the Lord of Water, which is not separately observed in Malaysia), the Hungry Ghosts' Festival is celebrated with zeal and pomp locally by the fishing fraternity and traders of marine products and other goods in all market places, with the Chinese *wayang* and puppet show in performance. In Singapore, notably, these celebrations last, in the aggregate, the whole month, when some streets in the Chinese quarter are blocked by temporarily erected stages with feasting and rejoicing in the pavement or five-foot way — a spectacular China Town scene in a cosmopolitan modern city.[11] This pattern of observance is almost the same in every market place, and the difference is merely the difference in scale and grandeur, depending on the available funds. Sea-farers and those associated with the sea, directly and indirectly, euphemistically allude to the ghosts as *hao hsiung ti* (好兄弟), "good brethren", for fear of unwittingly offending the shades, especially water spooks, who could play havoc with them in the stormy sea. To them the 7th Moon is the month for honouring or appeasing their "good brethren".

Taoists priests too keep the *Chung Yuan* festival going, for they recite incantations with their small coteries of adherents in such areas as Jelutong and Perak Roads, Penang — to bring blessings to the populace in localities which are relatively remote from the main Buddhist temples in the city.[12] More often than not, a puppet show is staged in celebration, and a big banner bearing the words "In Celebration of the *Chung Yuan* Festival" is hung up to attract notice. According to our friend, Alan Young, when he was the Secretary for Chinese Affairs, Negeri Sembilan, some years ago, the Chinese in Seremban seemed to lay more emphasis on the Taoist aspect of the festival, for there was inevitably a realistic and impressive gigantic paper ship on display and the service was conducted by Taoist priests.

Secular Observance   In recent years, however, certain sections of the celebrants do not appear to take the religious function, either Buddhist or Taoist, of the festival seriously. In fact, with

10. 道经 and 道藏经 in 岁时 , *op. cit.*, vol. iii, ch. 29, pp. 331–332.
11. The magnitude of Singapore's celebrations may be gauged from reports in 南洋 , 8th, 9th & 10th August, 1964, which say that more than 1,300 Chinese theatrical troupers were engaged for performances in the various sectors of Singapore to celebrate the Ghosts' Festival. (See pp. 00–00 above regarding sacrificial offerings to the San Kuan before putting out to sea for fishes.)
12. See 星槟 , 25th August, 1958. A well-documented feature, entitled 中元节与盂兰会 , appears in its supplement, though its writer tends to be too opinionated on the Penang celebrations.

many it has become noticeably a secular observance. This is substantiated by a report in an English newspaper, which covered some of the celebrations in 1958:[13]

"The Chinese Seventh Moon Festival celebration at the various markets and clubs in Penang this year saw yet another departure from the traditional wayang performances staged for the benefit of the spirits from the other world . . . . . Since the advent of singing cafes and musical parties, the modern touch was added to the festival by engaging a party or troupe of musicians and singers to render modern Mandarin songs. Then, as there were requests for English songs, these were also sung. Now, in addition to cha-cha-cha and rock'n'roll numbers for the ghosts, Malay songs were also included in the programme . . . . . Yesterday saw a Sunday of heavy rain in the morning, which spoilt the holiday for thousands of labourers and office-workers, but the rain did not prevent the wayangs and the musical parties from continuing their entertainment at the markets."

13. *SET*, 8th September, 1958.

CHAPTER 14:
The Moon Festival

A t no other time of the year, it is believed, is the nocturnal luminary so round and bright as on the 15th night of the 8th Moon. Hence the ancient maxim: "When mid-autumn comes, the moon is extraordinarily brilliant" (月到中秋 分外明). It was this unusual brightness that had inspired Hsu Wang-Chien (徐王建), a famous poet of the T'ang period, to compose this verse:[1]

> Tonight the moon is clear and bright,
> At it everyone gazes with delight.
> Where's the family, no one knows aught
> That gives Autumn a serious thought?
> (今夜月明人尽望，不知秋思在谁家。)

Following in his footsteps were even more famous poets like Li Po (李白, the poet-laureate of T'ang), Pai Hsiang-Shan (白香山), Han Ch'ang-Li (韩昌黎), Liu Ho-Tung (柳河东), Tu Fu (杜甫) and Su Tung-P'o (苏东坡), who vied with one another to extol the magnificence of the silver disc. But 'tis a pity that the seductive beauty of the moon was said to have lured Li Po to a tragic end. On one moonlight night, according to tradition, Li Po, who had several drinks with his friends, boarded a boat to have a cruise on the Yang-Tze River (扬子江). Fascinated by the moon's brightness, he leaned out too far to embrace its reflection in the water, and fell into the water to meet an untimely death.[2]

The T'ang Myths   The T'ang myth-makers, however, did a better job. They invented fanciful tales about the grandeur of the Moon Palace (月宫) wherein the fairy Ch'ang-O (嫦娥) and other bewitching angels tread in and out. Ch'ang-O was the wife of Hou-I (后羿), a skilful archer. One day the archer secured an elixir of immortality from Hsi Wang Mu (西王母), Queen-mother of

Chinese children play with lanterns in accordance with an ancient 8th Month tradition. All kinds of lantern are on sale at this time of year.

1. 历俗 · *op. cit.*, ch. 39, p. 445.
2. James Lee, p. 19. But Seeger, p. 195, says this legend has been discredited by some authorities; and Latourette, p. 208, points out that "unfortunately for romance, he (Li Po) seems to have died, in most prosaic fashion, in 762, while living with a kinsman in the present Anhui."

Western Paradise; and Ch'ang-O stole and ate it. To evade the pursuit of her husband, she fled to the moon, where she remains to this day.[3] This and other enchanting stories, which captivated the minds of the common people, still live with many Chinese in China and abroad — this, in spite of modern science, orbiting space craft and moon rockets.

One legend says that on the 15th night of the 8th Moon in about AD 678, Lo Kuang-Yuan (罗公远), a magician, inquired of His Majesty Ming Huang (唐明皇) whether he would like to see the Moon Palace. The magician threw his walking-stick into vacant space and a silver bridge immediately took shape. His Majesty mounted the bridge and, after an hour's walk, arrived at the destination. There Ming Huang feasted his eyes on hundreds of fairies dancing elegantly in flowing robes in the courtyard. The music that accompanied the dance was so melodious that His Majesty committed it to memory. The next morning, His Majesty repeated the tune and composed the famous "Rainbow-Dress and Feather-Skirt" (霓裳羽衣曲) song.[4]

Another legend states that in about AD 830, in the mid-reign of T'ai Ho of T'ang (唐太和中), a number of friends gathered in the house of Chou Sheng (周生), a noted magician, on the 15th night of the 8th Moon. In the course of their conversation, the topic turned to the visit of Ming Huang to the Moon Palace, to the envy of everyone present. "This my master has taught me as well," said Chou Sheng to his friends. "I too could do it." Whereupon he collected some hundreds of chopsticks and transformed them into a rope ladder. "I shall climb up this ladder to take down the moon," said Chou Sheng, who then sent all his friends out of the house. After a while, the party was asked to come into the room. "The moon is now in this coat," announced Chou Sheng, pointing to the coat. "Please watch." Chou Sheng then raised the coat about two finger-breadths high, and the whole room was flooded with moonlit brightness, with the audience feeling cold in its muscles and bones. After the performance, Chou Sheng sent his friends out again. Whilst they waited outside, there was pitch darkness, but after a while, the moon shone in the sky once more.[5]

And yet another legend relates to the reign of Hsien T'ung (咸通辛卯岁 , *circa* AD 860). The nocturnal orb had been concealed by clouds from the 1st to the 14th of the 8th Moon. Rain had been heavy and the weather chilly. On the 15th night, the weather was still inclement and the evening was dull. To Chao Chih-Wei (赵知微), a Taoist priest from the Chiu Hua Shan (九华山), a sacred mountain in North China, the evening became intolerable. So he was determined to scale the "Sky Pillar Peak" (天柱峰) to "play with the moon" (翫月). And this he did, in spite of the pitch darkness and the pouring rain![6]

As we have shown, there was no actual celebration of the moon during the T'ang dynasty (AD 618–906). It was merely a period of "playing (or flirting) with the moon", with the poets capping verselets and myth-makers creating myths.

The Harvesting Season   It was in the reign of Emperor T'ai Tsung of the Sung dynasty (宋太宗 , AD 976–995) that the 15th day of the 8th Moon became the Mid-Autumn Festival (中秋节) — a harvesting season; and its celebration was confined principally to the Mandarins below the third grade. During the festival, these

3. 后汉书天文志 in 子史 , *op. cit.*, vol. i, ch. 2, p. 8. Originally the name of this moon fairy was Heng-O (姮娥), but it was changed to Ch'ang-O because of a taboo of the name of Wu Ti during the Han period.
4. 唐逸史 in 月粹 , *op. cit.*, vol. iii, ch. 12, p. 8.
5. 宣室志 in 岁时 , *op. cit.*, vol. iii, ch. 32, p. 361.
6. 三水小牍 in 图书 , *op. cit.*, vol. xxi, ch. 73, p. 38; and 太平 , *op. cit.*, vol. vi, ch. 85, pp. 5–6.

officials were obliged to make gifts of mirrors (representing the moon) and "dew-collecting basins" (承露盘 , to forestall wet weather) to senior officials.[7] In addition to this, they celebrated the event by consuming what was called "flirting-with-the-moon broth" (翫月羹). There was no moon cake. Eventully, the celebration was taken up by the people, who feasted and rejoiced heartily over their harvests.

In the Yuan dynasty (元朝 , 1280–1366), when China was under Mongol rule, the Chinese became unhappy, furtively resenting the alien domination, and on festive seasons like the Mid-Autumn Festival, drowned their griefs in wine-drinking and feasting. This time the myth-makers became serious-minded and created some realistic legends, said to be in circulation in the twenty-sixth year of Chih Cheng (至正), i.e. 1367, the last of the Mongol reign years.

One of these stories of 1367 says that during the Yuan dynasty, the Mongols formed the bureaucracy, and Mongol officials were sent out to every district, where they governed the Chinese with an iron hand. It was decreed that every ten families in the district had to support a Tartar official. This oppressive measure was detested by the people who dared not to speak out their mind. At the Mid-Autumn Festival, the Chinese applied themselves lustily to alcoholic drinks, and, emboldened by the stimulant, rose in unity to slaughter the Tartars on sight.[8]

The next year (1368), the Chinese re-occupied China with Chu Hung-Wu (朱洪武), originally an unknown novice monk, assuming the reign as Emperor T'ai Tsu of the Ming dynasty (明太祖). Henceforth the festival was celebrated with pomp and gaiety on a nation-wide scale. However, according to a Chinese source, it was in the Ts'ing period (清朝), when China was under the Manchus (1644–1911), that moon cakes (中秋月饼) were first mentioned in connection with the celebration of the Mid-Autumn Festival.[9]

The Moon Cakes   During the Manchu regime, there was a large exodus of Chinese to various parts of Southeast Asia in different periods of the Ts'ing history. So much so that the Manchus were perturbed and laws were issued to prohibit migration.[10] With them the emigrant Chinese carried abroad their culture and traditions, many of which have had their evolution on alien soil. One of these traditions was the moon cake, which forms the chief item of food offering purely in celebration of the moon, without any connection with the harvesting festival in China. Shaped like the surface of the moon, this delicious cake is seasonal and is only baked for sale by the restaurants during the festive season.

To attract customers, present-day Cantonese restaurants, which make moon cakes and sell fanciful lanterns, exhibit revolving and novel miniature effigies and pictures, portraying legendary accounts of the Moon Festival, and decorate and illuminate their buildings with artistic posters, neon lights and coloured bulbs every night for three or four weeks prior to the festival day. There are several varieties of cakes. There is the *tou-sha* (豆沙 , black-bean paste) variety; the *lien-yung* (莲蓉 , brownish lotus paste) variety; the *tou-yung* (豆蓉 , yellow-bean paste) variety; and also the "golden trotter" (金腿 , lotus-seeds mixed with sweetened paste). Very often the yolk of a preserved duck's egg is

7. 太宗纪 and 膳夫录 cited in 历俗 ' *op. cit.*, ch. 39, p. 445.
8. 野史 cited, *ibid.*, p. 447. There is in circulation a similar legend centred on the moon cakes. Take the brief account in CJ, Sowerby, "Calendar", p. 243, for instance, which says: "It is said that during the Mongol dynasty when a Mongol soldier was quartered on every family in China, a secret message was circulated hidden in these cakes which resulted in the wholesale massacre of the hated Mongols by the people, and the ultimate overthrow of the dynasty." We are doubtful of this "moon-cake" legend, because if our Chinese source is correct (see mn.9), moon cakes were not in vogue until the Manchu period (1644–1911), and as a corollary, the story about a secret message being hidden in the cake is an anachronism. However, if we accept the theory of Wolfram Eberhard (p. 122 and mn.20 above), this "moon-cake" legend is probably one of the many folktales originated in the Manchu period. Hence the anachronism. As an interesting tail-piece, we may add that the moon-cake story inspired an English woman in Malaya to buy moon cakes and hide dollar notes therein for presentation to her servants during the Moon Festival (Sim, *Malayan Landscape*, p. 181).
9. 历俗 ' *op. cit.*, p. 448.
10. MacNair, p. 1.

A. *A Moon Festival biscuit in the shape of a sheep.* **B.** *Bright lanterns adorn a Singapore shop.*

stuffed in the moon cake to increase its flavour. Besides the moon cake, there are the wheat-flour cakes moulded into different shapes to represent the fish, the crab, an old man, the lion and the dragon. There are, in addition, the Hokkien-made moon cakes of diverse sizes, filled with ingredients of preserved pumpkin and sweetmeat.

During the festive season, Chinese families make gifts of the moon cakes to "foster close relationship between man and man" (取团圆之义). When the moon cakes are offered as sacrifice to the silver disc on the 15th night, the theory is to "promote harmony between man and moon" (取人月双圆意). This is preceded or followed by feasting and rejoicing.

In the exchange of gifts, there are, besides the cakes, paper lanterns, dragons, elephants, tigers, tortoises, phoenixes, butterflies, carp, rotating globes, aeroplanes, tanks and other fanciful articles of postwar invention that delight adults and children alike. When the celebration takes place on the 15th night, lanterns of the "galloping horse" variety are conspicuously exhibited in many households, whilst children disport themselves with the lighted

lanterns and fanciful contrivances in group parades. As we have shown in a previous chapter, this lantern display is a transference of the former *Chap Goh Meh* tradition to the Moon Festival night — a marked evolution of local custom, which has been noted by Chinese writers since the 1930s. It may be stressed that the lanterns have now become a feature of the Moon Festival in Malaysia.

Sacrifices to the Moon   When the nocturnal orb is shining in all her brilliance, the senior members of the family, particularly members of the fair sex, make sacrificial offerings in the open air, usually on a terrace. Upon the open-air altar is placed a plate of moon cakes.[11] Besides the cakes, there are fruits like melons, pomeloes, ground-nuts, yam (*keladi* or taro especially from China), water-calthrops and cups of tea. The ceremony is accompanied by the customary lighting of joss-sticks and red candles and the burning of joss-papers of the gold-leaf variety. With some families, the presence of a lighted "galloping-horse" lantern is a *sine qua non* because it represents the picturesque moonlight. At this ceremony,

11.   In China the number of moon cakes is usually thirteen of varying sizes, which are piled up like a pyramid, to signify a complete Chinese lunar year plus a intercalary month, making a total of 384 days, and likewise a complete cycle of happiness (Eberhard, p. 104; and Ayscough, p. 57). But in Malaysia, the number of moon cakes is flexible, though we have interviewed some families following the thirteen-cake tradition. It is possible that the majority of Malaysian Chinese have been influenced by the "unlucky number" tradition of the West.

the cakes, fruits and nuts acquire a special significance, indicating the fullness of family life, vigour and youth, longevity, and numerous progeny. With other families, boxes of face-powder and cosmetics are also placed on the altar, and after the prayers these articles are believed to be endowed with the secret of beautifying the complexion. At the same time, the moon is invoked to bless the female devotees with handsome, robust and intelligent offspring.

This child-anticipatory tradition may possibly have its root in "moon dream" (梦月) stories. In the Han dynasty, the mother of the Queen of Yuan Ti (元后 , 48–33 BC) once dreamt that the moon made an ingress into her womb at the Mid-Autumn Festival and a child destined to be the wife of Yuan Ti was eventually born.[12] And in AD 222–264, the wife of Prince Sun Chien (孙坚) dreamt of the moon coming into her womb and subsequently gave birth to Sun Ts'e (孙策). Later, whilst she was pregnant, she dreamt that the sun entered her womb, and Sun Ch'uan (孙权) was born. When Prince Sun Chien learnt of the dreams, he remarked, "The sun and the moon come from the essence of Yang and Yin — emblems of rank and nobility. Our sons and grandsons will indeed flourish."[13]

Moonlight Serenades   There are also group celebrations in connection with the festival. According to a report in a Penang Chinese newspaper of 1963, the Penang Peng Seah (槟榔屿平社), which then had its fifteenth anniversary celebration of the moon, held a tea-party in the spacious flower garden of the Rubber Trade Association at Anson Road, Penang, where amateur vocalists in Peking dialect regaled the audience with songs from the Peking repertory. The youths of the Hainanese Association at Muntri Street played harmonica numbers at their moonlit tea-party; whilst members of the Hakka Association at Burmah Road entertained themselves with moon cakes and modern tunes. And last but not least, the Nightingale Musical Party went round the city in a decorated vehicle to serenade in the gay moonlight.[14] These musical parties are reminiscent of the T'ang period when the bohemian Ming Huang made the charming courtesans dance in the open terrace. It was Ming Huang again, according to another legend, who caused the "jade flute" (玉笛) to be expropriated from the Moon Palace through the magician Yeh Fa-Shan (叶法善) for serenading in moonlight romance.[15]

The Moon Legends   Moon legends are not exclusive to China. In years gone by, the Britons of old believed that the silver disc was the home of a man who cut faggots on Sunday and was consequently banished thereto. A legend from the Jews claims that Jacob resides in the moon, whilst the Maoris of New Zealand believe that a certain Rona fell into the moon and stays there to the present day.[16] A parallel fable also exists in China, which tells of a man constantly cutting the cassia tree (because whenever an incision is made, it instantly closes when the axe is lifted). He is Wu Kang (吴刚), who, in the course of acquiring the secret of immortality, committed a breach for which he was deported to the moon.[17]

Whilst the American Indians imagine that a mystical hare inhabits the orb of the night,[18] the Chinese have already fabricated the existence of a hare as well as a three-legged toad, the

12. 汉书 in 事类 , *op. cit.*, vol. i, ch. 1, p. 7.

13. 搜神记 in 图书 , *op. cit.*, vol. 387, ch. 32, p. 59.

14. 星槟 , 27th September, 1963.

15. 集异记 in 图书 , *op. cit.*, vol. 21, ch. 73, p. 38.

16. Hammerton, vol. iii, pp. 941, 942.

17. 酉阳杂俎 in 说郛 series, *op. cit.*, vol. xix, ch. 36, p. 1.

18. Hammerton, vol. iii, p. 492.

latter being the transformation of Ch'ang-O. Once upon a time, says a legend, Buddha transformed himself into a hungry old man who approached three creatures for food. The fox produced a carp, whilst the baboon brought in some fruits. Having nothing to offer, the hare jumped into the fire and roasted himself for the starving man. In recognition of such a supreme sacrifice, Buddha instantly transferred the hare to the moon in order that he be known to posterity.[19]

Marriage Months   And to repeat, there's the legend of the divine matchmaker, whom we have met earlier. With such a heritage of fairy-tales, the Malaysian Chinese may perhaps be excused for choosing the 8th Moon of the lunar calendar as one of the most auspicious months for marriages — a bold departure from China's Chou tradition of preference for the 2nd Moon.[20] "The month in mid-spring (2nd Moon) is the appropriate time for the union of boys and girls," says the *Chou Li Ti Kuan* (周礼地官), "and elopers should not be restrained from entering into matrimony" (中春之月 , 令会男女 , 于是时也 , 奔者不禁). The reasons are not far to seek: first because the climate in China in mid-spring is warm and cosy, and secondly, it is the time for pink peaches (symbolic of long life) and green willows (the agency against evil spirits and bad luck) to blossom forth in elegance.

If the Malaysians have appropriately adopted the 15th evening of the 1st Moon as the night of moonlight romance, it is a logical sequence for them to have selected the Moon Festival month as one of the seasons for propitious marriages.

As a matter of interest, we may conclude that the other popular nuptial months are the 11th Moon and the 12th Moon. This season is a tradition of China, where winter was the natural time for celebrating marriages because "once the harvest is in and cold weather automatically stops field-work, people have money and leisure to attend to their family affairs."[21] In Malaysia, this season is chosen probably because it is nearer the New Year when the newlyweds look forward to parading themselves in limousines in the mammoth car procession at the *Chap Goh Meh.* Significantly, the nuptial months are also the season in which loyal Malaysian families and their relatives and friends make intangible contributions to the coffer of the central government (without the benefit of income tax reliefs); for in recent years, it has been the fashion for wealthy parents to give sizeable donations, including monetary wedding gifts received, to hospitals and educational and charitable institutes instead of wasting enormous sums of money on traditional nuptial feasts and other marital rituals.

19. 西域记 in 事类 , *op. cit.*, vol. i, ch. 1, p. 7.
20. 历俗 , *op. cit.*, ch. 19, p. 234. See also 日知录 , *op. cit.*, vol. ii, p. 8; and also Granet, p. 258, in which it is quoted that the *Chou Li* fixes the spring equinox (2nd Moon) for "the great festival of marriages".
21. Bredon & Mitrophanow, p. 499.

CHAPTER 15:
Nine Venerable Sovereigns

On the summit of the Paya Terubong Hill at Ayer Itam, Penang, there stands a well-known Taoist temple denominated Ch'ing Kuan Ssu (清观寺 , the "Temple of Clear View"). It is dedicated to the Kiu Ong Yiah (九皇爷), the "Nine Venerable Sovereigns".

In Chinese mythology, these nine sovereigns were the sons of Tou Mu (斗母), the Goddess of the North Star, who is also called T'ien Hou (天后), Queen of Heaven. Tou Mu is the Taoist counterpart of Kuan Yin, having a deep compassion for the suffering of mankind. She is believed to have control over the books of life and death, and all who wish to live long may offer prayer to her.[1] A native of India, Tou Mu was married to Ch'en Chi-Ts'ung (辰祭从), king of the realm of Chou-Yu (周御), by whom she had nine sons who were later deified as *jen huang* (人皇 , "human sovereigns"), Their names were T'ien-Ying (天英), T'ien-Jen (天任), T'ien-Chu (天柱), T'ien-Hsin (天心), T'ien-Ch'in (天禽), T'ien-Fu (天辅), T'ien-Ch'ung (天冲), T'ien-Jui (天芮) and T'ien-P'eng (天蓬).

In Malaysia, these deified brothers are known as Kiu Ong Yiah in Hokkien, and are believed to confer luck, riches and long life, and effect cures for ailments. There are statues enthroned in an annexe of the Kuan Yin Temple at Burmah Road — ten statues in all, representing the nine deified brothers and their mother, which will be discussed at a later stage.

A Local Legend However, only one statue, representing the ninth of the deified brothers, is enthroned in the Ch'ing Kuan Ssu at Paya Terubong. With bushy beard and horn-like hair standing erect behind each of the temples of his fierce round face, this statue is believed to have a face capable of four changes. Seated on

A. *T'ien Hou, Queen of Heaven and Taoist counterpart of Kuan Yin. T'ien Hou leads the procession at the Ma-Chor P'o festival staged annually in Kota Tinggi on the 23rd day of the 3rd Moon.* **B.** *Women devotees make offerings to the spirits of the Nine Venerable Sovereigns, or Kiu Ong Yah.*

1. Werner, *Dictionary*, p. 511; and 槟城 *op. cit.*, pp. 24–27, in which its author, citing two other sources with running comments, supports Werner's allusion to the 九皇 ·

a lotus pedestal, the statue has four pairs of hands. Two hands are clasped in meditation. Each of the six remaining hands holds respectively the sun, the moon, a big seal, a sword, a spiked club, and a bow and arrows. This is how it came to pass, according to a local legend (presumably a variant of Werner's version). Of the nine brothers, seven have ascended to Heaven, the eighth is halfway up, whilst the ninth has decided to remain on earth to protect the people.

This ninth brother revealed himself to five Chinese of the Taoist persuasion in a vision about eighty-five years ago in Penang. The five Chinese had decided to look for a secluded place to meditate like the famed recluses in China. In their search, they saw a vision — the vision of the ninth brother — which ultimately led them to a site on the Paya Terubong Hill, upon which they built the Ch'ing Kuan Ssu in about 1880. When the Ch'ing Kuan Ssu — plank walls with zinc roof — was completed, the founders made a statue, resembling the vision, for enthronement in the main sanctuary.[2]

Soon after its completion, devotees visited the temple, and as their prayers were answered, more devotees were attracted. When and how the pilgrimage was first fixed from the 1st day to the 9th day of the 9th Moon, we are unable to find out. At an interview with Wong Nyook-Chong (黄玉涨), a present-day trustee and a great-grandson of Wong Kim-Mun (黄锦文), one of the founders of the Ch'ing Kuan Ssu, the explanation given was this: "Devotees make an annual religious pilgrimage to the temple for a succession of nine days in the 9th Moon because Kiu Ong Yiah stands for the nine deified brothers; hence nine days in the 9th Moon."

The Pilgrimage   As the temple is situated on a summit, the pilgrims have to scale the height of this hill, which has a winding, undulating path of "one-thousand-and-two-hundred steps" (千二层). On a Sunday, a mammoth crowd — mainly youths and maidens — surge their way up, and the arduous up-hill climb is relieved by a number of resting stations — roofed shelters. The pilgrims fall under three main categories: those who have recovered from serious illness; those who have made a new fortune, such as winning a lottery prize; and those who desire to have their wishes fulfilled. In other words, the pilgrims make this strenuous journey to perform votive offerings either in anticipation, or after fulfilment, of some promise; though, in recent years, their number is considerably swelled by large bands of pleasure-seeking picnickers.

At the temple, the trustees and a number of female vegetarians who have gone up to sleep therein during the season offer voluntary service, whilst devotees donate oil, rice, vermicelli and other items of necessaries for the purpose of serving free meals to the pilgrims, who, almost exhausted by the steep climb, and invigorated by the refreshing mountain air, partake of the vermicelli and broth with exceptional appetite. As is customary with Chinese temples, devout believers, after offering prayers to the deities (besides the "ninth brother", there are other deities enthroned in another sanctuary), make voluntary cash gifts, called *hsiang iu* (香油), the fees for incense and oil for burning at the shrines. In return, each of the donors is given three sets of amulets. The largest set contains a portrait of the Kiu Ong Yiah, printed on a yellow-faced paper — 45 cm × 26 cm — which is for posting up

2. Interview on 21st December, 1964, with Wong Nyook-Chong, a trustee of the temple. See also *ST*, 16th October, 1963.

at home; the second set, also printed on yellow-faced paper — 30 cm × 8 cm — and which is for wearing on the body, invokes protection from the Jade Emperor; and the third set, also printed on yellow-faced paper — 18 cm × 8 cm — and which is for consumption, exempts the five internal organs from disease or sickness. As regards consumption, the amulet is first burnt to ashes, and the ashes are diluted in a cup of water or tea, which is gulped down by the believer.[3]

It is believed that devotees who have observed meat-abstinence may reach the temple without mishap. Stories were once current about pilgrims fainting halfway or falling off the cliff for not having restricted themselves to vegetarian dishes.[4]

Teng Kao Custom   This Penang pilgrimage is unique in Malaysia. Whatever may be the explanation or views of some local residents, we believe that it is the survival of the custom of mounting the heights, called *Teng Kao* (登高) in China, which takes place on the 9th day of the 9th Moon. The word *teng* means to count. The word *kao* (meaning height) implies promotion, and also rhymes with the word for cake (糕). Therefore the expression *teng kao* metaphorically refers to a promotion; and eating the cake is symbolic of attaining success in the official career. The word "ninth" is *chiu* (九), which puns with the word meaning a long time (久). From the words *ninth* day of the *ninth* Moon comes the expression *chiu chiu* (九九), which is homonymous with the term meaning a very long time (久久) — metaphorically, a very long span of life.

It also happened that in China the climate was nice and the sky was clear on the 9th day of the 9th Moon — an ideal time to scale the heights to relax at a picnic and enjoy the panoramic view. For these reasons, the *Teng Kao* tradition was very popular with the elite of imperial China, especially in the T'ang and Sung periods, during which Mandarins and scholars went on excursions, ate special cakes, and drank chrysanthemum wine. As this was the time for bacchanalian gusto, elaborate feasts were also held.[5] This double-ninth festival is also called *Ch'ung Yang Chieh*, when a second visit to the cemeteries was observed in China on a lesser scale — a tradition also followed in Malaysia.[6]

According to the *Book of T'ang* (唐书), Wei Hsiu (韦绶), who had invited the court officials to dine in festive mood at the Ch'u River (曲江), also extended it to the sages and savants of his time.[7] And there was also the story of Wang P'o (王勃), whom we have met before.[8] When he was fourteen years old, he attended a magnificent feast given by Governor Yen Kung (都督阎公) at the T'eng Wang Pavilion (滕王阁). In order to make a show of his son-in-law's talent, the Governor passed round papers for the honoured guests to compete in extemporaneous essay-writing. Everyone declined, but Wang P'o swiftly composed his piece and was awarded five hundred pieces of water-proof silk.[9]

The origin of *Teng Kao* is traceable to the Eastern Han (206 BC – AD 219) when Fei Ch'ang-Fang (费长房), a Taoist magician and eccentric, advised his friend Huan Ching (桓景) to take his family with him to the mountain to avert a calamity. It was the 9th day of 9th Moon, and Huan Ching and family spent the whole day up the hills. When they returned home in the evening, they found that their dogs and poultry had died as their substitutes.[10] And a few decades after, during the Wei dynasty

3. The actual amulets imprinted on yellow-faced paper were kindly supplied by Wong Nyook-Chong.
4. The same type of story was current relating to climbing the flights of steps leading to the Batu Caves near Kuala Lumpur. In China, there was the famous story of the mausoleum of Prince Liang Hsiao, which was buried underground, access to which was through a long granite tunnel. Legend says that anyone going though the tunnel had to observe meat-abstinence, otherwise his feet would be bitten by an unknown animal. (See 子史 , vol. vi, ch. 112, p. 52.)
5. 干宝 , in 子史 , *ibid.*, vol. viii, ch. 151, p. 4; and 历俗 , *op. cit.*, ch. 39, p. 445.
6. See "Homage to the Ancestors", pp. 129–143 above.
7. 唐书 in 事类 , *op. cit.*, vol. i, ch. 7, p. 54.
8. See p. 134 above.
9. 摭言 in 说库 , *op. cit.*, vol. viii, p. 4; and 事类 *ibid.*
10. 续斋谐记 in 逸史 , *op. cit.*, vol. 55, p. 4.

(魏朝 , AD 220–264), the celebration of the double-ninth festival came into vogue.[11]

Vegetarian Cult   It is remarkable that the China tradition of special cakes, chrysanthemum wine and feasting has been supplanted on Malaysian soil by a pious observance — the consuming of maigre food for a stretch of nine days from the 1st day to the 9th day of the 9th Moon, or in some cases, for a whole month, making it the most important and longest vegetarian season of the lunar year, principally because of its association with the *Kiu Ong Yiah* festival.

Equally remarkable is the coincidence that both the Muslim *Hari Raya Puasa* and the most important Chinese vegetarian (partial fasting) festival fall on the ninth month of their respective calendars, the *puasa* falling in Ramadan.

Next in importance to the 9th Moon is the New Year's Day when many Chinese serve breakfast[12] with what is called "the Life Redemption Maigre Food" (续命斋). The favourite maigre dish among the Cantonese is the *fuat choy* (发菜), a black, dry, vegetable product, resembling human hair, imported from China. This vegetable is fried (or boiled, as the case may be) with other vegetable products, such as dried bean-curd and mushrooms. The more conservative Cantonese invariably eat the *fuat choy* — at least a morsel of it — as the first food that enters the mouth, before they apply their chopsticks to any other kind of dish at the breakfast table. The word *fuat* means hair; and the word *choy* means vegetable. The combined words form the expression *fuat choy* which is homonymous with the term meaning to grow prosperous (发财). For this reason, to consume *fuat choy* first is tantamount to receiving blessings, at the first instance — an omen that augurs well for the day and for the whole year.

History of Cult   The first recorded case of fasting or meat-abstinence in Chinese history is that of the legendary Emperor, Huang Ti (2737 BC), who was told that the secret of attaining long life was to "fast".[13] After he had killed the rebel Ch'i Yu (蚩尤), Huang Ti "fasted" for three days to report to the God of Heaven. This, on the authority[14] of *Nui Chuan* (内传), was the origin of *chai ch'iai* (斋戒). In the early era, *chai ch'iai* was the exclusive domain of the elite, the *chun tzu* (gentleman), who "fasted" in order to acquire the "power of the perspicacity" (精明之德).[15]

It was not until the advent of Buddhism, formally introduced into China from India in the reign of Emperor Ming of the Eastern Han (汉明帝 , AD 58–76), that vegetarianism became widespread. Buddhism preaches against killing, and, to meet this religion halfway, Chinese take maigre food on certain days in the month — on 1st and 15th (the City God cult, 城隍斋), on 1st, 15th and 24th (the Kitchen God cult, 竈王斋), or on 2nd, 6th and 9th (the Kuan Yin cult, 观音斋). This Chinese compromise is called by Lin Yutang the application of the "Golden Mean".[16]

The vegetarian cult has since assumed such importance to the devout that many vegetarians regard meat-eating as a great sin. This theory is dramatized in the popular story of Mu-Lien (whom we have met before[17]) and his mother, which is presented periodically by the Cantonese *wayang*. A pious vegetarian, Mu-Lien's mother took a dish of meat-soup, prepared and offered to her by her son, without her knowledge. She had been suffering

A. *Devout believers receive amulets smeared with blood taken from the tongue of a spirit medium.* **B.** *"Kuan Yin" leads her vegetarian devotees in a 9th Moon procession.* **C.** *An altar is prepared for a nine-day vegetarian festival in Penang.*

11. 汉旧俗 cited in 历俗 , *op. cit.*, ch. 39, p. 438.
12. 四时宜忌 , *op. cit.*, p. 1.
13. 春秋命诚图 in 原纪 *op. cit.*, vol. i, ch. 2, p. 49. The character for "fast" is 斋 We have used "fast" as its equivalent in the modern sense in order to stress the origin of meat-abstinence. In the original ancient text, the correct translation should most probably be "self-purification" — the translation used by Soothill, *Hall of Light*, p. 36, in connection with the Shang rituals. An elaborate explanation of 斋 is given by the translator Homer H. Dubs (Pan Ku, vol. ii, p. 78 fn.21.4), which says: "Whenever (it is necessary to) abstain before sacrificing to Heaven and Earth, (the Emperor should abstain for) seven days; (before sacrificing) in the ancestral temple or to the mountains and streams, five days; (before) lesser sacrifices, three days. (During) the days of abstinence (he should remain) within (the house or room. If he should commit any) impurity or uncleanness (during the period of abstinence, it would) dissolve the abstinence . . . . . The fundamental idea about abstinence in Han times was not the avoidance of particular foods as at present under the influence of Buddhism, but the purification of the celebrant by ablutions and the avoidance of contamination from others' uncleanness."
14. 内传 *ibid.* See also 古今事物考 , 王三聘 in 丛书 , 商务 , June 1936, vol. i, ch. 5, p. 87.
15. 礼祭统 in 故事 , *op. cit.*, ch. 3, p. 182.
16. Lin Yutang, p. 120.
17. See p. 162 above.

from an acute illness, and the soup soon made her well. When Mu-Lien heard of this, he told his mother about the soup. Unaware of what had happened, she denied it, declaring: "If I have eaten meat, I pray that all the gods may cast me down into the deepest hell!" In an instant she was seized by Yen Lo's lictors and taken to Hades.

In order to save his mother, Mu-Lien offered to take all the punishments. As Mu-Lien was placed in a cauldron and about to be dismembered and cooked, Buddha revealed himself and came to his disciple's rescue.[18]

Practice in Malaysia   In Malaysian practice, Chinese vegetarian food is, generally speaking, subdivided into two classes: (a) the uncooked variety, and (b) the cooked variety.

The uncooked variety is called *cheng chai* (净斋 — Cantonese, meaning pure fruits and vegetables). Mainly confined to pious nuns and monks, who are striving to acquire supernatural power, *cheng chai* is the extreme form of meat-abstinence. Pure, cold water and fresh vegetables and fruits form the daily diet, year in and year out.

The cooked variety is eaten by vegetarians in general. Though the food is usually simple, there are elaborate dishes to whet the appetite, prepared on festive occasions. Made purely from cereals, especially wheat-flour and the by-products of soya beans, the vegetarian food offers, amongst others, imitation shark's fin, imitation chicken curry, imitation pig's trotters, and even imitation *satay babi* (barbecued pork) of Malaysian origin.[19]

It is believed that, by living intermittently on vegetarian diet, and by devotion to occasional meditation or prayer, a person may go to the Buddhist paradise, or may be re-born in a better or richer state. Because of this belief, there is a considerable number of partial or full-fledged vegetarians among the laity, especially members of the fair sex.

As a class, the best-known vegetarians are the vegetarian nuns, who are venerated as *chai koo* (斋姑 — Cantonese). They reside in the Little-publicised vegetarian institute, denominated *chai t'ong* (斋堂 — Cantonese).[20] Unlike the Catholic nuns who devote their life to educational work, or health and social services, vegetarian nuns believe that it suffices to lead a life of absolute retirement and religious piety. They have "renounced the temporal affairs of the world" (出家), to use the Chinese idiom; and, apart from meditation, prayer and some domestic chores, there is no need for them to have anything to do with the sordid affairs of mankind. There is a tincture of Taoist philosophy *wu wei* (道德经) 无为 , "do nothing") in this negative attitude towards life. Perhaps there's some wisdom as well — depending on how you look at it.

Shrines and Rituals   In the city of George Town, there are many other Kiu Ong Yiah temples and shrines, and devotees flock to the temple or shrine of their choice to make sacrificial offerings during the nine-day festive season. A well-known shrine in the heart of the city is located in the left annexe of the Kuan Yin Temple at Burmah Road. In the main shrine of this annexe are twelve statues: the central and big statue, with four pairs of hands, representing Tou Mu; and nine other statues of uniform size and make-up, representing the deified brothers; whilst the remaining

18. Reichelt, pp. 80–81, from which our abridgement is made.
19. *JMBRAS*, Topley, "Religion", p. 107, fn.64, wherein the writer, who has partaken of a fourteen-course vegetarian meal, testifies that Chinese vegetarian food is far from being the often tasteless fare that it is in the West. It is possible to dine very sumptuously indeed on completely vegetarian Chinese food.
20. The term *chai t'ong* is translated as "maigre feast hall" in Reischauer, *Ennin's Diary*, p. 396, fn.1497. Those interested in such institutes are referred to *JMBRAS*, Topley, "Vegetarian Houses", pp. 52–67.

two, each at one end of the topmost tier, without the Mandarin cap, are the Northern and Southern Constellations. When you pass this temple (at the junction of Madras Lane), you will be attracted by a lighted mammoth incense-stick (about a man's height) poised outside the annexe. Made of fragrant sandalwood sawdust, this artistically manufactured joss-stick is designed to burn for a duration of three days. For the whole season of nine days, three gigantic sticks are sufficient. These incense-sticks are presented by some devotees whose names are inscribed thereon; and as the givers are blessed by the deities, devotees regard it a privilege to present a set of these sticks for burning.

Some other shrines are located at Hutton Lane, Noordin Street Ghaut, Magazine Road and Hong Kong Street. By "shrine" here, we mean a shrine enthroned in a section (usually the rear portion on the ground-floor) of a private dwelling house, normally tenanted by ordinary people and sometimes with subtenants. In all these shrines, no statues or images of the Kiu Ong Yiah are enthroned.[21]

The Hong Kong Street shrine is believed to have a history of more than one hundred years and is acclaimed as the oldest Kiu Ong Yiah shrine in Penang. It was originally set up at the Seh Tan Court, where there was once a portrait of the Kiu Ong Yiah (now non-existent), later transferred to the Kien Tek (建德) Kongsi at Armenian Street, and again to Malay Street and finally to Hong Kong Street.[22] On 24th December, 1964, Goh Kim-Seng (吴金成), a devout believer, and the author visited the Hong Kong Street shrine. Except for a rectangular wooden board and a pair of big lanterns bearing the words *Tou Mu Kung: Chiu Huang Ta Ti* (斗母宫九皇大帝), meaning the Nine Great Sovereigns (another name for Kiu Ong Yiah) of the Tou Mu Palace, the house looks like a private residence. At the far end of the hall of this residence is an altar with a few urns and statuettes thereon, and behind this altar is a shrine with a wooden niche, about 60 cm × 60 cm, wherein a few statuettes are enthroned, *none representing the Kiu Ong Yiah.*

According to our informant, the Kiu Ong Yiah come to this shrine only during the festival from the 1st day to the 9th day of the 9th Moon inclusive. An invitation ritual is held on the eve of the 1st day of the 9th Moon. In this process, a Kiu Ong Yiah urn is taken out from the altar to the roadside. The urn is then deposited in a special wooden niche, which is placed on the roadside altar. A Taoist priest, specially engaged for the service, then recites incantations to invite the Kiu Ong Yiah, in the course of which amulets, incense-papers and sandalwood slabs are burnt in the Kiu Ong Yiah urn. Lighted incense-sticks are also planted in this urn. Meanwhile, two kidney-shaped divining blocks are cast on the road in order to signify the deities' assent or otherwise. If assent is indicated, the urn, now filled with sacred ashes, is believed to be spiritualized by the arrival or presence of the Kiu Ong Yiah. As soon as this happens, the Kiu Ong Yiah urn and the special niche are respectfully removed back to the original altar inside the building. This holy niche is then screened off from public gaze by a huge yellow curtain. During the whole festive season, devotees are normally not allowed to peep at the holy niche and the spiritualized urn, to which they make sacrificial offerings on the other side of the curtain, as if they were worshipping the deities. Whenever the urn or part of the ashes from the urn is carried about, it is wrapped up in a piece of yellow

21. This is generally true of Hokkien-sponsored Kiu Ong Yiah temples and shrines in Malaysia. When we were on research in Kuala Lumpur in January 1965, K.K. Lam of the *Straits Times* confirmed that "there are no statuettes of Kiu Ong Yiah" in the famous temple at Ampang which makes headline news during the annual festival. (See also *ST*, 16th October, 1961.) Similarly, there are no Kiu Ong Yiah statuettes in the temple at Upper Serangoon Road, which claims to be the biggest and oldest of its kind in Singapore.
22. Courtesy of Lim Teong-Aik, a well-known Buddhist lay preacher of Penang.

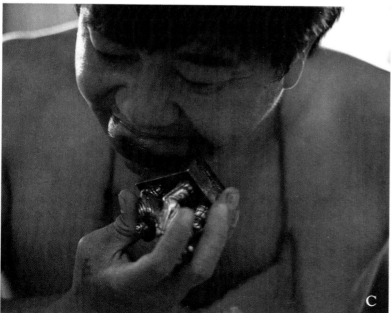

A. *A spirit medium displays in lurid detail the thirty-six spikes inserted through the skin of his arms — without apparent bleeding.* **B.** *A medium of the Leng Hyam Twa temple, North Boat Quay, Singapore, is possessed by the spirit of Twa Ya Peh: his tongue has been cut to produce the blood necessary for the preparation of amulets.* **C.** *Another medium licks the base of a magisterial seal before preparing an amulet.* **D.** *Mediums paddle red-hot iron balls in Penang during the 9th Moon festival.* **E.** *A medium assists an elderly devotee in a fire-walking ceremony during the Kiu Ong Yah festival in Singapore.* **F.** *A special boat is loaded during an* au revoir *ceremony to the Kiu Ong Yah.*

cloth. An assistant holds a huge drum-shaped cylindrical umbrella made of yellow fabric aloft, as if to protect the urn or ashes from the sunlight or rainwater — a process reminiscent of a touring monarch of imperial days.

The Fire Ceremonies   At some of these shrines during the festival, a medium or two entrance themselves to dispense charms for their believers to avert misfortune and usher in luck. At others there is, in addition, a "fire-ball" display held a couple of days before the 9th day. An iron ball, about ten centimetres in diameter, is heated to incandescence in an improvised furnace on the street. Then the incandescent ball is kicked about by four or five mediums with their bare feet, as if they were playing an ordinary football game. This is followed by the spiked iron-ball display undertaken by a single medium. The spiked ball is about seven or eight centimetres in diameter and heated to incandescence. The incandescent ball is tied to a chain with a handle, and the medium, holding the handle, swings the heated ball like a pendulum, occasionally swinging it over his shoulder to strike at his back. Before the blow hits the bare back, an aide tries to cover up the back with a triangular black pennant to cushion off the impact. This performance and the kicking of the iron-ball game last for several minutes to the amazement of the gaping spectators. At other times there is the fire-walking ritual, during which the devotees, led by a medium, walk across the scorching fire-pits filled with burning charcoal.[23] According to popular belief, fire-walking is a "cleansing" ritual, an act of purification. Only devout believers who have abstained from meat may walk over the flames without mishap.

"Au Revoir" Processions   On the evening of the 9th day, this festival ends, and under the aegis of the Kiu Ong Yiah temples and shrines in George Town, two or three separate processions are held in their honour. Each procession consists of a set of lanterns and banners; a drum-and-cymbals band; a spirit-medium, possessed by the Kiu Ong Yiah; a rocking-chair, carried on the shoulders of two aides, one in front and the other behind; and a special boat, conveyed in a decorated chariot. Inside the boat are deposited the sacred ashes representing the nine deities. Two long ropes are tied to each side of the chariot in front, and devout participants (each holding a cluster of lighted joss-sticks in one hand) zealously pull the long ropes with their empty hands to set the chariot in motion.

Each procession passes through an approved route and terminates at the nearest beach or shore. At the terminus, usually at about the time of the receding tide, a religious service, conducted by the medium, is held, with the congregation of devotees kneeling and praying. The special boat is then put on the shallow water, set on fire and allowed to drift away with the retreating waves. This constitutes an *au revoir* ceremony to the Kiu Ong Yiah until their return on the last day of the 8th Moon in the following year.[24]

In pre-war years, when Malaya was enjoying a period of peace and prosperity, the procession was a spectacular event, and was headed by a *Chingay*, with a few parties carrying the huge variegated-coloured triangular flags, for which Penang is famous. The main feature was the mediums parading the streets in a

23.   Courtesy of Goh Hee-Kong, who was an eye-witness to these "fire" ceremonies in the postwar years at the Magazine Road Shrine and the Noordin Street Ghaut Shrine, Penang.

24.   We have witnessed the procession and the *au revoir* ceremony in pre-war as well as postwar years. According to a report in the 星檳，8th October, 1962, Ooi Theam-Siew, the Mayor of Penang, took part in a ritual in honour of the Kiu Ong Yiah held at Noordin Street, Penang. Similar ceremonies were also held at the Kiu Ong Yiah temples at Hutton Lane, Hong Kong Street and Magazine Road. Probably it is this "sending-off sea ritual" that has influenced Dr Victor Purcell, p. 138, to identify the Kiu Ong Yiah with the Lung Wang or Dragon Kings — a theory we are unable to endorse.

trance, with self-inflicted wounds on their bodies caused by brandished swords, and slit tongues caused by sharp instruments. With blood stains all over the semi-naked trunk, partially covered by an undersized sweat-soaked apron, and with dishevelled hair and distorted feature, the mediums were frightfully weird, and it was no surprise that they did excite a certain amount of awe, if not veneration. The seals of the mediums, dipped in vermilion ink, were used to chop amulets on the dress worn by the devotees, thus bringing luck to the wearers and driving away evil spirits.

Spirit-mediums are a common sight in the Orient. Whether you believe or disbelieve in them, there are things reported to have been achieved by them, either by fluke or through miracles, which are often perplexing to the layman.[25]

25. A good study on the subject of spirit-medium cults is Elliott.

CHAPTER 16:
Au Revoir to the Kitchen God

On the 24th day of the 12th Moon, Malaysians make an *au revoir* offering to the Kitchen God, denominated Tsao Chun (竈君), who is also known as the Prince of the Oven.[1] For on this day, he takes leave of the mundane world and soars skyward to Heaven on his annual furlough. With him he carries a report of the merit and demerit of every Chinese during the past twelve months for submission to Yu Huang, the Jade Emperor.

The departed Prince of the Oven is believed to come back to earth any time between New Year's Eve and the evening of the 15th day of the 1st Moon to resume his sovereignty over the household, though, in practice, devotees extend him a return ovation on New Year's Eve.[2] For this reason, the Festival of the Kitchen God is associated with the New Year, either as a prelude to, or as a terminal of, the twelve-month cycle of festivals. We have placed the Kitchen God in the last chapter of this book advisedly, for should he condescend to make a report about this publication, he would have had an opportunity of appraising its merit and demerit.

The Kitchen God is one of the most popular deities in Chinese polytheism. Every home must have a kitchen, and every kitchen may have a Kitchen God. Besides, it is easy to set up a Kitchen God. He can be represented by a slip of red paper inscribed with the necessary characters, a wooden board, a piece of zinc-plate, or a portrait, at a convenient nook near the oven. There the Kitchen God faithfully abides, and through him your prayers to the Jade Emperor may be transmitted and favourably answered.

In the *au revoir* offering, the motive is common, namely, everyone tries to muzzle the mouth of the celestial agent. Hence

Tsao Chun, the Kitchen God. His au revoir should be as sumptuous as possible, so he will make a good report of his family to the Jade Emperor.

---

1. In Tientsin and other parts of North China, the ritual is generally held on the 23rd of the 12th Moon. (See 全国 · *op. cit.*, pt. ii, ch. 1, p. 80; and Bredon & Mitrophanow, p. 73.) There is a prevalent belief in Malaysia that the 23rd was reserved exclusively for the Mandarin (bureaucratic) class.
2. 清录 · *op. cit.*, p. 118.

the common ritual is to sweeten the lips of the Kitchen God. Some use honey, and some use sugar candy. If the mouth of the Kitchen God is sweetened — thus the devotees argue, rather naively, perhaps — only sweet and flattering words can come out of his mouth. This is in conformity with the practice in Peking[3] where devotees, after smearing the Kitchen God's mouth with sweets, entreated him to "say more about our good deeds and say less about our bad deeds" (好话多说 , 不好话少说).

Other Malaysians are more thorough: they use glutinous rice cakes to seal the lips of the Kitchen God so that he becomes dumb and nods assent only to all that is favourable to his votaries.

An important item in the sacrificial ritual is the paper-made hat, shoes and garments, purporting to be the property of the Kitchen God. They are later set ablaze together with the incense-paper. Candles and incense-sticks are lighted, often accompanied by the popping and crackling of fire-crackers. If the shrine is made of paper, and if it is an old portrait, or rusty zinc-plate, or decaying wooden board waiting for replacement, it is destroyed in the bonfire of the paper articles. The burning act, with or without the shrine, signifies that the deity is being sent skyward in a pall of smoke. Not long afterwards, the shrine is put up again in preparation for the deity's return after his furlough.

A Post-Sung Legend   There are several versions of the origin of the Kitchen God. But there is one legend, obviously an invention of the post-Sung period (any time after AD 1207), which has a bearing on the practice of "gagging" the deity. In the 1930s Fei Hsiao-T'ung (费孝通) made a field study of country life in the Yang-Tze Valley and uncovered this post-Sung myth.

At a certain time, when a foreign power had conquered China, says the Yang-Tze Valley story, every house was ordered to support a foreign soldier as its inspector. In course of time, the people found it intolerable to continue this extra burden, especially the domineering conduct of the spy. Finally, they decided on a plot to kill the sentinels. On an agreed date, glutinous cakes were prepared and offered to the soldiers, whose mouths were glued together after the repast. In consequence, when they were being attacked, they could not raise an alarm.

This plot was triumphantly carried out on the 24th day of the 12th Moon. But the people soon realized the danger of reprisals. To appease the spirits of their victims, they paid homage to them in the kitchen as the deity of the household in order that they might continue their function of inspectors.[4]

In venerating the Kitchen God, the villagers took great pains to score merit in their daily life. So they introduced a set of taboos for observance. These taboos were summarized and classified by Fei Hsiao-T'ung under three categories: (i) There was great reverence for rice, it being the staple food. No rice was to be wasted, nor trampled underfoot. If there was any left over and the rice turned rancid, it was cast into the river to feed the fish. (ii) All things and activities connected with sex were not to be brought into the kitchen, and women during menstruation were forbidden to touch anything on the platform of the Kitchen God. (iii) Great respect was always shown to learning. On no account was any paper containing written characters, including newspapers, to be burnt in the kitchen. Such articles were invariably burnt in an open space or in a special furnace at the temple.[5]

3. 北京辙轩录in 全国 , *op. cit.*, pt. ii, ch. 1, p. 24.
4. Fei Hsiao-T'ung, pp. 101–102.
5. Fei Hsiao-T'ung, p. 100.

Origin and Evolution   The history of the worship of the Kitchen God is very much older, and it is necessary to allude briefly to the origin of some Chinese festivals from the ancient days in order to follow its evolution. In the days before the Chou dynasty (1122 BC), when people lived in small groups, a social unit consisted of twenty-five households, called a *li* (二十五家为一里，a town). At that time of their history, there were only two sacrificial festivals in a year. The first festival was in spring and the second in autumn. At each festival, bulls and sheep were slaughtered for the sacrificial offering, after which the participants divided the meat amongst themselves. A grand banquet was held, and the inhabitants, who had refrained from work for the day, ate, drank and danced to relax themselves.[6]

Then about the Chou period (1122–255 BC), a third festival, called *La* (腊祭百神, the "Festival of Thanksgiving Offering to the Hundred (All) Deities"), was added towards the end of the year (10th Moon); and from Confucius' time (*circa* 550 BC) it was celebrated with gusto on a country-wide scale. But no definite date was yet fixed for this festival. An incident illustrates this point. In about 255–249 BC, Prince Hsiang of Ts'in (秦襄王) fell seriously ill, and the people, who were gravely concerned, prayed devoutly for him and he recovered. In gratitude, the people slaughtered bulls to make a thanksgiving offering. Kung-Sun Yen (公孙衍), who witnessed the ceremony, commented, "But this isn't the time of the *La* festival — why kill the bulls for sacrificial offering?"[7]

It was some years after this incident that the *La* festival was fixed on the "third day after the winter solstice" (冬至后三戌为腊，22nd December),[8] and down through the decades the people observed this date as the Festival of Thanksgiving Offering.

In all religious matters, sincerity is an important factor. There was the case of Yin Tzu-Fang (阴子方), well known for his filial piety, charity and religious devotion. In the reign of Hsuan Ti (宣帝, 73 BC) of the Han dynasty, Yin Tzu-Fang made sacrificial offerings to the hundred deities on the *La* festival day. Because of his intense sincerity, the Kitchen God manifested himself. Soon after this, Yin Tzu-Fang slaughtered a yellow lamb to add to the items of food offered to the deities. For his faith and devotion, he was subsequently showered with riches, owning more than seven hundred pieces of arable land, with a vast number of chariots, horses, servants and serfs, which could easily rival the possessions of a local prince. Tzu-Fang used to say that his descendants would multiply, and even at the third generation their prosperity would continue to grow.[9]

Down through the centuries, the *La* festival was gradually relegated to the background, with *La Yueh* remaining to signify the 12th Moon. By the time of the Sung period (AD 960–1126), the important association with the *La* was the *La Pa Chu* (腊百粥) held on the 8th day of the 12th Moon, with the mutual gift of a special porridge. This porridge was prepared on the 7th day when dates were first boiled in soup form. On the 8th day, many ingredients such as rice, walnut, chestnut, and water-calthrop were added to the "date" soup to cook into a porridge. This was first offered as a sacrifice to Buddha and then consumed by all members of the family. It was also distributed to, and received from, friends and relatives who vied with one another to cook the most palatable dish.[10]

This custom was still in vogue in North China in the third

6.   历俗, *op. cit.*, pp. 433–434. Though the land system in the ante-Chou period is not an important factor in our discussion of festivals, the word *li* (里) used in 历俗, which we have rendered as "town", is indicative rather than definitive. It seems that during the ante-Chou, i.e. the Shang, and also during the Chou era, according to a school of thought, the land system called the "well-field" (井田) was constituted thus: eight families were a "well"; four wells were a "town" (邑); four towns were a *ch'iu* (丘); four *ch'iu* were a county (甸); four counties were a district (县); and four districts were a *tu* (都). However, the existence or non-existence of this so-called "well-field" system has been a subject of much controversy by modern scholars, and its definite knowledge is not yet conclusive. According to another authority, it was in the later Wei period (AD 386–535) that the word *li* came into vogue in the *san chang* (三长, "three local heads") system. In this system, five families constituted a *lin* (邻), five *lin* constituted a *li* (里), and five *li* constituted a *tang* (党), (E-Tu Zen Sun & de Francis, pp. 5–17, 158–159.)

7.   韩非子, ch. 14, p. 253 in 诸子, *op. cit.*, vol. v. The *La* festival is termed *Pa Cha* (百蜡？) in Granet, pp. 168 ff, where he says that "the celebration had all the characteristics of an orgy", which originally included "sexual rites" which were later banned. An interesting sketch of the ancient celebration of the *Pa Cha* is reconstructed in this work.

8.   岁时, *op. cit.*, vol. iii, ch. 39, p. 421; and 历俗 *op. cit.*, p. 434.

9.   干宝 ch. 4, p. 8 in 学津书, *op. cit.*, vol. 149; and 后汉书阴兴传 in 子史, *op. cit.*, vol. vi, ch. 3, p. 47. Whereas in the 搜神记 in 续道藏 series, *op. cit.*, Yin Tzu-Fang is said to have offered a "yellow puppy" and not a "yellow lamb". The "yellow lamb" version is confirmed in 风俗通义 (written in the Han period), 应劭 in 丛书, 商务, December 1937, ch. viii, pp. 195–196, and in 逸史, *op. cit.*, vol. vii, ch. 3, p. 3. For our purpose it is immaterial whether it was a "yellow lamb" or a "yellow dog" that was offered; but it may be pointed out as an historical fact that the dog was eaten and sacrificed in considerable numbers in those days. (Creel, *Birth of China*, p. 77.)

10.   图书, *op. cit.*, vol. xxiii, ch. 94, p. 17; 京兆辂轩录 in 全国, *op. cit.*, pt. ii, ch. 1, p. 64; and 梦华录 cited in 历俗, *op. cit.*, 3rd ed., May 1941, p. 448. As the 8th day of the 12th Moon coincides with the traditional birthday of Lord Buddha, the Buddhists observed *La Pa Chu* as a dual festival, with emphasis on the ritual of "Bathing the Buddha" (浴佛) to avert possible disaster. In Fukien Province, the ritual of "Bathing the Buddha" was eventually transferred to the 8th day of the 4th Moon. (See 全国, pt. i, ch. 4, p. 41.) In Penang the Fukien tradition had been followed. But some years ago, when Wesak Day (the calendrical birthday of Buddha) came into prominence, the bathing ritual was transferred to the 15th day of the 4th Moon and has since remained so.

A

B

C

A, B, C and D. *A Mercedes Benz is burned and so transferred to a deceased member of the family. Luxuries as well as essentials may be transferred in this way: if the deceased drove a Mercedes during his lifetime, then he is entitled to one after his death.* **E.** *A family group prepare paper objects for burning in an* au revoir *ceremony.*

11. Bredon & Mitrophanow, p. 71; and *CJ*, vol. xii, no. 1, January 1930, p. 3.

12. 清录，*op. cit.*, p. 101.

13. 荆楚，魏志管辂传 and 辂 cited in 杜神考，杨坤 in 汉学，北京中法汉学研究所，1944, vol. i, p. 113.

14. 古史考 and 管子 cited, *ibid.*, p. 128. See also 津沽春游录in 全国，*op. cit.*, pt. ii, ch. 1, p. 80.

15. 搜神记 in 续道藏，*op. cit.*, vol. 高下，ch. 6, pp. 14, 15.

16. 诺皋记，段成式 in 说郛，*op. cit.*, vol. xix, ch. 36, pp. 6, 7; and 抱朴子，ch. 6, p. 27 in 诸子，*op. cit.*, vol. viii. However, 抱朴子 gives a different version on the punishment of sins: "For a serious sin, a man is to be deprived of 300 days from his span of life; for a minor sin, 3 days (or 1 day)."

decade of the century, according to *The Moon Year* in which a legend is recounted. The first *La Pa Chu*, says this legend, was prepared by a poor mother whose unfilial son drove her to ask for food from the neighbours, one of whom supplied her some grains, another a basket of fruits, and yet another a cup of beans. From these ingredients she cooked the special porridge, "still eaten by high and low with the underlying idea of brotherhood." Describing this special porridge as "the Chinese equivalent to our Christmas pudding", Arthur de C. Sowerby, writing in 1930, said the 8th day was the most important date in the 12th Moon to the Chinese.[11]

On the other hand, the Kitchen God continued independently to gain popularity. His popularity was high-lighted by a new ritual, called *T'iao Tsao Wang* (跳竈王 , the "Leaping Oven Prince"). This ceremony took place between the 15th and the 24th of the 12th Moon, during which beggar-boys gathered into groups of three or five to impersonate the Kitchen God and the Kitchen Goddess. They paraded the streets, each leaping with a bamboo-stick, and went from door to door begging for money.

As this performance was regarded as an act of dispelling pestilence towards the close of the year, it was welcomed by all and sundry.[12] It was probably from this ritual that the 23rd or the 24th day of the 12th Moon eventually emerged as the Festival of the Kitchen God.

Various Versions As we have said earlier, there are many versions of the Kitchen God legend. One source claims him to be Su Chi-Li (苏吉利), another source says he was the elf of Sung Wu-Chi (宋无忌), who was led into the oven, and a third source states that when the wife of Wang Chi-Chia (王基家) gave birth to a baby, it entered into the oven straightaway.[13] Others attribute the origin of the Kitchen God to the fabulous ruler Sui Jen (燧人 , said to have discovered fire); to Shen Nung (神农 , 2737 BC), another fabulous ruler, said to have taught the people to cook rice on a burning rock; to yet another mythical ruler, Huang Ti (黄帝 , 2697 BC), said to have introduced cooked food to prevent belly-aches.[14]

A theological source tells us that the Kitchen God was born on the 3rd day of the 8th Moon (year not given). His name was Chang Tan (张单) alias Chang Tzu-Kuo ((字) 子郭), who had the appearance of a beautiful woman. His wife was Ch'ing-Chi (卿忌), and she bore him six daughters, whose names were Ch'a (察).

They became supervisory angels in Heaven and on earth, and their duty was to report on the sins committed by mankind at the beginning of every month. For a serious sin, a man was to be deprived of two hundred to three hundred days from every twelve years of his destined span of life. For a minor sin, a period of one hundred to two hundred days was to be deducted from his destined span of life.[15]

A T'ang source states unequivocally that it was the Kitchen God himself who was to ascend to Heaven to report the sins of human beings. For a serious sin, a man was to be deprived of three hundred days from his span of life; for a minor sin, one hundred days. This is corroborated by a much older version in *Pao P'o Tzu* (抱朴子) by Ko Hung (葛洪) of the Eastern Han (AD 25–220) and has been accepted by the people down through the ages.[16]

The God's Functions   From the T'ang and the Sung periods onwards, the reputation of the Kitchen God for answering prayers increased daily and his influence became more widespread. By now, he had become a deity of the temple, not merely a family deity; he had become one of the patriarchs of the seventy-two trades, not merely a home monitor.[17] This is evident from the multifarious functions of the Kitchen God embodied in the *True Canon of the Prince of the Oven* (竈王府君真经), which reads as follows:

"The venerable Prince of the Oven is in full charge of the kitchen on the east and thus the monitor of the entire family. He watches clearly what every member of the family does. Whoever does good and whoever commits evil — this he observes truthfully and carefully and reports to the Court of Heaven on the last day of each month. Scholars who venerate him will score high places in the Civil Service Examinations. Farmers who respect him will reap rich harvests. Technicians who honour him will become skilful in all technical works. Traders who hold him in high esteem will flourish in business. Home-keepers who show devotion to him enjoy health and peace. Travellers who adore him find safety everywhere. Aged persons who revere him have clear eye-sight and fast-moving limbs. Youngsters who glorify him remain energetic and robust.

"Oh, ye men of the human world, why should ye forsake what's near and seek what's far, scaling mountains and crossing the seas, making a journey and voyage of thousands of miles? What ye need to do is to pray to the Kitchen God with a devout heart, and whatever may be thy problem, it shall be resolved. Ye have only to keep a kind heart and do good, and I will transmit all this to the Court of Heaven. If ye want honour, I guarantee thy name shall be glorified; if ye want riches, I guarantee ye shall prosper in gold; if ye want to get well, I guarantee ye shall recover from the most serious sickness; if ye want long life, I guarantee ye shall live to over 90 years; if ye want male children, I guarantee ye shall have noble sons; if ye want a wife, I guarantee that Heaven shall send thee a pretty girl.

"When I interview the Jade Emperor, I will add a few good words for thee. What ye pray for shall receive divine response; what ye ask for shall be favourably answered — ye shall be gratified in everything."[18]

The Food Offerings   In the earlier days, there was no attempt to gag the Kitchen God, and elaborate meat food was offered. In the wake of Yin Tzu-Fang, yellow lamb was offered. Later, chicken and wine supplanted the lamb; whilst others offered pig's head and pork.[19] In the course of evolution the Kitchen God, originally a *shen* (神 , deity of Confucian and/or Taoist cult), was elevated to a *fu* (佛 , Buddha). As a result, meat food was replaced by vegetarian dishes.[20] This practice, if observed by devout Buddhist adherents, is not uniformly adopted in Malaysia, where meat is also offered, though not on an elaborate scale. In fact, simple fare suffices, and judged by a stanza from Lo Yin's "Poem on Sending-Off the Kitchen King" (罗隐送竈诗), even a simple tea service is acceptable to the deity. The stanza reads as follows:[21]

> In all sincerity,
> With a cup of pure tea
> and a small pall of smoke,

17. 灶神考，*op. cit.*, pp. 138, 166, fn.160.
18. *Ibid.*, p. 139.
19. 白虎通，荆楚，东坡纵笔 and 范石湖祭灶诗 cited in 清录，*op. cit.*, p. 63.
20. *Ibid.* According to 江震旧志，also cited *ibid.*, there was in China a votive offering to the Kitchen God on the 4th, 14th and 24th of the 6th Moon, consisting of marble-like rice balls (like those offered at the Winter Solstice Festival) and four dishes of vegetarian food. To our knowledge, this is not observed in Malaysia.
21. 罗隐送灶诗 cited in 灶神考，*op. cit.*, p. 138.

O Kitchen King, please look,
I'm sending thee on high
to yonder azure sky.
（一盏清茶一缕烟，竈君皇帝上青天．）

At one time, it was the duty of man to pray to this deity, for according to a maxim, "Men don't glorify the moon; women don't sacrifice to the kitchen" (男不圆月，女不祭灶). The reason was that since the Kitchen God was primarily the household monitor, it was but fitting for man, being the head of a family, to pay homage to him. In Malaysia, the Kitchen God is popularly believed as a home monitor and celestial agent; but both the man and woman may worship him. As we have shown, the Kitchen God is ever ready to lend you his sympathetic ear and can be persuaded to make nothing but favourable reports about you. Furthermore, there is legendary evidence to show that the Kitchen God might also come to your timely rescue if you were harassed by supernatural beings.

The Yang Family   In the southern city was a Mr Yang (杨氏), a man of moderate opulence. As his eldest son was an unworthy boy, Yang drove him out of the house. The weather was icy cold. Since the boy had no place to go, he took shelter in his father's cow-shed and lay on the grasses (hay). The night was moonlit, but as he was cold and lonely he could not sleep a wink. Of a sudden, a tiger leapt into the shed, followed by a few tiger-bitten ghosts. They took hold of some grasses, and, in frolic, began to prance and dance. The boy was so frightened that he withheld his breath. Then suddenly, dark clouds and strong winds swept into the shed. As if being chased, the tiger dashed off in fright, hurriedly followed by the dispersal of the tiger-bitten ghosts.

A divine voice then cried out, summoning the God of Earth (土地), in answer to which an old man appeared and bowed to the divinity. Reprimanding the old man, the divinity said, "You've been receiving sacrifices from the Yang family for years and yet you permitted the tiger to play havoc here. Yang's boy was nearly eaten up until I sent out divine soldiers to repulse it. You've committed a breach of duty. Did you know that I'm the Kitchen God of the Yang family?" The God of Earth admitted his fault, thanked the Kitchen God and left. On the next day, a survey revealed the footprints of a tiger and the disorderly condition of the grasses. Later Mr Yang's anger subsided, he pardoned his son, and brought him back to the house. When this incident was recounted, the family became more devout to the Kitchen God.[22]

22. 异闻总录 in 不详人 in 丛书，商务，June 1937.

Epilogue

In looking back, we realize that we have shared, with pleasant memories, the festivals with the Malaysian celebrants in the twelve-month cycle — a cycle of festivities and of life itself in nearly all its facets: hope and despair, happiness and sorrow, courage and fear, generosity and greed, wisdom and folly, charity and unkindness, romance and love. Hope when they pray for blessings, and despair when they muzzle the mouth of the Kitchen God. Happiness when the family reunion feast is held, and sorrow when the rain prevents the Cowherd and the Weaving Lady from meeting. Courage when they honour the heroic death of patriotic Ch'u Yuan, and fear when they imagine the presence of lurking devils. Generosity when they insist on your *yam seng*, and greed when they scramble for the possessions of the Spirit of Luck. Wisdom when they make New Year wishes and let the deities fulfil them, and folly when they create a boisterous din to frighten off some imaginary monster in an eclipse. Charity when they make food offerings to the straying ghosts and burn for them thousands of Hell Bank Notes, and unkindness when they drink their guests under the table by unfair means. Romance and love in the *Chap Goh Meh*, in the festival of the two star-lovers, and in the Moon Festival.

With the celebrants we have also traversed a kaleidoscopic world of make-believe, wherein the friendly deities of Heaven, the fairies of the moon, the flower nymphs, the snake-fairies and the evil spirits from Purgatory fraternize, without superiority, or inferiority complex, with human beings on earth. In this make-believe, there is nothing irreconcilable for the Chinese to welcome the Kitchen God into their household as the celestial agent and to gag or sweeten his mouth upon sending him off to Heaven; to offer passports for the ghosts to come up on earth and to scare

An elderly man takes down, for the last time, the red festival banner that has proudly adorned the entrance to his temple compound. For the bulldozer of urban renewal has destroyed more than half his village, and there will be no festival at this temple next year.

them off with the detonating fire-crackers during New Year's Eve and other festival days; to create romance and love with the fairies and spirits and accept their stories as gospel truth; and to canonize or deify the dead and pray to them as powerful gods. It is poetic fancy at its acme — perhaps the best and cheapest form of escapism, which the Western men and women, tired of the matter-of-fact or realistic existence in this humdrum world, try to seek, at enormous expense, at the Hawaiian beaches, the skating rinks in the Alps, or the dizzy heights of the Himalayas. To the masses, especially the hard-working and frugal Chinese of the medium and lower income groups, who seldom make good use of their Sundays and public holidays, the time of the traditional festivals is the time for release from irksome routine and toil — for feasting and rejoicing, carefree living, for unleashing of the purse-strings and for whole-hearted indulgence. To the devout, even the same type of food, with the same cooking, is said to taste better on festive days, especially after the sacrificial offering to the deities.

Two Salient Features　As we try to analyse the cycle of festivities, two salient features emerge pre-eminently. The first is the religious piety of the celebrants. It is this piety that motivates them to make sacrificial offerings to the deities of Chinese polytheism. As a scholar has aptly explained, "The average Chinese layman believes in the friendly and ordered coexistence of all gods, regardless of their religious identification. The layman's spiritual world comprises gods and spirits from Taoism, Buddhism, the worship of Heaven and its associated cult of Yin-Yang and the Five Elements, ancestor worship, and numerous local cults of magic animism. In this grand pantheon, the boundary between religions hardly exists, and the gods and spirits are arranged in a hierarchy according to their magical powers."[1] Ruling over this hierarchy is a Supreme Being (the God of Heaven, the Jade Emperor or what you will), and the god-fearing devotees make annual offerings to Him and members of his hierarchy to express their gratitude for the blessings they enjoy, ask forgiveness for their errors in life's perilous journey, and pray for protection and the better things of life, year in and year out.

The second is the family cult, in which it is essential to pay homage to the ancestors. According to Wolfram Eberhard, this homage is "the acme of all religious services" which unites the living members with their divine ancestors who lived hundreds of years ago . . . and laid the foundations of the power and glory of the family. In the Chinese family cult, comprising the ancestors of the past and the present and future members, "everyone has his definite place in this never-ending chain of generations." In the Western world, the family is but an economic unit, where a child from the early days of childhood feels itself alone in this world, growing up with a deep-seated feeling of insecurity. But in the Chinese framework, every member has his definite position and has security from the time of birth. He is a member of the community, come what may, and will remain a member even after his death. He will take part, even then, in the family reunion on New Year's Eve.[2] As we have shown in the text earlier, the family group underlies the fabric of society, and, extended in application, recognizes that all mankind is but one large family, which ambitious and jingoistic politicians of the present day tend to tear apart.

1. Kang, p. 287.
2. Eberhard, pp. 41–43.

The sum total of their being god-fearing and their desire to keep the family escutcheon free from stain plus the eternal fear of reprisal or punishment from the numerous ghosts lurking around cannot but make the celebrants model citizens. Besides, if they believe, as they do, in the amicable and ordered coexistence of all deities of whatever religious identification, then little or no persuasion is needed for them to accept and put into daily practice the concept of brotherly coexistence in our multi-racial society.

Causes for Survival   The question may now arise: how is it that whilst these festivals continue to survive on alien soils like Malaysia, they are relegated to the limbo of the past in Communist China? The answer to the second part is simple: there is no freedom of worship in a godless and totalitarian state. The answer to the first part is equally simple: in Malaysia, as in all democratic countries of the free world, the fundamental principle is toleration. This enlightened policy was first introduced by the British administrators of the Straits Settlements through the three well-known Charters of Justice of 1805, 1807 and 1826, in which the "religions, manners and customs" of all races are recognized. This was later extended to the British-guided Malay States and became the fundamental policy of Malaya. When the independent Federation of Malaya came into being on 31st August, 1957, the same pattern of tolerance was written in the Constitution with Islam as the religion of the Federation. Similarly, the provisions of toleration constituted the fundamental principle of the Federal Government of Malaysia when it was formed on 16th September, 1963.[3]

This is manifestly carried out, in practice, in the latest list (1965) of public (religious) holidays: Solar New Year on 1st January (Europeans, Eurasians, principally); Ramadan beginning on 5th January (Malay Muslims principally); Lunar New Year on 2nd February (Chinese); Hari Raya Puasa on 3rd February (Muslims); Hari Raya Haji on 13th April (Muslims); Good Friday on 16th April (Christians); Wesak in May (Buddhists); Prophet Mohammed's Birthday on 12th July (Muslims); Deepavali in November (Indians); Christmas Day on 25th December (Christians of all races).

Chinese Conservatism   Another fundamental cause is the proverbial Chinese conservatism. Traditionalists by nature, most Chinese adopt the easy attitude of "What was good enough for my ancestors is good enough for me." So in spite of an attempted calendar reform a few decades ago the bulk of the populace in Malaya continued to observe the lunar New Year and the festivals as their forefathers had done before them.

Briefly this is how it happened. When Dr Sun Yat-Sen and his colleagues founded the Republic of China in 1912, the lunar calendar was abolished in favour of the solar calendar; but it was in 1927 that a vigorous campaign was launched by the Nationalist Government. This reform was taken up by a few enthusiastic supporters in Malaya through the Chinese press and the Chinese schools. Brushing aside the lunar New Year, the Chinese press published New Year supplements on the first day of January and observed a four-day holiday. (This practice is still in vogue.) The Chinese schools, which were not so rigidly controlled by the Education Department then, also declared holidays during the

3. Braddell, *Law*, pp. 1–61; Sheridan, pp. 4, 17, 18; and Groves, pp. 190, 212.

solar New Year, whilst continuing to open their schools during the lunar New Year, thereby rousing strenuous protest from many parents. Solar New Year greeting cards were sent out and received by reformists and their supporters. This went on for a few years.[4]

Meanwhile, the Nationalist Government was beaten in the attempted change of the calendar and, as a compromise, altered the name of the lunar calendar to *Nung Li*, the farmers' calendar, and the name of the lunar New Year to "Spring Festival" (春节), whilst retaining the solar calendar for official use. This trend was followed in Malaya by the reformists, the Chinese press and the Chinese schools, which also changed the name of the calendar to *Nung Li* and the name of the lunar New Year to "Spring Festival". These new names are still maintained in the Chinese press. The outcome of this short-lived attempt at abolition is the observance of two New Years by many Chinese: sending out and receiving greeting cards for the solar New Year and resuming the traditional observance of the lunar New Year (including the sending out and receiving of greeting cards the second time), with even greater pomp and more grandeur in postwar years.

Temples and Other Institutes   As a result of the liberal policy of democratic Malaysia, there are scattered all over the states hundreds of temples and shrines of the Buddhist and Taoist religions. The facilities offered by these temples and shrines in the urban and suburban areas contribute immensely to the observance of some of the festivals: New Year's Eve, the New Year, the *Chap Goh Meh*, the Ghosts' Month, and so on. For the Taoists, there are the *Shang Yuan Chieh* and the *Chung Yuan Chieh*.

Besides, there are other religious festivals directly connected with some of the temples and shrines: the birthday anniversaries of Kuan Yin, Ma-Chor Po (妈祖婆 , goddess of mariners and the fishing fraternity), Kuan Ti (关帝), the Monkey God (齐天大圣), the T'ai Shang Lao Chun (太上老君 , Lao Tzu), and a host of deified heroes and gods too numerous for inclusion. A good illustration is the Kiu Ong Yiah Temple at the fifth milestone (eight-kilometre stone) of Upper Serangoon Road, the biggest of its kind in Singapore, owning its own stage. In 1964, a Tiechiu *wayang* performed on its stage for a stretch of seven consecutive days commencing from the 1st of the 9th Moon, followed on the 8th and 9th by a puppet show. In better years, there were alternate performances by a Tiechiu and a Hokkien *wayang* for nearly a fortnight. This temple originated from a small wood shack built in 1902 at the fifth milestone of Paya Lebar to which sacred ashes were invited from Penang for the enthronement of the Kiu Ong Yiah. When funds poured in, it was removed to the new temple erected in 1921 at the present site. Another good illustration is the ninety-year-old "Ipoh Old Temple" (坝罗古庙), in Perak, dedicated to Tuah Peh Kong, which holds an anniversary celebration on the 26th day of the 2nd Moon with a *wayang* in performance for four or five days. An unusual feature of this temple is that it runs a Chinese school (坝罗古庙义学) under its own name for the free education of over-age boys of poor parentage. According to a Penang Chinese newspaper, the *Sing Pin Jih Pao* of 28th February, 1965, there are two sets of funds during the festive season: one is for the *wayang* and the other is for the school, to which the more affluent residents subscribe liberally.

Then there are the clan temples and territorial associations

4.   The author was one of the staunch supporters of this abortive reform, entering into a prolonged controversy in the English press.

which hold joint celebrations at such important seasonal festivals as the Winter Solstice, the *Ch'ing Ming*, the Spring Festival, the Summer Solstice and the Autumnal Festival; whilst dozens of guilds hold similar celebrations in addition to observing the birthday anniversaries of their patron saints. Amongst these patron saints is Lu Pan (鲁班), annually commemorated in Malaysia on 13th of 6th Moon by contractors and artisans of the building trade. A contemporary of Confucius, Lu Pan (born in 606 BC) is said to have been a sort of Leonardo da Vinci, around whom numerous stories have been woven. Once a Yuan monarch decreed a summer house of original design to be constructed, and when the contractor was at a loss, Lu Pan, in the disguise of an old man, conveyed the idea to him through the structure of a bird's cage.[5]

The Family Cult   Yet another fundamental cause is the preservation of the Confucian family cult. Confucianism was consciously revived at about the turn of the century through the founding and forming of Confucian Associations and Confucian Schools in the principal towns of Malaya, the first Confucian Society being established in Singapore in 1898. But the dissemination of Confucianist teachings was confined to members of the Confucian Associations and a number of teachers and a greater number of students, and, in English, through such publications as the *Straits Chinese Magazine*, edited by Dr Lim Boon-Keng (林文庆), Song Ong-Siang (宋旺相), Dr Wu Lien-Teh, and Dr S.C. Yin (殷雪村), father of Leslie Charteris of *The Saint* series fame, in the first decade.[6]

In reality, the sustenance of the family cult is due primarily to the annual homage to the ancestors observed, without interruption, from generation to generation. A typical example comes from the well-known Heeren Street of Malacca where generations of Chinese families have resided. In a family house we visited, we noticed, at the ancestral shrine, spiritual tablets representing four generations of ancestors of the Ong Sek-Pek (fifth generation) family. In other houses at Heeren Street there are even more generations represented, we were told. The presence of these generations of ancestral tablets, coupled with the generations of tombstones at the renowned Bukit China Burial Ground, reveals the history of continuous and uninterrupted observance of the various festivals of the lunar year — this, in spite of the fact that most Malacca *Baba* have been Malayanized or assimilated, speaking the National Language (Malay), eating *Nonya* (Malayanized) food, wearing shirts (European influence) and sarongs (Malay influence) at home, day in and day out. The same practice of ancestral veneration is noticeable throughout Malaysia in many old-fashioned homes with a long history of domicile.

Commercialization   And yet another fundamental cause is the commercialization of the festivals by industrialists, traders and artisans. At every festival Chinese traders offer topical commodities for sale: special *Ch'ing Ming* incense-papers and *Nonya*-made *Ch'ing Ming* cakes; the triangular pulut-rice cakes and evil-expelling plants and flowers in the 5th Moon; paper contrivances and articles for celebration in honour of the star-lovers; seasonal fruits, Hell Bank Notes, imitation passports, more varieties of incense-paper and paper articles during the Ghosts'

5. Burkhardt, vol i, pp. 31, 144; vol. ii, pp. 118–119; and vol. iii, p. 157.
6. L.E. Williams, p. 55; Tregonning, p. 177; and SCM, vol. i (1897) to vol. xi (1907), in most of which issues there are articles on Confucianism principally contributed by Dr Lim Boon-Keng.

Festival; moon cakes, China-imported taro and water-calthrops, and large assortments of lanterns for the Mid-Autumn Festival; big quantities of fresh vegetables and dried maigre food, forcing the prices of meat and fish to come down during the nine-day *Kiu Ong Yiah* festival; and special paper hats, shoes and costumes and sweetmeats for the Kitchen God on his furlough.

Commercialization is at its peak during the New Year season when trades of almost every sort experience a transient boom and when every Chinese unleashes his purse-strings. There are flamboyant banners, colourful Chinese lanterns, and neon lights put up by Western and Oriental firms to attract customers. The press publish Chinese New Year supplements with New Year messages from ministers of the governments and leaders of the various communities. Then there is palatable fare at the restaurants, extensions of time at the cabarets and night-clubs, decorated with the traditional dragons and phoenixes and meaningful Chinese characters, special numbers by attractive singers and prize-giving dance programmes, topical festive displays or exhibitions put up in the various Parks of the Shaw Organization — all this tends to engender an atmosphere of warmth, gaiety, glamour and conviviality that few normal human beings could resist. And bonuses are distributed by flourishing firms and advances are given by business houses and, in certain years, by the governments to their employees to promote such celebrations and the seasonal boom. In recent years, the broadcasting stations, Rediffusion and latterly the television programmes provide enchanting talks and stories relating to the New Year, thus dramatizing the already buoyant atmosphere.

Influence of the Housewives   Last but not least is the dominating influence of the housewives. According to the traditional way of life, it is the duty of the husband to produce the income whilst it is the duty of the wife to run the household, to spend the income or a large portion of it. As the household duties include the worship of all deities and homage to the ancestors at the family shrine, it is mainly the woman who keeps all the festivals going.

It is the woman who consults the Chinese almanac, who knows the dates of all the festivals, who buys and prepares the seasonal cakes, fruits and food for sacrificial offerings, who seeks counsel from the fortune-calculators, the spirit mediums, the priests and the nuns. It is she who purchases topical commodities for each festival from the shops and it is she who makes all the preparations for the New Year: "spring-cleaning" of the house, the choice of a new limousine, especially the colour, the purchase of glittering jewels and fashionable bracelets, the latest wristlet watch (for herself), the new dresses and shoes for the children and perhaps a carton of cigarettes for her husband.

It is she who exerts considerable influence on her husband and on members of the younger generation, and it is she who transmits verbally the host of formalities and customs, in minute details, connected with the celebrations of each festival. It is she who goes to the temples (except the clan temples and guilds which are normally for men), and it is she who donates liberally to keep the temples going, to renovate them and even to build new and magnificent ones. And she it is, who is amongst the most zealous in the observance of meat-abstinence for the expiation of sins.

In short, without the housewives, the festivals are doomed to oblivion, even in a tolerant and democratic country.

Disintegrating Forces Simultaneously, there are disintegrating forces tending to affect the survival or continuation of the festivals. The most destructive is the law. The first is a judicial decision by the Supreme Court against the owning and holding of property in perpetuity, which nullifies any attempt by the rich to leave their property indefinitely for the purpose of ancestral veneration.[7] The second is the Estate Duty Law, which expropriates a large portion of the estate left by the affluent. No sooner is a multi-millionaire dead than his property is cut down by half or even more than half in payment of estate duty in cash, not in kind. This is especially so when the value of an estate is appraised on the date of death and when the property has to be disposed of in slump years. The third is the Income Tax Law, which does not permit reliefs for aged parents and other needy kin. The combined effect of these legal provisions tends to shake the foundation of the traditional family ties, which, in turn, disrupts the continuation of homage to the ancestors involving the observance of some traditional festivals.

Western Education An equally important factor is Western education, which lays more stress on conjugal love than filial piety and which inculcates the Western ideal of the husband-wife-and-children unit, which is diametrically opposed to the Chinese traditional practice of large family-ism. The result is the breaking-up of group living with aged parents and grandparents and a host of kinsfolk. When this happens, as it has happened and is still happening, there is less incentive to promote or continue the ancestral cult and to observe the traditional festivals.

Many graduates who have returned from Western universities with professional or academic degrees — and without degrees — are inclined to adopt a superior attitude and to dissociate themselves from the old cultural traditions, resulting in a new pattern of life that is neither Western nor Oriental. Some clan temples honour the scholastic achievements of graduates of the same clan, offering them monetary gifts and putting up honorific boards at a prominent section of the temple in their honour, on condition that they do homage to the ancestors; but many graduates have refused such an offer because they consider the condition repugnant to their Western education.

However, there is a large section of the English educated from secondary and primary schools who are forced to leave school in their early teens and who are not economically independent because of their lower income. This large group of Chinese is less determined to break away from the big family ties and the old traditions which are advantageous to them as a whole.

Modern Chinese Schools Similarly, modern Chinese education is a potent force in rupturing the old traditions for two major reasons. First, most of the writings of scholars of the latter part of the nineteenth century and this century are anti-traditional in character. As they are expressed in the *Pei Hua* (白话) language and are of high literary merit, they are read with avidity in China and abroad and their influence on the readers is incalculable.[8] Second, Malaya was the cradle of China's revolution in the first decade of the century, and the speeches and writings of political

7. See p. 79, fn. 17 above.
8. Even today amongst the most popular sets of books in the National Library of Singapore are 饮冰室全集，中国新文学大系，and 鲁迅全集.

reformers like K'ang Yu-Wei (康有为) and Liang Ch'i-Ch'ao (梁启超), and of revolutionaries like Sun Yat-Sen, Hu Han-Min (胡汉民) and Wang Ching-Wei (汪精卫), have left their mark on Malaysian soil.[9]

This is one of the reasons why when the calendar reform was attempted in Malaya a few decades ago, the Chinese press, the teachers and the students of the modern Chinese schools were amongst the most enthusiastic supporters. Though the attempted calendar reform eventually fizzled out, the tendency to cast overboard the old traditions is still dominant. But this applies only to the highly sophisticated, the extremists and the intellectuals who constitute the minority.

Like their counterparts from the English schools, the majority of the Chinese youths from the secondary and primary schools are faced with the economic problem of making a livelihood as soon as they are compelled by circumstances to cease schooling. Generally, they find employment in less important jobs with remuneration barely adequate for subsistence. As a result, they become more amenable eventually to the continuation of the traditional way of life which offers them the security of the family. Moreover, the observance of the festivals with their secular feasting and rejoicing affords them the escapism they need badly in the grim battle of life.

Influence of Other Religions The influence of other religions in disrupting the family and the old traditions is equally considerable. Christian movements in the East have a very old history and their influence on the Chinese in China produced such early Christian bi-lingual scholars as Yung Wing (容闳 , the first Chinese to be trained in Western education in the United States in the 1870s).[10] In Malaya, it was Robert Morrison of the London Missionary Society who launched the first Chinese monthly in Malacca on 5th August, 1815, which continued publication till 1821.[11] At the same time, the teachings of the Bible were disseminated with help from Liang Fa (梁发), the first Chinese convert, and others.[12]

Christian influence was so widespread that a Chinese scholar, writing about Singapore in 1887, complained that there were more than twenty churches of different sects in Singapore whereas there were relatively few temples and Chinese associations. He further observed that "ill-bred" Singapore-born Chinese were arrogant of their British status and became worse when they grew up to be Christians. There were some whose relationship with their parents was estranged because of the customs.[13]

To belittle Chinese polytheism, early Christian missionaries coined a phrase *ang kong* (红公 (仔), "idols") for Chinese images and statuettes. Literally, the term means "red-faced images", for images representing deified heroes are traditionally typified by a reddish facial complexion to indicate loyalty and righteousness, two of China's cherished virtues; but metaphorically it implies idolatory, calculating to degrade the Chinese form of belief and worship. Ancestral veneration was also deprecated.

There are many Islamic Chinese converts, especially in the rural areas where the Malays predominate and where the influence of Islam is almost without rival. But these Islamic adherents are relatively too few to produce any visible influence on the prevalent

9. This aspect of Malaya's history is dealt with in Chinese books such as 华侨与中国革命， 黄福銮，香港亚洲出版社，2nd ed., March 1955, Nanyang Section; and 华侨革命开国史， 冯自由，台湾，商务，August 1953, Nanyang Section. There are also two interesting monographs in English: *JSS*, Wang, "Sun Yat Sen and Singapore"; and *JSAH*, Png, "The KMT in Malaya".
10. Latourette, pp. 373–374.
11. [Robert Morrison was based in Canton, and did not visit the Malay Peninsula until 1823. The first mission press in Malacca was established by William Milne, also of the LMS and a protege of Morrison.]
12. 马来亚丛谈，许云樵，新加坡青年书局，1961, pp. 31–37; 星槟银禧纪念册， 1939–1964, Leith Street, Penang, p. B58; and 梁发传，香港基督教辅侨出版社， May 1955.
13. 新加坡风土记，李钟珏，(Reprint) 星洲南洋书局， 1947, pp. 9, 10, 12.

traditions. About a year ago, a Chinese Muslim of Kedah, a certain Mr Ma (马领事) who was one-time Chinese Consul in Malaya, smashed to pieces a Tuah Peh Kong image in Penang to show that no harm could come to him, but his act was interpreted as "sacrilegious" and his intolerance was attacked in the press by Koh Sin-Hock (辜承福), a prominent leader of Penang.

Evolution and Assimilation   In the final analysis, the disintegrating forces are insufficiently overwhelming to cause any drastic form of upheaval. When one community is allowed to coexist in peace and harmony, and in prosperity and contentment, with other communities, there is no impelling desire for any change, nor is there any need for an ardent and forceful leader to arise with the banner of reformation. What applies to Chinese traditions applies also to those of other communities. This is a healthy sign and an everlasting tribute to the good sense of the Malaysian leaders.

But though customs die hard, they are not static, and in a multi-racial society a fusion of inter-communal cultures or assimilation is inevitable, though the process is slow and often imperceptible. Already the *Chingay* of Penang and the *Wangkang* of Malacca, two of Malaya's most outstanding events, are fast dying out, if not becoming extinct. Of recent changes, the *Chap Goh Meh* is significant. It is a religious-cum-secular festival. On the religious side, the worship of the Tuah Peh Kong and the T'ien Kuan remains purely Chinese in character; whereas on the secular side, when the Chinese go out on a motorcade, it is joined in by other residents, irrespective of creed, race or colour, to make it into a truly cosmopolitan event with occasional *lagus* and *pantuns* sung by a Chinese *kronchong* party. The ubiquitous fire-crackers introduced by the Chinese into Malaya are now used by the Malays in Hari Raya Puasa, the Indians in Deepavali, and the Christians of all races in celebrating the Christmas festival. Also, in the Ghosts' Month, originally a solemn religious event, the festival is observed by large groups of celebrants amidst musicians and singers who sing English, American and Malay songs in addition to anglicized Chinese melodies. Even in sacrificial offerings to the deities, a notable modification is the offer of certain dishes of cooked food prepared in Malaysian style. And at the *Kiu Ong Yiah* festival, when devotees are led by entranced mediums to walk over the scorching fire-pit, the ritual is traceable to an Indian origin.

The Chinese New Year season is even more cosmopolitan in character with New Year greeting cards pouring in from friends of every race and creed. In the old days, a red or pink envelope was a *must*, it being an auspicious omen, though a danger sign of Westerners; whereas nowadays even white envelopes — white being a Chinese traditional mourning colour — are used in enclosing the greeting cards. When you make New Year calls and when your host shakes hands with you, instead of clasping his own hands in Chinese fashion, that is Western; and if your host holds out his right hand to touch both your hands, without any grasp or handshake, and then raises it to touch his forehead and then the breast lightly, that is a Malay heritage.[14] During the season, Chinese homes are visited by persons of many races — the Filipino bands playing Western tunes, instead of the traditional Chinese flageolet, gong and cymbals; the Indian labourers claiming

14. Sheppard, pp. 1, 2; and 马来风俗与文化，梅井，Ministry of Culture, Singapore, 1963, p. 18.

the Chinese *ang pau*; and the Europeans, the Japanese, the Malays, the Indians, the Eurasians and even the Indonesians who make social calls on you for a *yam seng* amidst a Western atmosphere of beer, whisky-and-soda, gin-and-tonic, and brandy-and-ginger-ale in an Oriental setting — all this is Malaysian, isn't it?

Since Merdeka on 31st August, 1957, there is a tendency for liberal-minded politicians to participate in secular celebrations during Chinese festivals such as the Moon Festival. In 1964, politicians from both the Socialist Front and the Malayan Chinese Association convened dinner parties at some festivals to win the goodwill and support of the voters in their constituencies. There were tea parties, served with the traditional moon cakes, Malayanized home-made cakes as well as restaurant-made sponge cakes, pastries and tarts of Western origin. At some parties, Malay-prepared chicken curry and rice formed the chief menu in lieu of the traditional Chinese roast pig. As Lee Kuan-Yew, Singapore's enlightened and farsighted Prime Minister, has correctly observed, "Each of the cultural groups in Malaysia has a special contribution to make to the life and culture of our new nation . . . . Slowly, over the years, we will develop an identity of our own, provided nobody tries to enforce his particular customs or religious practices on others." His observation is fully substantiated by the trend of evolution and assimilation discernible in the Chinese traditions; and what is true of Chinese traditions is equally true of the traditions of other races or communities.

Sino-Malay Solidarity   In 1965 when the Chinese New Year and the Hari Raya Puasa fell on 2nd and 3rd February respectively, ministerial heads of the governments considered this coincidence an auspicious omen for Sino-Malay unity and took the opportunity to appeal to members of these two major communities (forming about 85% of the entire population) to further strengthen their relationship in the face of external threat from Indonesia and the communists.[15] As a matter of fact, there has been similarity of observance between the Chinese and the Malays annually when the former abstain from meat (partial fasting) in the 9th Moon and the latter begin fasting in Ramadan (the ninth month in the Muslim calendar).[16] Again, the pilgrims who go to Kusu Island annually pray to a Chinese deity as well as a *kramat* of Malay origin on the same day — a harbinger of Sino-Malay solidarity. Furthermore, a legend narrated by Professor Hsu Yun-Ts'iao, a former Professor of History of the Nanyang University, has already laid the foundations for Sino-Malay brotherhood, for better or for worse.

According to this legend, in years gone by a sailing boat foundered near Kusu Island and went down with the waves. Only two persons — a Chinese and a Malay — managed to swin ashore on the island where they had to share the shrubs and wild fruits to keep themselves alive. As they found one another's company cordial, they became sworn brothers, living in harmonious co-operation until death. Later on, a ship, contaminated by an epidemic, happened to cast anchor on this island and through a miracle the epidemic disappeared and the sick recovered. It transpired that the Tuah Peh Kong deity had manifested himself to come to the timely rescue of the afflicted. Thereafter, Kusu Island became a holy place of worship to the people of Singapore.[17]

Finally, as these last lines are being written in the first week

15. *ST*, 2nd & 3rd February, 1965.
16. A Chinese writer has publicised in his work on Malay customs that the Islamic fasting month is held in the ninth month of the Muslim calendar. (See 马来人风俗，梅井，星洲马来亚文化协会出版，1957, pp. 51–54.)
17. 龟屿的传说，许云樵，南洋学报，vol. xiii, pt. i, June 1957, pp. 68–69.

of February, 1965, the holiday period for both the Chinese and the Malays, we conclude with a double greeting: A Happy Chinese New Year and Selamat Hari Raya Puasa.

Explanatory
Notes

Usage of Words   Malaysia was constituted on 16th September, 1963, and its citizens are all Malaysians, regardless of racial origin. In pursuance of this new trend, the word "Malaysians" is often used, where unambiguous, to indicate Malaysians of Chinese origin. The word "Chinese" is used to represent the Chinese of China, and, where distinction is necessary, the Chinese of Malaya or Malaysia.

The words "Malaya" and "Malaysia" and their derivatives are used to indicate the different periods of Malaysia's history — "Malaya" to denote the period prior to 16th September, 1963, and "Malaysia" the period between 16th September, 1963, and 9th August, 1965.

The term "multi-racial" is used in our work to indicate more than one race or community, not in the same political sense as that propounded by Professor K. G. Tregonning, when he says that "a multi-racial population is not necessarily a plural society, where groups of marked difference to the resident community establish and preserve their identity and resist assimilation. The USA is multi-racial . . . there is no plural society . . . . . In South Africa force has established and maintained a plural society and a divided state . . . . . The Malay Peninsula in the 1870's was multi-racial, but by the 1910's it had become a plural society." (Tregonning, *A History of Modern Malaya*, p. 173.) At any rate, we do not subscribe to this debatable distinction insofar as Malaya is concerned.

Translations   Where Chinese sources are concerned, the translations are ours, unless otherwise indicated. In our rendition, our primary aim is intelligibility and readability, and to pursue that aim precis or abridged translations or even paraphrases are sometimes given. At other times, the original versions are embellished. But fidelity is invariably maintained.

Romanization　We have not adopted any standard system of romanization, because the spellings are used to represent the phonetic equivalents of five different dialects — Mandarin, Hokkien, Tiechiu, Hakka and Cantonese — which defy any unified system of romanization. Besides, such terms as *Kiu Ong Yiah* and *Chap Goh Meh* are already accepted as the norm in the everyday vocabulary of most Malaysians, and any attempt to change them is likely to cause confusion. Experience shows that the most satisfactory solution lies in providing Chinese characters for the names and terms — a device followed by us in this book.

Bibliography

In the course of our research, we have covered a wider field than the sources cited in this volume, but it would be pretentious to include more than the works actually alluded to or mentioned in the notes or to suggest a longer list for reading.

Chinese Sources   Where Chinese sources are concerned, the titles are given in Chinese without romanization, for the simple reason that those who examine these items are presumably students of Chinese themselves and any romanization is superfluous. Dozens of sources published in such encyclopaedic volumes as the 事类，岁时，图书，子史，格致，群芳，故事 and 月粹，which are cited by us, are omitted in this bibliography, as their details are already given in the marginal notes.

Chinese publishers seem to have had a rough time a few decades ago: for instance, The Commercial Press originally printed a vast number of books in Shanghai; during the Japanese occupation, many works were undertaken in Changsha; and in post-Communist China, in Formosa (Taiwan) or Hong Kong. Hence the reader will find The Commercial Press mentioned at different addresses. The same applies to a few other publishers.

As hundreds of Chinese characters are used, many of which are repeated again and again in the marginal notes, it is imperative for us to resort to abbreviations:

史记(汉)司马迁(一百三十册)，涵芬楼影印，乾隆，ed.
中国年历总谱(二册)董作宾，Hong Kong University Press, 1960
增补事类统编(十二册)道光，上海文盛书局石印
岁时广记(宋)陈元靓(三册)，丛书集成，长沙商务印书馆，December 1939
前汉书，班固(八史经籍志)光绪九年，镇海张寿荣刊本· (a)艺文志
元史纪事本末，陈邦瞻原编，国学基本丛书，上海商务印书馆，(n.d.)

Annotated Chinese Annual Almanac 香港天宝楼，1964 ed.

霞外捃屑，平步青(三册)，明清笔记丛刊，上海中华书局，November 1959

诸子集成(八册)，北京中华书局，上海印，1954

     i. 淮南子

     ii. 老子道德经

     iii. 论衡，王充

     iv. 抱朴子，葛洪

     v. 管子

     vi. 韩非子

     vii. 论语

     viii. 颜氏家训

     ix. 荀子

     x. 世说新语，(宋)刘义庆

蠡海集，(宋)王逵，丛书集成，长沙商务印书馆，December 1939

聊斋志异，蒲松龄(二册)，香港商务印书馆，January 1963

古今图书集成(清)(八百零八册)，上海中华书局影印，October 1934

子史精华(雍正)(八册)，上海锦章图书局，1922

格致镜原(雍正)陈元龙(十八册)

说库(六十册)，王文濡编，上海文明书局，民国四年

     i. 江南余载(宋)郑文宝

     ii. 开元天宝遗事(五代)王仁俗

     iii. 摭言(唐)王保定

幼学故事琼林(宋)，香港广智书局，(n.d.)

古今怪异集成，周敥肃，(四册)，上海中华书局，(n.d.)

历代小史，陈文烛(三十三册)，景明刻本，上海涵芬楼影印

     i. 王子年拾遗记(前秦)王嘉撰，萧绮(梁)录

说郛(明)陶宗仪辑(四十册)，明抄本，上海涵芬楼藏版，民国十九年，上海商
    务再版

     i. 广州记(晋)顾微

     ii. 荆楚岁时(晋)宗懔

     iii. 唐乐史，段成式

     iv. 诺皋记(唐)段成式

四时宜忌(元)瞿祐，丛书集成，长沙商务印书馆，December 1939

续道藏(六十三册)，上海涵芬楼影印，April 1926

妙法莲华经(大正新修大藏经)第九卷，第一页

广群芳谱(清)圣祖敕(二十四册)，万有文库，上海商务印书馆，March 1935

李开先集(明)(三册)，北京中华书局，December 1959

清嘉录(清)顾铁卿，笔记小说丛书，上海新文化书局，2nd ed., October 1943

槟城散记，邝国祥，星洲世界书局，1958

民间故事新集，黄华，上海正气书局，May 1948

民间异俗，上海国光书店 May 1949

苏轼诗，宋代名著选辑，香港绿窗书屋，December 1954

春秋左传(僖公二十四年)，十三经注，光绪十三年脉望仙馆石印

民间说怪，上海国光书店，November 1948

历代社会风俗事物考，尚秉和，长沙商务印书馆，April 1938

古文观止(三册)，上海商务印书馆，November 1946

美术丛书(三辑，共六十册)，邓实编，上海神州国光社，民国十七年覆印

中华全国风俗志(四册)，胡朴安等，上海广益书局，October 1923

董勖问礼俗，玉函山房辑佚书(清)马国翰(一百册)，光绪九年，长沙琅嬛馆

事物纪原(宋)高承(四册)，上海商务印书馆，June 1937

陶渊明，梁启超，万有文库，上海商务印书馆，1929

节令风俗图，龙先生，(n.d., Singapore Archives)

月令粹编(清)秦嘉谟(六册)，琳琅仙馆，嘉庆十七年

古今逸史(明)吴琯辑(五十六册)，上海涵芬楼，景明刻本

茶余客话，阮葵生(二册)，明清笔记丛刊，上海中华书局，May 1959

杜甫诗，傅东华，上海商务印书馆，October 1949

李白，作家与作品丛书，香港上海书局，July 1962

中国文学家大辞典，谭正壁编，香港文史出版社，October 1961

贵妃醉酒，梅兰芳主演，许原来编，上海新美术出版社，June 1955

红楼梦(清)曹雪芹(曹沾)北京作家出版社，1953

十四经新疏(第一期书，世界文库四部刊要)，台北世界书局，February 1956
玉烛宝典(隋)杜台卿(二册)，丛书集成，长沙商务印书馆，December 1939
端午礼俗史，黄石，香港泰兴书局，April 1963
屈原，作家与作品丛书，香港上海书局，July 1962
屈原，陆侃如，上海亚东图书馆，民国廿二年六版
续齐谐记(梁)吴均，古今逸史
广东新语(康熙)屈翁山(十册)，水天阁绣版，1680
大正新修大藏经，日本高楠顺次郎(四百册)，东京大正一切经刊行会，
　　　6th year of Showa
古今事物考(明)王三聘，丛书集成，上海商务印书馆，June 1936
风俗通义(汉)应劭，丛书集成，长沙商务印书馆
异闻总录(宋)阙名，丛书集成，上海商务印书馆，June 1937
太平广记(宋)李昉主山房主人(四十册)，小说丛书大观，上海扫叶山房印行，
　　　1924
五行大义(隋)萧吉，常州光哲遗书，武进盛氏汇刊
搜神记(晋)干宝，学津讨原(二百册)(清)张海鹏辑，琴川张氏藏版
小方壶斋舆地丛抄(清)王锡祺辑，上海著易堂排印
闽杂记(清)施可斋(四册)，申报馆印，光绪戊寅
吴趋风土录(清)顾禄，小方壶斋舆地丛抄
民间笑话，沈文华，香港国光书店，(n.d.)
新年风俗志，娄子匡，上海商务印书馆，1935
日知录(十二册)，顾炎武，万有文库，上海商务印书馆，1919
中国节令掌故，孟寻，香港中华书局，1954
瑜伽焰口施食要集，会陵校刊，闽中鼓山涌泉寺，(reprint, n.d.)
民间传说，严殊炎，上海国光书店，March 1948
民间恨事，严殊炎，上海国光书店，March 1949
中华民族抗战史，陈安仁，上海商务印书馆，3rd ed., February 1947
清代史，萧一山，上海商务印书馆，3rd ed., February 1947
清朝野史大观(十二册)，小横香室主人，上海中华书局，5th ed., September 1930
华侨与中国革命，黄福銮，香港亚洲出版社，March 1955
华侨革命开国史，冯自由，台湾商务印书馆，August 1953
梁发传，香港基督教辅侨出版社，May 1935
马来风俗与文化，梅井，新加坡国家语文局，1963
马来人风俗，梅井，星洲马来亚文化协会，1957
饮冰室全集(廿四册)，上海中华书局，June 1941
鲁迅全集(十册)，北京人民文学出版社，August 1958
中国新文学大系(十册)，香港文学研究社，(n.d.)
马来亚潮侨通鉴，潘醒农，Singapore, 1950
叶德来传，王植原，新加坡艺华出版印刷有限公司，March 1958
新加坡风土记(清)李钟珏，Reprint 星洲南洋书局，1947
马来亚丛谈，许云樵，新加坡青年书局，1961
南洋三月记，郑健庐，上海中华书局

English Sources　　As regards English sources, the accepted
practice of quoting the authors in alphabetical order is followed.
Abbreviations in the marginal notes employ the surname of the
author; in cases where an author is attributed with more than one
title, the distinction is made by using the author's surname and an
abbreviated form of the book's title, for example: Creel, *Birth of
China*, and Creel, *Studies*. Journals and casual publications are
abbreviated as initials; in the marginal notes, the author's surname
(where applicable) follows the publication's initials.

Allen, Bernard M., *Gordon of China*, MacMillan & Co., London,
　　1933
(Anon.), *Reminiscences of a Chinese Official*, Tientsin Press, Tientsin,
　　1922
Arberry, A.J., *The Romance of the Rubaiyat*, George Allen & Unwin,
　　London, 1959

Ayscough, Florence, *A Chinese Mirror*, Jonathan Cape, London, 1925

Balfour, Frederic Henry, *Leaves from my Chinese Scrapbook*, Trubner & Co., London, 1887

Ball, J. Dyer, *Things Chinese*, 5th ed., Kelly & Walsh, Shanghai, 1925

Beal, Samuel, *A Catana of Buddhist Scriptures from the Chinese*, Trubner & Co., London, 1871

Beighton, John T., *Betel-Nut Island*, The Religious Tract Society, London, 1888

Bilainkin, George, *Hail Penang!*, Sampson Low, Marston & Co., London (1932?)

Birch, Cyril, *Chinese Myths and Fantasies*, Oxford University Press, London, 1961

Braddell, Roland, *The Law of the Straits Settlements* (2 vols), Kelly & Walsh, Singapore, 1931

——————— *The Lights of Singapore*, Methuen & Co., London, 1934

Bredon, Juliet and Igor Mitrophanow, *The Moon Year*, Kelly & Walsh, Shanghai, 1927

Britton, Nancy Pence, *East of the Sun*, William Blackwood & Sons, Edinburgh & London, 1956

Burkhardt, V.R., *Chinese Creeds and Customs* (3 vols), South China Morning Post, Hong Kong, vol. i, 13th impression, 1959; vol. ii, 6th impression, 1959; vol. iii, 3rd ed., 1960

Chang Chi-Yun, *The Essence of Chinese Culture*, The China News Press, Taiwan, 1957

Chen Ta, *Emigrant Communities in South China*, Kelly & Walsh, Shanghai, 1939

Chen Te K'un, *Archaeology in China*, W. Heffer & Sons, Cambridge, 1960

Chiang Yee, *A Chinese Childhood*, Methuen & Co., London, 1953

Chou Hsiang-Kuang, *A History of Chinese Buddhism*, India, 1955

Couling, Samuel, *The Encyclopaedia Sinica*, Oxford University Press, London, 1917

Crane, Louise, *China in Sign and Symbol*, Kelly & Walsh, Shanghai, 1926

Creel, Herrlee Glessner, *The Birth of China*, Jonathan Cape, London, 1936

——————————— *Studies in Early Chinese Culture*, American Council of Learned Societies, 1948

Cronin, Vincent, *The Wise Man from the West*, Rupert Hart-Davis, London, 1955

de Bary, W. Theodore, Wing-Tsi Chan and Burton Watson, *Sources of Chinese Tradition*, Columbia University Press, New York, 1960

de Groot, J.J.M., *The Religion of the Chinese*, MacMillan Company, New York, 1912

——————— *The Religious System of China* (6 vols), Leyden, 1892–1910

Douglas, Robert K., *Confucianism and Tauism*, Pott, Young & Co., New York, 1879

——————— *Li Hung Chang*, Bliss, Sands & Foster, London, 1895

Dyson, Verne, *Forgotten Tales of Ancient China*, The Commercial Press, Shanghai, 1934

Eberhard, Wolfram, *Chinese Festivals*, Henry Schuman, New York, 1952

Elliott, Alan J.A., *Chinese Spirit-Medium Cults in Singapore*, London School of Economics and Political Science, 1955

E-Tu Zen Sun and John de Francis, *Chinese Social History*, American Council of Learned Societies, Washington, D.C., 1956

Fei Hsiao-T'ung, *Peasant Life in China*, Kegan Paul, Trench, Trubner & Co., London, 1943 (reprint)

Fletcher, W.J.B., *More Gems of Chinese Poetry*, The Commercial Press, Shanghai, 1929

Frazer, James George, *Balder the Beautiful*, vol. ii, "Golden Bough" series, MacMillan & Co., London, 1930

———————————— *The Golden Bough*, abridged ed., MacMillan & Co., London, 1949

Freedman, Maurice, *Chinese Family and Marriages in Singapore*, Her Majesty's Stationery Office, London, 1957

Fung Yu-Lan, *A History of Chinese Philosophy* (2 vols), tr. by Derk Bodde, George Allen & Unwin, London, 1952

Giles, Herbert A., *Civilization of China*, Williams & Norgate, London, 1919 (reprint)

Giles, Lionel, *A Gallery of Chinese Immortals*, John Murray, London, 1948

Goodrich, L. Carrington, *A Short History of the Chinese People*, 2nd ed., George Allen & Unwin, London, 1957

Gowan, Herbert H. and Joseph Washington Hall, *An Outline History of China*, D. Appleton & Company, New York, 1933

Granet, Marcel, *Festivals and Songs of Ancient China*, George Routledge & Sons, London, 1932

Groves, Harry E., *The Constitution of Malaysia*, Malaysia Publications, Singapore, 1964

Hammerton, J.A., *Manners and Customs of Mankind* (3 vols), Amalgamated Press, London (n.d.)

Hearn, Lafcadio, *Selected Writings*, The Citadel Press, New York, 1949

Hirth, Friedrich, *The Ancient History of China*, Columbia University Press, New York (1907?)

Hsiao Ch'ien, *A Harp with a Thousand Strings*, Pilot Press, London, 1944

Hu Shih, *The Chinese Renaissance*, University of Chicago Press, 1934

Hume, Edward H., *Doctors East Doctors West*, George Allen & Unwin, London (n.d.)

Johnston, Reginald Fleming, *Buddhist China*, John Murray, London, 1913

———————————— *Confucianism and Modern China*, Victor Gollancz, London, 1934

———————————— *Lion and Dragon in Northern China*, John Murray, London, 1910

Kang, C.K., "The Functional Relationship between Confucian Thought and Chinese Religion", in *Chinese Thoughts and Institutions*, ed. John K. Fairbanks, 2nd impression, University of Chicago, 1959

Krappe, Alexander Haggerty, *The Science of Folk-Lore*, Methuen & Co., London, 1930

Kyshe, J.W.M., *Cases Heard and Determined in Her Majesty's Supreme Court of the Straits Settlements, 1808–1884*, Singapore, 1885

Latourette, Kenneth Scott, *The Chinese: Their History and Culture*, MacMillan Company, New York, 1947

Lee, Edward Bing-Shuey, *Modern Canton*, The Mercury Press, Shanghai, 1936

Lee, James Zee-Min, *Chinese Potpourri*, 2nd ed., The Oriental Publishers, Hong Kong, 1951

Liang, Ch'i-Ch'ao, *History of Chinese Political Thought*, Kegan Paul, Trench, Trubner & Co., London, 1930

Lin Yutang, *My Country and My People*, William Heinemann, London, 1948

Low, James, *A Dissertation on the Soil and Agriculture in the British Settlement of Penang*, Singapore Free Press, Singapore, 1836

MacDonald, Malcolm, *Borneo People*, Jonathan Cape, London, 1956

MacNair, H.F., *The Chinese Abroad*, The Commercial Press, Shanghai, 1933

McKie, Ronald, *Malaysia in Focus*, Angus & Robertson, Sydney, 1963

Needham, Joseph, *Science and Civilization of China* (7 vols), Cambridge University Press, 1954 and later

Nourse, Mary A., *A Short History of the Chinese*, Williams & Norgate, London, 1938

Pan Ku, *The History of the Former Han Dynasty*, tr. by Homer H. Dubs, Waverly Press, Baltimore (n.d.)

Parker, E.H., *China, Her History, Diplomacy and Commerce*, John Murray, London, 1901

Purcell, Victor, *The Chinese in Malaya*, Oxford University Press, London, 1948

Reichelt, Karl Ludwig, *Truth and Tradition in Chinese Buddhism*, The Commercial Press, Shanghai, 1927

Reischauer, Edwin O., *Ennin's Diary*, tr. from the Chinese, The Ronald Press Company, New York, 1955

——————————— *Ennin's Travels in T'ang China*, The Ronald Press Company, New York, 1955

(Rogers, Samuel), *Recollections of the Table-Talk of Samuel Rogers*, Edward Moxon, London, 1856

Schlegel, Gustave, *Thian Ti Hwui*, Lange & Co., 1866 (reprint, Government Printer, Singapore)

Seeger, Elizabeth, *The Pageants of Chinese History*, 3rd ed., Longmans, Green & Co., New York, 1947

Sheppard, M.C.ff., *Malay Courtesy*, Donald Moore, Singapore 1956

Sheridan, L.A., *Federation of Malaya Constitution*, University of Malaya in Singapore, Singapore, 1961

Shu-Chiung (Mrs Wu Lien-Teh), *Yang Kuei-Fei*, The Commercial Press, Shanghai, 1923

Sidney, Richard J.H., *Malay Land*, Cecil Palmer, London, 1926

Sim, Katharine, *Journey out of Asia*, Robert Hale, London, 1963

————— *Malayan Landscape*, 2nd impression, Michael Joseph, London, 1957

Siren, Osvald, *The Imperial Palaces of Peking* (3 vols), G. van Oest, Paris & Brussels, 1926

Skinner, Charles M., *Myths and Legends of Flowers, Trees, Fruits and Plants*, J.B. Lippincott Company, Philadelphia, 1925

Solomon, Bernard S., *The Veritable Record of the T'ang Emperor Shun-Tsung*, Harvard University Press, 1955

Song Ong-Siang, *One Hundred Years of the Chinese in Singapore*, John Murray, London, 1932

Soothill, W.E., *The Hall of Light*, Lutterworth Press, London, 1951

————— *The Three Religions of China*, 3rd ed., Oxford University Press, London, 1929

T'ien Ju-K'ang, *The Chinese of Sarawak*, London School of
Economics and Political Science, London (1953?)

Townley, Susan, *My Chinese Note Book*, 2nd ed., Methuen & Co.,
London, 1904

Tregonning, K.G., *A History of Modern Malaya*, Eastern Universities
Press for University of London Press, London, 1964

Vaughan, J.D., *The Manners and Customs of the Chinese in the Straits*
Settlements, The Mission Press, Singapore, 1879

Werner, E.T.C., *A Dictionary of Chinese Mythology*, Kelly & Walsh,
Shanghai, 1932

——————— *Myths and Legends of China*, George C. Harrap,
London, 1922

Wieger, Leo, *China Throughout the Ages*, tr. from the French by
Edward Chalmers Werner, Hsien-hsien Press, China, 1928

Wilhelm, Richard, *I-Ching* (2 vols), tr. from the German by Cary
F. Baynes, Routledge & Kegan Paul, London, 1951

——————— *The Soul of China*, Jonathan Cape, London, 1928

Williams, C.A.S., *Outlines of Chinese Symbolism and Art Motives*,
2nd revised ed., Kelly & Walsh, Shanghai, 1932

Williams, Lea E., *Overseas Chinese Nationalism*, The Free Press,
Glencoe, Illinois, 1960

Williams, S. Wells, *The Middle Kingdom* (2 vols), Charles Scribner's
Sons, New York, 1883

Withers-Payne, C.H., *The Malayan Law Digest*, Malayan
Law Journal Office, Singapore, 1936

Wong, C.S., *A Gallery of Chinese Kapitans*, Ministry of Culture,
Singapore, 1963

——————— *Temple of Paradise*, Malaysian Sociological Research
Institute, Singapore, 1963

Wong, K. Chimin and Wu Lien-Teh, *History of Chinese Medicine*,
2nd ed., National Quarantine Service, Shanghai, 1936

Wu Lien-Teh, *Plague Fighter*, W. Heffer & Sons, Cambridge, 1959

Wylie, Alexander, *Chinese Researches*, Shanghai, 1897

Yang Lien-Sheng, *Studies in Chinese Institutional History*, Harvard
University Press, 1963

Journals, Magazines, Newspapers and Occasional Publications

汉学，北京中法汉学研究所

星槟银禧纪念册，Penang

星洲十年，关楚璞(主编)，新加坡星洲日报社，1940

南洋年鉴，郁树锟(主编)，新加坡南洋报社，1951

南洋学报，Singapore

南洋杂志，Singapore

南洋商报，Singapore

星槟日报，Penang

星洲日报，Singapore

光华日报，Penang

CJ   *The China Journal*, Shanghai
            Sowerby, Arthur de C.,"The Chinese Lunar Calendar",
                vol. xiii, no. 6, December 1930
                ——————————— "The Chinese Calendar",
                vol. xiii, no. 5, November 1930

CJSA   *The China Journal of Science and Arts*, Shanghai
            Sowerby, Arthur de C., "Crossing the Year", vol. iii,
                February 1925

CR	*The Chinese Repository*, Canton
CSA	*China Society Annual*, Singapore
	Cheng Hui-Ming, Homer, "Chinese Religious Festivals in Singapore", 1949, pp. 21–26
	Kluenter, Beatrice, "Chinese Music", 1952, pp. 49–59
JMBRAS	*Journal of the Malayan Branch, Royal Asiatic Society*, Singapore
	Farrer, R.J., "A Buddhist Purification Ceremony", vol. xi, pt ii, 1933
	Middlebrook, S.M. and J.M. Gullick, "Yap Ah Loy", vol. xxiv, pt ii, July 1951
	Topley, Marjorie, "Singapore Chinese Paper Charms and Prayer Sheets", vol. xxvi, pt i, July 1953
	—————— "Chinese Women's Vegetarian Houses in Singapore", vol. xxvii, pt i, May 1954
	—————— "Chinese Religion and Religious Institutions in Singapore", vol. xxix, pt i, May 1956
JNCBRAS	*Journal of the North China Branch, Royal Asiatic Society*, Shanghai
	Billas, F.X., "K'u Yuan, His Life and Poems", vol. LIX, 1928, pp. 231–253
	Kingsmill, Thos. W., "The Chinese Calendar: Its Origin, History and Connections", vol. xxxii
	Mayers, W.F., "The Use of Gunpowder and Firearms among the Chinese", (new series), no. vi, 1871
	Read, Bernard E., "The Dragon in Chinese Medicine", vol. LXX, 1939
JSAH	*Journal of South-East Asian History*, University of Singapore
	Png Poh Seng, "The KMT in Malaya", vol. ii, no. i, March 1961
JSS	*Journal of the Southseas Society*, Singapore
	Wang Gungwu, "Sun Yat Sen and Singapore", vol. xv, 1959
KL	*Kuala Lumpur 100 Years Centenary, 1859–1959*, Kuala Lumpur Municipal Council, 1963
MCM	*Mesny's Chinese Miscellany*, Shanghai
MG	*The Malacca Guardian*, Malacca
MM	*Malay Mail*, Singapore
NCR	*The New China Review*, Shanghai
	de Saussure, Leopold, "The Lunar Zodiac", no. 6, vol. iii, December 1921
NM	*Nanyang Miscellany*, Singapore
NYB	*Nanyang Year Book*, Singapore
PG	*Pinang Gazette*, Penang
SCM	*Straits Chinese Magazine*, Singapore
	Pun Lun, "Wangkang Procession in Malacca", vol. ix, no. 3, September 1905, pp. 119–123
SEM	*Straits Echo*, (Mail Edition), Penang
SET	*Straits Echo and Times of Malaya*, Penang
SG	*Sunday Gazette*, Penang
	Wu Liu (pseud. of C.S. Wong), "Matters Chinese", weekly column
SM	*Sunday Mail*, Singapore
ST	*Straits Times*, Singapore
STA	*Straits Times Annual*, Singapore

General Index

A

Chinese Traditions and Beliefs: A Record for Posterity

by Steve Thompson

The Tiger Balm Gardens

Chinese traditions and beliefs are largely verbal legacies passed down through many generations: the more famous of these may have been written down or dramatized in traditional Chinese opera. But in the 1930's, one man decided that this precious legacy must be preserved in a more permanent form. His idea was to take Chinese deities and historical and legendary figures from the pages of books, and re-create them more vividly in tableaux of concrete painted in brilliant colours.

And so, in 1931, the Tiger Balm Gardens — one in Singapore, one in Hong Kong — were created. Known also in Singapore as the Haw Par Villas, in Hong Kong as the Haw Par Mansions, these gardens stand today as treasure houses of Chinese history, folklore and mythology, as well as recreational parks popular with both tourists and local residents.

The Singapore Tiger Balm Garden is located on eight acres of land in Pasir Panjang Road, on a hill overlooking the sea. It was built at a cost of S$300,000. Curved paths guide the visitor through a collection of Buddhas, deities, demons and mortals, who in stone weave tales of good and evil, and expound the familiar themes of filial piety, diligence and honesty. A highlight of the garden is the Ten Courts of Justice, the Taoist vision of purgatory, each of which portrays the punishments that await the wicked and sinful.

Mammals and reptiles are not excluded, which is no surprise as they have always played important roles in Chinese mythology. The presence of other animals, however, is merely to illustrate the typical fauna of a particular area.

Lessons in good self-conduct, matrimonial advice and warnings against temptations such as gambling and cabaret are also part of this fascinating garden.

A. *Two memorials to the Aw brothers at the centre of the Haw Par Villas in Singapore.* **B.** *The Aw brothers in an old print.*

Tiger Balm and the Tiger King

The moral code evinced in the Tiger Balm Gardens was important to their creator, who saw himself as a social reformer. He was Aw Boon Haw, the elder of two empire-building brothers who themselves achieved legendary status. Stories of the two brothers continue to fascinate as much as their gardens to this day.

Born in Rangoon, Burma, in the 1880's, Aw Boon Haw and Aw Boon Par were the sons of a Chinese herbalist. Haw means "tiger" in Chinese, Par "leopard", and the brothers later chose the tiger as their emblem: it was to bring them more fame and wealth than could be imagined.

Success began in 1926 when the Aw brothers arrived in Singapore with their revolutionary balm, called Tiger Balm. They also brought other potions and ointments on which they had patents.

The tiger and the mystical powers with which it was credited helped to spread the fame of the balm that carried its name. A popular belief for many years was that some portion of the animal was actually included in the balm — a tiger's hair, perhaps, ground into a fine powder.

Superstition and mysticism notwithstanding, Tiger Balm soon became a popular cure-all. Loyal users maintain that it gives effective relief from such ailments as muscular aches and pains, sprains, rheumatism, insect bites, itching, lumbago and headaches.

An astute marketing man long before his time, Aw Boon Haw appreciated the effectiveness of advertising and embarked on aggressive campaigns to sell his products. He even made his own posters and roamed the streets of Singapore at night, looking for blank walls on which to display them.

A. *The Monkey God in his celestial court robes.* **B.** *A female participant in the mythological epic, The Eight Immortals Crossing the Ocean.*

*Part of a morality tableau depicting the
decadence of the idle rich.*

Even his car bore the livery of the tiger. A Fiat, it was a familiar
sight in the 1930's with its tiger's head mounted on the bonnet and
its body painted in bold black stripes over orange and white. As it
raced through the streets of Singapore, its driver would sound the
horn and a pre-recorded tiger's roar would scatter pedestrians in its
path.

Aw Boon Haw's promotional ideas were equally ingenious, and
these, of course, included the revolutionary idea of the Tiger Balm
Gardens. Although he undoubtedly intended them to be primarily
cultural in content, parts of the gardens served as an advertisement
for his trade. The name "Tiger Balm Garden" is displayed
prominently on one of the main arches; a ferocious tiger stands
guard at the gates; and Tiger Balm and other medical products
manufactured by the Aw brothers can be seen on display in the
gardens.

Considering that the gardens were created in the 1930's (when
the idea of Disneyland has not even been conceived), and because
entry was free, this promotional idea was a great success and spread
the name of Tiger Balm far and wide. Branches to market the
product were soon open in Penang, Jakarta, Bangkok, Hong Kong
and China.

Today, Tiger Balm is a household name throughout the region,
and the advent of modern medicine has in no way affected its
popularity. In Malaysia and Singapore, the product is found in the
first-aid kits of not only Chinese homes but also of Malay and
Indian homes. Its popularity has prompted countless imitations, but
none has achieved the success of the real thing.

Established and accepted as is Tiger Balm, the aura of mystique
still remains. Its proponents (who use it for many diverse ailments

A. *The evils of gambling depicted in a morality tableau.* **B.** *Mu Lien resists temptation in the epic tale* The Journey to the West. **C.** *Animals are also depicted at the Haw Par Villas.*

not even suggested on the pack) are largely unable to explain exactly how it works: it is enough for them that it does work. And to Westerners its distinctive Eastern packaging, which has hardly changed at all since Tiger Balm first appeared on the market, is at once all things mysterious and Oriental.

The men responsible for the success of Tiger Balm became as famous as their product, and their fame continues to this day. Aw Boon Par died in Rangoon in 1944, and it was left to his elder brother to continue building their empire. This was precisely Aw Boon Haw's intention, as a fortune-teller's prediction had warned him that, if he ever stopped building, he would die and lose his empire.

By the time of Aw Boon Haw's death in 1954, the Aw empire had diversified to include real estate, insurance, banking and newspapers, such as the Singapore *Standard* (founded in the 1950's), and the *Tiger* (now the Hong Kong *Standard*) and the *Sing Tao Jit Poh* in Hong Kong.

One of the most generous philanthropists of his time, Aw Boon Haw's legacy to schools and hospitals is almost incalculable. One of his traditions is continued today by his daughter Sally Aw: each Chinese New Year, she visits old people's homes in Hong Kong with gifts and *ang pau*.

The Jade Collection
Another Aw legacy as famous as the Tiger Balm Gardens is the Aw Jade Collection — perhaps the largest private collection in the world.

The collection began with the building of the famous Jade House, the Aws' stately home in Singapore, in 1927. The architecture of this beautiful white building is strangely Western, considering the importance of Chinese traditions and culture to its owner.

To grace his new mansion, Aw Boon Haw collected the finest *objets d'art*, and his jade and jadite carvings were in a great variety of shapes and sizes. There were jade gods, goddesses, animals, birds, bowls and many other designs. The collection grew into a priceless investment and pride of possession prompted its owner to open the collection to public viewing.

Aw Boon Haw's family continued to exhibit the collection after his death until it was moved in 1979 to the National Museum of Singapore, where it remains open to public viewing.

Tiger Balm, the Tiger Balm Gardens, the Jade Collection... all have their roots in Chinese traditions and beliefs, and all are today very much part of the culture and lifestyle of Malaysians and Singaporeans.

A. *A leaping tiger on one of the many stone benches at the Haw Par Villas.*
B. *A range of Tiger Balm products, now a household name throughout the region.*